Stuck in the Middle with Ewe

Stuck in the Middle with Ewe

Published by The Conrad Press Ltd. in the United Kingdom 2022

Tel: +44(0)1227 472 874
www.theconradpress.com
info@theconradpress.com

ISBN 978-1-914913-67-9

Printed and bound in Great Britain by Clays Ltd, Elcograf S.p.A

Typesetting and Cover Design by The Book Typesetters
www.thebooktypesetters.com

Illustrations by Susan Reed

The Conrad Press logo was designed by Maria Priestley.

Stuck in the Middle with Ewe

Or how I lost my heart and found my flock in Northern Ireland

Holly Crawford

To my gorgeous husband Paul: The love of my life and best friend. Thank you for supporting and believing in me. It's an honour to be your wife. I will love you forever and a day.

To Mum and Dad. Thanks for your love, support and for believing that one day, I would write a book! I will love you always.

To the sheep: for letting me into your flock.

Beginnings

This is the start
Of a story you will long remember,
In the heart of
Every girl, there is a dream,
Of a person and a place
But she does not know
Upon first meeting,
That love has finally found her

By H.A.Crawford

(Using the cento technique of poetry based on words from *The People's Friend* circa 1953.)

Prologue

Like most new mums, I'm still in my pyjamas at midday.

Bleary-eyed as I make up bottles for my bawling babies, I have no idea if it's Tuesday or Christmas. My hair hasn't seen a comb since I don't know when and to top it all, the postman has just arrived. Normally, I'd be mortified that anyone should see me like this. Today, I couldn't care less.

My arms are aching from all the whisking, and I'm squinting to see the 500-millilitre mark because I have no idea where my glasses are.

In my haste, I pour out more milk power, miss the jug and am suddenly engulfed in a haze of white. Coughing and spluttering, I emerge looking like an abominable snowman.

The noise coming from the nursery is intensifying. 'Mumma's coming,' I call out in a bid to pacify them.

Paul and I have only been married four months and we already have fifteen babies, with more on the way.

I stagger under the weight of the bottles, making my way through the kitchen, out to the yard and into the sunshine.

The babies, who are all expectantly peering out of their pens, crank up the volume as I enter the room until I can't hear myself think.

Their big, beautiful eyes follow me around as I get things set up and ready to serve the milk.

Every time I walk past the pens, they rush forward and then cry forlornly when I don't give them their milk straight away, like I'm the worst mother in the world who has abandoned them.

'I haven't forgotten you, I promise,' I coo as I pour and carry. 'I'm going as fast as I can.'

Something of a silence descends as I serve up the first helping to the hungry babies, who merrily suck away, making contented gurgling noises.

Happiness wraps itself around me like a blanket at this beautiful sight and I lean forward to stroke their heads. I see myself in the reflection of their huge, brown, blinking, kind eyes, and smile. They don't look anything like me, of course. Nor Paul. Probably just as well.

Had someone been watching, they'd probably comment that I have that gooey-eyed look that most new parents have. The one which says, 'I'm exhausted but this is worth it. You are worth it.'

I take a step back with hands on hips and then move to massage my aching muscles. This is heavy work, but the most rewarding job I've ever done.

There's a tear in my eye as I consider how fast they have grown. It seems like only yesterday that they were born and now they're standing up and drinking for themselves.

One day, my babies will be bigger than me. And a time will come when they won't remember me. But I will remember them and know that I gave them the best start in life.

These are my children. They are huge. They are calves.

My name is Holly Crawford. I'm a farmer's wife, a foster mum to lambs and calves and a milker of cows.

But my life wasn't always like this.

I used to be a journalist with a fast-paced job in a city in England. It was all business suits, meetings, trekking to London for conferences, hitting deadlines, battling it out with other reporters for scoops (the front-page story of a publication) and asking probing questions to bring important issues to the fore. It was stressful, unpredictable, demanding and I loved it.

I've always found it ironic that someone as shy and nervous as me (no sniggering at the back), went into journalism. After all, it's a cut-throat, hectic and unpredictable job. But I've always thrived on pressure and challenges.

So, how did I go from being a journalist in England to milking cows and caring for animals in the lush countryside of Northern Ireland in just over a year? It's a very good question. Read on, and I'll tell you. But first, feed this calf for me, would you? Ta.

A note from the author

I refer to humans as hoomans at various points. This is not an error, but the way in which I think the sheep would address us. All will become clear. I think.

1. Trailers and tribulations

'Why aren't you getting out of the trailer?' Paul asks.

I want to reply, but I'm a bit preoccupied trying to extract myself from underneath the six ewes that are currently using me as a bouncy castle.

My face is pressed up against the trailer wall and I have sheep to the left of me and sheep to the right. I am literally stuck in the middle with ewe (and I apologise to the rock band Stealers Wheel for the appalling pun).

Today, we're moving some sheep from one field to the other because they've stripped this one bare.

When we arrived at our destination, I jumped out of the car and opened the gate while Paul started getting the trailer open and ready.

I went ahead with my bucket of bribes (sheep nuts) to tempt the ewes and their many, many lambs up from the bottom field.

The idea being that I would call them and shake my bucket (as it were) and they would come galloping up the hill and follow me, *à la* The Pied Piper of Hamelin; out of the field, over the road and up into the pen which Paul had made earlier when channelling his inner *Blue Peter* presenter. No doubt it was being held together with bits of binding string and sticky back plastic.

11

Things had started out well. I had the advantage over the opposition because I was at the top of the hill, much like Harold Hardrada perched on Battle Hill on that fateful day in Hastings in 1066. (In retrospect, that was a bad example to give, as things didn't end well for him. But anyway...)

I saw the sheep dotted below, standing like fluffy map markers with their heads down as they diligently chewed the grass. Then I shook my bucket for all I was worth, watched and wait. I've seen the ewes react to the food bucket many times now, but it always makes me smile.

One sheep will hear the rattling bucket and her ears will twitch. A couple more shakes and she'll look up and over at you as she assesses the source of the noise. Once she's ascertained that yes, you are a friend and you do indeed have food on your person, she'll call out to her mates.

Then, one by one, heads will bob up in response and they'll turn as one to look at you. The ewe who spreads the word will move off slowly towards you, then break into a run and any lambs around her will quickly pick up the pace and follow.

The vibration of her hooves on the firm ground will ring out across the field, a signal for the others to follow.

They 'baaa' all the way up the hill, their hooves clattering the earth so it feels as if the very ground is vibrating, having been tapped with thirty little tuning forks.

It doesn't take them many minutes to go from tiny dots on the horizon to big fluffy balls of wool right in my face.

Pleased with my obvious sheep whispering efforts, I turned smugly and walked on as they followed, the sound of their hooves slapping the wet grass and their bleats ringing in my ears.

Then suddenly, in a strange and unexpected turn of events, *I* was following *them*.

They were so keen to be fed that they picked up the pace and surged forward, making it look as if I was being carried forth on a huge, fluffy and very low cloud.

I don't know why they always act as if they're poor, starved creatures, which is what they would have you believe if you met them. They'd be all big, sad eyes and mournful bleats, as if they are never given anything to eat. Indeed, they'd certainly give Dickens' *Oliver* a run for his money.

And they're certainly not starving. I mean, they literally stand in their dinner all day. That would be like me covering my office carpet in chocolate bars, which isn't a bad idea.

'Er, girls, I'm here,' I shouted, 'you aren't going to get any food while I'm behind you.' But my words fall on deaf, fluffy ears and they charged on regardless. Safe to say, Paul found the fact I was outrun by his sheep hilarious.

Eventually, I made it into the pen, and, feeling like The Child Catcher from *Chitty Chitty Bang Bang*, shouted, 'come on sheepies, come and get your lovely treats,' as I walked up the tailgate and into the trailer. The plan was that I would lead them all inside in a calm and orderly manner and then exit via the side door with my bucket of food intact.

The sheep, however, were having none of it and barrelled straight in behind me, one after the other much faster than

I was expecting, so before I could make my grand exit, they had the bucket and me on the floor. And that, dear reader, is where you came in.

From the outside, it must look like we have a TARDIS for a trailer, because that's the only way such a large number of sheep could possibly pile into such a small space. But sadly for me, the trailer really is smaller on the inside, making it a very rubbish TARDIS, and I'll be complaining to Jodie Whittaker or whoever it is now, just as soon as I get this sheep's hoof off my trachea.

'Why aren't you coming out?' Paul shouts again.

My response is carried off on the wind and thus, will not be recorded in the annals of history.

After about fifteen years, the side door opens and Paul peers in. 'Stop playing with the sheep and get out,' he says, smiling as he reaches in and pulls me out. I remove the lamb which was nesting in my hair and put it back in the trailer. It bleats in a miffed kind of way.

I close the door and wait until Paul is out of earshot before turning to the ewes who are peering at me smugly through the window of the trailer, mouths stuffed with their ill-gotten gains.

'Woolly little beggars,' I whisper, 'I'll get you later.'

Today's score: Holly: zero. Sheep: 125,000.

2. Fields of opportunity

As a journalist, I'm more used to chasing deadlines than sheep. At least, I was.

Now, I'm standing in a field with sweat pouring down my face as the woolly wonders run rings around us. This is a different batch of sheep who we're trying to round up so we can move them to a new location. For the past few weeks, they've been lawnmowers-for-hire, eating the grass up before this field is ploughed for crops.

The sheep are having a strop and so am I. In fact, it's a toss-up as to who has thrown the biggest hissy fit today, but I think it's me.

For the last hour, they've been refusing point-blank to get into the pen we've erected in the corner of the field, let alone pile into the trailer.

The ewes are such teases, and they know it. They amble over to the pen, sniff around it and will occasionally put a hoof through the open gate, before removing it again in some bizarre ovine version of the 'Hokey-Cokey'.

Sometimes, they'll even lick the silver gates and peep over the top as if they're on a house viewing, looking for all the world as if they're about to trip merrily inside, like good little sheep. Then they turn at the last second and gallop back across the fields as one woolly mass.

If you listen carefully, you might be able to hear what they're saying in their own language. Translated, it means this: 'Sure, we'll come inside in our own sweet time when we're good and ready, and not a second before. Ha-ha!'

I'm quickly coming to the conclusion that sheep are a bit like children. What's that old rhyme? *There was a little girl who had a little curl, right in the middle of her forehead. When she was good, she was very, very good, but when she was bad, she was horrid.*

Well, it's a bit like that with our sheep (not all sheep, of course, I won't stereotype) in that on the whole, they're wonderful and gorgeous and life-enhancing.

But if they've gotten out of bed (or off of the straw) on the wrong side, they show off, just like toddlers, and if they don't want to do something, they ain't gonna do it, so there.

We finally get them in after cajoling, calling and flapping our arms about as if we're guiding planes into land.

Exhausted, Paul and I lay on the grass and hold hands.

'How has my life changed so much in such a short space of time?' I ask, smiling.

It's Wednesday afternoon. In my old life, about this time, I'd be chained to my desk, frantically writing a news article and trying not to miss my deadline. Then, I'd stagger to the gym, go on the treadmill, not actually get anywhere and go home to a microwave meal for one before watching some rubbish on television.

Now, I spend my afternoons chasing sheep around lush green fields in Northern Ireland with Paul, before heading to our farm to tuck the lambs in and have a nice home-cooked meal with vegetables from our greenhouse. I know which one I prefer.

Rolling on my back, I look at the sky, close my eyes and enjoy the feel of the sun on my face. I can smell the salt from the sea and hear the waves crashing against the rocks on the beach below the field we are in.

I squeeze Paul's hand and smile. It's amazing how quickly my circumstances have changed.

'It feels as if it was only last week that we were coming back to Northern Ireland from our honeymoon,' I muse.

'It *was* only last week.'

'Oh, right. That's why then.'

I grin at the memory and the chain of events that brought me to this point.

3. Returning from honeymoon

The moonlight dances on the water as the ferry comes into the shore. I'm holding my coffee cup while admiring my engagement ring and the shiny, lovely new wedding band below it. Then I grab Paul's hand and admire his wedding band, too.

The crossing from Scotland to Northern Ireland takes about two hours and the journey was relatively smooth, well, at least that's what the seasoned travellers said.

Personally, when I saw the stools in the café twirling around on their own accord due to the ferocity of the waves, I thought otherwise, but what do I know?

When we pulled away from the mainland, I had tears in my eyes. For the journey signalled the start of a new adventure but also the end of an era for me. I wasn't just leaving the country behind for a holiday but sailing towards a new life as the wife of a wonderful man, which of course was exciting, but also nerve-racking. It felt so grown up, and I've never been very good at being an adult. I've always admired Peter Pan in that respect; stay young and childlike, that's what I say.

My thoughts are interrupted by the thump of the tannoy and the announcement that we can return to our transport.

The *Just Married* banner on our car has held out well, despite having been attached for more than a week and enduring all weathers.

Our original honeymoon to Italy had to be postponed and so instead, Paul organised a stay in Whitby, one of my favourite places in the world on account of it being beautiful, but also because it was where Bram Stoker got inspired to write *Dracula* and where the 1990s television series *Heartbeat* was often filmed.

We also stopped off in Thirsk, another favourite place of mine, where the author and veterinarian James Herriot (AKA, Alf Wight) lived and worked.

I took a photo of Paul outside the front door of The World of James Herriot, a museum housed in the building in which Mr Herriot used to practice. I did this as I thought it was a nice quirk of circumstance that as a child, I devoured the adventures of James Herriot and his wife. And now all these years later, I'm a vet's wife and we get to have animal adventures all of our own!

James Herriot is one of my favourite authors. I first discovered his books when rooting through a box in a charity shop in Winchester, when my dad and I were on one of our weekend adventures.

I couldn't believe my luck when I pulled a gorgeous hardback from the box of dog-eared and tea-stained paperbacks. Nor could I understand why anyone would want to part with it. To my mind, giving books away is akin to tying a dog to a lamppost and walking off. Ergo, it isn't right and shouldn't be allowed.

The cover was adorned with lovely ink drawings of animals, and I knew I had to have it. I'd never heard of this James Herriot, but suddenly I wanted to know all about him.

On the way home, I read bits of the story out to my dad, and I had the book finished within a week.

As a result of those stories, I wanted to be a vet myself, but for numerous reasons (not being able to do numbers, chief among them), I had to pursue other interests.

Despite this, when I worked as a newspaper reporter in Yorkshire, I volunteered at The World of James Herriot and met his children, the wonderful Jim and Rosie, via The Friends of James Herriot Fan Club.

That my career as a journalist would mean I would end up working in the veterinary sphere too, albeit on the fringes, was a nice touch. But I would have hardly believed that my job as a veterinary reporter would, in turn, lead me to meet my future husband. A beautiful bit of serendipity.

I'm pulled from my thoughts by the revving of engines as everyone on the passenger ferry starts to disembark.

When Paul and I checked in, the sweet lady on the desk clocked the *Just Married* banner and gave us priority passes, meaning we were at the front of the queue to get off, and begin our new chapter as 'Mr and Mrs.' We were very grateful for this act of kindness, as it had been a long day, for Paul especially, as he'd done all the driving.

'It will be nice to get to your house,' I yawn as we venture into the night.

'It will be nice to get to *our* house.'

'Oh yes,' I say, the penny taking a moment to drop. 'You're my husband now,' I grin, waving my wedding ring at him. 'It's official. No getting out of it.'

He smiles. 'And we've got the certificate to prove it.'

Rectangles of light emanate from the upper windows of houses as we pass through town; thousands of people are already tucked up in their homes for the night.

It's strange seeing the area in the dark and knowing that on this occasion, I don't have to be thinking about returning home after the weekend. This is my home now. I shiver with nerves and excitement.

'Don't go backwards,' I squeal an hour later as Paul lifts me up to carry me over the threshold. 'And be careful you don't hurt your back.'

We giggle as he puts me down and I take a moment to look around our house.

'I can't believe we can stay here tonight,' I gasp, taking in the scene.

Paul has been building his own house for many years and it has only recently been completed. But I didn't know it would be in a fit state for us to begin our married life when we returned from honeymoon. Indeed, I thought we'd be staying at my mummy-in-law's for a few months.

But unbeknownst to me, workmen had been in the house around the clock for weeks. So, while we were tucking into fish and chips and ice cream in Whitby, they'd been working hard so we had running water and electricity when we got back.

Mummy-In-Law takes a photo of us and then says goodnight. Mind you, she hasn't got far to go, as her house is opposite ours. Paul's mum and dad also moved into their house straight after their honeymoon, which was more than forty years ago. I squeeze her hand, wishing her beloved husband were here too, but I don't say anything. I don't need to.

I loved being carried over the threshold, but it was a surreal moment because I didn't think I'd ever be anyone's wife. So I'm amazed, proud and confused all at once.

As we unpack, I have a little moment. I miss my parents even more than usual and I suddenly feel every one of the five hundred miles between us.

I have no deep-rooted history here, and no idea where I am geographically (my GCSE in geography isn't going to help me out with this one).

My friends and family are in a different county, despite me still being in the United Kingdom. I can't just jump in the car and be in my parents' kitchen enjoying a cuppa in fifteen minutes. It dawns on me that future visits are going to require a lot of planning. Suddenly, the wind seems even colder, and the sky extra dark.

I shake off the fear. I don't have anything to be afraid of.

I have Paul and we are a team, a starter kit family. I can combine my roots with his and we will make new memories.

But it doesn't stop me from wishing my parents lived just around the corner. Still, I've lived away from home before, so it's not like that's something new to get my head around.

I bring in some suitcases and then go back for an extra bag I tucked under my seat.

Back in our room, I pop it on the bed and smile as I open it. A pair of high heels glisten inside; my journalist shoes which I wear for interviews. They cost a fortune but are so smart and comfortable and when I put them on, I walk taller and look confident, even if I don't feel it.

Nestled next to them is my 'reporters kit,' consisting of my Dictaphone, shorthand notebook and pen, as I fully intend to become a freelance reporter in this new chapter of my life. Writing is my passion, and so I've bought the basics with me.

I've also managed to squeeze in a pair of new Wellington boots (complete with fake diamonds, well, I wanted to bring a bit of bling to the yard). I step back and look at the contents: my old life juxtaposed with the new.

Then I hear the cattle calling and the sheep bleating, so I pull out the boots and close the bag. My new life and my new role beckons.

4. Every day's a Holly-Day

I t takes a while to realise where I am when I open my eyes.

I frown at the unfamiliar ceiling and the silence which wraps itself around me like a blanket. Then I recount the last few days. No, I'm not dreaming. I really did marry the love of my life and I am here, in our house, all safe and warm. I smile like I have a boomerang in my mouth.

Softly and gently, birdsong floats through the open window on a sea-salt breeze.

I would like to say I stirred gently and greeted the day with a smile and a swish of my long, glossy locks like a Disney princess, but that would be a lie.

In truth, I fall out of bed, run a hand haphazardly through my knotted hair and retrieved the alarm clock from the bin, which is where it landed after I threw it across the room. I then open the curtains to find a cow pressed up against the window. I squeal, totter backwards and fall onto the bed in a crumpled heap.

'Ah I see you've met the neighbour,' Paul says, coming in with a cup of tea in my new *wifey* mug.

I smile weakly, sit up, take a glug and then proffer it to the cow. 'Would you like a cup?'

'I think she'd prefer her breakfast. The farmer will be along in a minute to feed her and her friends.'

'What will she have?' I ask innocently. 'How about corn flakes? She could provide her own milk, couldn't she?'

He laughs. 'Not quite. She'll have meal. And cows don't drink their own milk. It's meant for their calves. She'll just stick to water'

'Oh, I see.' It seems I have got a lot to learn.

I turn and look back at the cow who is continuing to impersonate a window sticker.

'She's beautiful,' I whisper, admiring her big brown eyes, long eyelashes and black and white markings which run over and across her back, intricate and detailed, like a map.

I want to reach out and trace the patterns with my fingers. I imagine the feel of her warm skin and wonder if following the markings would reveal her journey, or perhaps kick up memories like dust? Would I learn about her ancestors, meet the humans who cared for them and unpick how they saw the world?

Paul leaves to feed our animals and my window sticker friend takes her leave, presumably to find her breakfast.

As I admire the stunning scenery, I suddenly get the excited feeling I used to get when I was on holiday with my parents. Do you know the sort I mean?

When you wake up on the first day of your holiday and hear seagulls tap-tapping their little feet on the roof, and you realise with a smile, that you're not at home, but somewhere new and, even more exciting than that, is the fact that you are there for a week!

Seven days of eating in cafés, exploring shops and buying trinkets. Seven days of chatting to the locals, writing postcards on the beach, getting sand between your toes, exploring rock pools and enjoying an ice cream or three. In short, being as happy as a seagull with a chip.

Back in our room, and for the tenth time in twenty-four hours, my brain reminds me that I'm not on holiday. Yes, I'm somewhere new and there *are* exciting, unplanned days ahead, but I'm not on holiday. This is a difficult concept for me to get my head around, especially given the view from our window.

Sunlight dances along patches of green and yellow grass; fields stretch out as far as the eye can see, each peppered with cows and sheep who are busy eating, which reminds me how hungry I am. Indeed, breakfast sounds like a good idea. Then I'll explore my new surroundings and get some more of that sunshine on my skin.

5. Tuning into a new life

People have commented on how quickly I've settled into my new life in Northern Ireland.

'You just take it in your stride,' they say with admiring looks. 'Sure, it feels like you've always been here.'

And that's lovely of them to say, but I didn't really have a choice, because Paul, the man I love, lives here.

Now, I'm not going to pretend that I wouldn't rather he lived just around the corner from my parents, because I miss them like mad. But seeing as we would've struggled to fit 200 sheep onto an easyJet flight (and they wouldn't have liked the in-flight meal options anyway), I had little choice but to up sticks and move country.

As I'm always saying, 'I'd rather be with him in his world than without him in mine.' Oh no, wait. That was Gladys Knight and The Pips. Yes, they said that. But you get the idea.

6. Milking it

I 've just been told that while Friesian (black and white) cows give white milk, brown cows give chocolate milk and red cows give strawberry. I believed this for longer than I should have. But just in case there is any doubt, this is not true. Do not repeat this lie, this propaganda. Although it would be great, wouldn't it?

7. The regeneration game

I stand looking down on a chess board of fields, squares of dark green and butter yellow.

Tractors in poster paint shades of red and blue sweep around in circles, before positioning themselves on opposite sides of the field and turning to face each other. Then, they race forwards like jousting knights, only to curve away at the last minute, causing the corn to tremble as they pass.

The surrounding fields are quiet now, but yesterday they were full of noise and activity, as tractors and balers drove up and down, packing the grass into squat, cylindrical parcels which are wrapped in black plastic. To me, it seems as if the grass has been cocooned and, like a butterfly, will burst forth in winter, having transformed into silage to feed hungry herds.

8. Flocky road

'The problem with sheep,' the farmer says, getting himself comfortable by leaning against the gate, 'is they're always finding new and exciting ways to die.'

I don't know what to say and so stay silent, which has to be a first.

'Take that girl over there,' he says, pointing to where Paul is tending to a sheep, 'She's been dithering over whether she's going to live or die for days now. Sure, I wish she'd make up her little woolly head about it all.'

I look across the field to where the patient is sitting on her bottom, her spindly legs sticking out in front of her. She wriggles as Paul struggles to keep her still while he jags (injects) her. From where I'm standing, she looks determined to live, which is good.

Paul walks slowly back up the field towards us, smiling

as he does. I always feel such pride when I see him at work and marvel at all the veterinary knowledge in his head.

When people say, 'Ah, you must be the vet's wife,' I almost burst with pride. In fact, I like the sound of it so much, I think I'll get it printed on a T-shirt.

9. Ballerina dreams

Sadly, I never realised my dream of being a ballerina. Mainly because I have all the grace of a fairy elephant. And I'm short. (I'm sure there are short ballerinas out there, but I was never going to be one of them.)

Yet this morning, the sheep tried to help me achieve my ambition, which was very sweet of them.

I had made my way into the sheep shed to check that they all had enough food and water. But instead of opening the gate and walking through, I decided to climb over, which turned out to be a mistake.

I clambered over the gate and placed one foot on the ground, which was good progress. But as I swung my other leg over, the sheep surged forward and so were suddenly right where I wanted to be. Not wanting to hit them over the head with my foot, I clung onto the fence as if it were a barre in a dance studio and kept still.

I believe barre work is great for the core and can improve strength and balance. And I would be more than happy to work on these things during a studio workout, but perhaps not in a shed while wearing my farm clothes.

Sadly, the sheep showed no sign of moving, so I was stuck in my ballerina pose until they got bored and shuffled off, giving me enough space to put my leg down.

'Thanks, guys,' I said, patting their woolly heads as I walked through the shed. 'Great workout.'

In addition to checking food and water levels, I can also, if needed, 'bed up,' by which I mean I can throw more straw into the pens.

One of my biggest worries is that they won't be warm enough on cold days or overnight, despite the fact they're covered in thick wool. (I sunk my fingers into a ewe's fleece once and was almost up to my knuckle in wool before I reached her body. I was surprised at how dense it was, but I suppose that is what keeps them nice and warm. Sheep look big but their bodies are quite small, it's all the wool that makes them look sturdy.)

Being a 'townie,' I'm all for bringing them in at night and tucking them up by the fire, or at least putting them in pyjamas. But Paul reassures me that they're perfectly alright in the barn, which is the equivalent of us checking into a luxury hotel, and besides, it's only temporary.

Usually, sheep are more than happy living in fields and sheltering under bushes if the rain gets too heavy, but mostly they're not bothered by it. They're hardy creatures and have everything they need to survive and thrive.

I'm also conscious of the fact that Paul is taking something of a risk by letting me loose among his treasured sheep. I hate responsibility of any kind and it makes me feel sick. I'm certainly not a managerial person. I know my place in life; I'm a follower, not a leader.

Another of my new jobs is to conduct basic sheep checks (Unofficial Farm Assistant Qualification Level One). That is, to ensure all four feet are pointing down and both ears are pointing up. Or to put it another way, to check they're not dead. Even I could spot a dead sheep. I think.

In addition, if a water bucket is empty, I fill it, and if a hayrack is out of hay, I replenish it. I've got this.

Once the ewes in the shed have been checked, I make my way to see those who live on the hill. To get to them, I must walk through a lovely orchard, which is always a treat. The air is sweet with the smell of apples and mint, which grows in abundance around the trees and the long grass is full of pretty little pink flowers which sway in the breeze, making it look as if they are waving in greeting.

I clamber over a gate and make my way up the steep incline. By the time I get to the top, my legs are burning, but on the plus side, I get the feeling I won't have to join a gym any time soon, as this outdoor life will be workout enough.

'Morning, girls.' The ewes, who are standing in a bunch and munching grass, look up momentarily, but as I don't have a bucket of nuts on me, they're not interested and go back to munching.

Checks complete, I pick my way carefully down the hill, as I am a little unsteady on the uneven terrain. I stop to get my balance, look up and catch my breath; the view is stunning. Straight ahead I can see the lough and beyond that, the blue-grey sea which stretches out until it kisses the deep blue sky. The picture is framed by a dramatic coastline of jagged cliffs and sweeping hills.

A mist hangs over one of the rock formations, which looks like a basking dragon. The long, curved section is his body, while the thin edge at the end looks like his head which is dipping towards the sea, as if he is about to take a drink.

The two smaller formations next to him look like smaller dragons. A whole family! Maybe they come alive when the town sleeps and take to the starlit skies to enjoy many adventures together, before returning as the sun rises and becoming part of the landscape once again. No wonder Northern Ireland and Ireland are built on legends and soaked in stories. The stunning scenery certainly stirs the imagination, bringing to mind mythical creatures and heroes intent on undertaking acts of derring-do.

Further on, the mist becomes thicker, casting shadows on the hills and rocks below. This only serves to make the scene even more mysterious and intriguing. I want to explore the hollows and follow in the footsteps of the ancient people who would have walked these parts, sowing stories and traditions as easily as crops.

The sound of the sheep in the yard shakes me from my thoughts and reminds me that they still need their breakfast, as does my lovely husband. I have a family to feed! I grin at the thought and make my way to the house. I will have to explore another day.

Later, I unpack some more of my belongings. Chief among them is my wedding dress, which I've bought with me in the hope that one day, we'll be able to have a blessing in the local church so that Paul's family and friends can celebrate with us. We hoped this might occur around our second anniversary, but the way this Covid-19 pandemic is taking hold, it may end up being our golden wedding anniversary.

But beggars can't be choosers.

I take the dress out of the bag and admire it, lovingly touching the beautiful folds of soft material. I can't believe I'm a married woman! I'm so lucky to have met Paul and that my parents were there to see me marry him.

Married women often tell the bride-to-be to enjoy every moment of their 'big day' because it goes so fast, but because we only had the ceremony (receptions in hotels were banned), it went doubly quick!

Oddly, for someone who worries about everything from the moment I get up until the second I shut my eyes (and then have nightmares), I didn't feel nervous at all on my wedding day. Part of me couldn't believe it was actually happening and I didn't want to get too excited, just in case Boris Johnson popped out of a wardrobe at the eleventh hour to say the rules had changed and we couldn't tie the knot after all.

It wasn't until I was actually standing outside the church with my dad and the bridal party that it actually began to sink in. My future husband was standing inside the church and I would soon be walking towards him. It was the best moment of my life, seeing Paul waiting for me at the top of the aisle. We both had tears in our eyes as I made my way to him. And I didn't fall flat on my face, either, which was a bonus and there was much rejoicing!

I carefully put the dress, which had done its job of making me feel like a princess, back in the wardrobe, hoping to wear it again at our reception, one day.

10. Wedding dress stress

Finding my dream wedding dress was easy. My parents and I visited one shop and the third gown I put on proved to be 'the one'. However, I did try on a fourth, a beautiful princess-style garment with a huge skirt and layers of frills and sequins, because that's what every little girl dreams about when playing weddings.

But because I'm short, the princess dress unfortunately just made me look like a 1970s toilet-roll holder. Still, it was nice to try it on.

The dress I picked was a gorgeous mix of medieval, Spanish and Grecian designs with a hint of 1920s glamour. The shapely dress was given a feminine and pretty twist via a pale pink outer skirt, which added an element of the princess dress I mentioned earlier. OK, so the description isn't really doing it justice, but trust me when I say, it was exquisite.

As I made my way out of the changing room, my dad, who isn't one for great shows of emotion, said, 'well, you aren't going to beat that, are you?' And that was how I knew it was the one for me.

'I must admit, I had a little cry when I saw you in it,' Mum confessed on the way out of the shop.

'I cried too,' Dad added, 'when I saw how much it cost.'

The only thing we wanted to add was sleeves, and seeing as we had to go to a tailor to get the dress fitted anyway, it didn't seem too much of a liberty to ask.

The tailor was talented and accommodating and all our appointments went swimmingly. Then Covid-19 reared its head, and my neatly plotted timeline went down the swanny, taking our dreams of a May wedding with it.

My dress was put back on its peg, and my beautiful white shoes were placed in their box and stored in a wardrobe. Everything seemed to go into hibernation, and we waited impatiently for hope to melt the fear and awaken our plans once again.

Six months after we'd initially seen the tailor, Mum and I were back with a new wedding date and plenty of enthusiasm.

The tailor looked me up and down, her eyes narrowed with suspicion, before whipping out her tape measure and wrapping it around my waist.

'Jesus, Mary and Joseph, you've lost so much weight,' she cried. 'Zara, get the pins, we're going to have to pull an all-nighter to get this done.'

I don't think they *did* work through the night, but such was the dynamic duo's dedication that I think they would have done had the occasion called for it. In fact, they said they could have the dress back to me within twenty-four hours if needed. They were truly amazing, but in the event, they actually had about two weeks to make the adjustments and the result was stunning.

I hadn't deliberately been trying to lose weight; however, I did do an awful lot of worrying, which was probably a contributing factor. But the main cause was due to all the farm work I was doing, which got me sweating far more than a gym workout ever did. From carrying feed bags and filling wheelbarrows with manure to lifting lambs and turning sheep, I was doing it all and enjoying every second. So, it wasn't long before I felt fitter than ever and had dropped a few dress sizes into the bargain.

When I tried the wedding dress on at the final fitting and saw myself in the mirror, I gasped. Not just because the elegant woman in the stunning gown didn't look like me, but because I was a bride-to-be, a role I never expected. I could hardly believe I'd found someone who wanted to marry me, who loved me just as I was and who didn't expect me to be some kind of performing seal.

When the ladies fluffed out the skirt and arranged the train, I had to hold back the tears. I turned and whispered, 'I scrub up alright, don't I?'

My friend Anna was the only one who got anywhere close to guessing what my wedding dress would look like. Hetty thought I'd go for the princess style and Ben said it would be some sort of Jane Austen getup. Hilariously, Liz, one of my oldest friends, thought I was going to rock up in a 1960s minidress because of my love for the television show *Heartbeat,* which is set in that era. A lovely thought, but no.

Liz still hasn't forgiven me for the time I took her on a *Heartbeat*-themed coach trip when we were eighteen, or, as she describes it, 'the longest three days of my life.' Now, I only have to say the word Yorkshire and she goes off on one. 'I'd have had more fun cleaning a drain out with my tongue. In fact, I'd have preferred it.' Well, that's gratitude for you.

We were teenagers and Liz was longing to get away for some nightlife and adventure. She wanted a trip to Ibiza where she could drink an obscene amount of alcohol, swim in a warm pool, stay in a posh hotel, dance until dawn and flirt with a lot of hot men.

What she *got* was a wet weekend in Whitby, three nights in a B&B, fish and chips wrapped in newspaper and a big cup of cocoa before bed at 9pm. Her fatal error, of course, was leaving me to make the arrangements.

So instead of boarding a cheap flight where she could drink her own bodyweight in vodka before we were even airborne, Liz found herself staggering up the steps of a coach, at 5am on a drizzly Friday in August, to learn that we were the youngest holidaymakers by about one thousand years. I had a great time. Liz, not so much,

'I got us a great deal,' I explained as we searched for our seats, 'just think, if we'd gone to Ibiza, we'd probably have spent all our money on duty-free before we got anywhere near the plane, but we don't have that problem now. Also,' I continued, despite the fact Liz was giving me daggers, 'there are lots of excursions included in the price, so it's educational *and* economical.'

The trip was really meant for fans of *Heartbeat*, which I may have forgotten to mention to Liz until we were on the coach. 'You've got to be joking,' she spat as she eyeballed the itinerary, which included the words 'museums' and 'tea rooms.'

Then she turned her gaze on me. 'I've been up since 3am, have paid £100 for the privilege and now I discover we have to visit,' she glared down at the list of activities, 'the *Heartbeat* museum?'

I grinned.

'I hate you,' she whispered as she pulled her coat over her head. 'Don't speak to me until we get to Yorkshire or wherever it is we're going. And don't wake me up unless it's for alcohol or food. I mean it. You're on thin ice, lady.'

Three hours later, deep in the Yorkshire countryside, the coach slowed to a stop outside a remote house with a neat front garden and sheep mooching in the background, which caused a ripple of excitement among the passengers. Liz awoke with a jump. 'Whaisit?' she mumbled, wiping her eyes, blearily. 'Is the coach on fire? I do hope so.'

'No,' I squealed, pointing out of the window. 'Look.' She looked. 'What? Is it a celebrity or something?' she enquired, craning her neck to get a better view.

'Better than that, my love,' one of the passengers said as she passed us, waving her camera excitedly. 'Come and see.'

We all piled off the coach and gathered on a grass verge, wrapping our coats around us against the blustery day. 'What are we looking at?' Liz asked, getting increasingly annoyed.

'It's *the* house,' camera lady whispered, her eyes as wide as saucers.

'Good,' Liz said, nodding her head philosophically. 'What house?'

'*The* house', camera lady repeated, as if emphasising 'the' would ram her point home. 'Don't you watch *Heartbeat*?'

Before Liz could say she'd rather walk across broken glass than endure a single episode (her words) camera lady continued, 'it's *the* house.' She grinned at Liz who stared at her blankly. 'Where Nick and Kate lived… *the* police house… the actual place where they filmed. And look,' she said, pointing in wonder, 'it's *the* blue door.'

I, too, was extremely excited by the iconic blue door and asked Liz to take a photo of me next to it.

'Do you want me to take a photo of you both?' camera lady asked.

'No,' Liz said at the same time as I chirped, 'yes please.'

'Come on,' I said, putting my arm around her. 'Smile, you're on holiday.'

'I'm in hell,' she said through gritted teeth. 'I'm standing in the middle of nowhere with a load of *Heartbeat* nuts, probably about to get arrested for trespassing outside some poor sod's house at ridiculous o'clock in the morning. *And* I'm freezing my tits off, all for the sake of some bloody blue door, the relevance of which, by the way, is still lost on me.'

Back on the coach, Liz threw her jacket over her head at the same time as the tour guide put a *Heartbeat* CD on full blast and everyone started singing. Except one, of course.

'Kill me now,' Liz muttered.

While she tried to pretend she was somewhere, anywhere, else, I looked again at the itinerary and smiled. Whitby was hosting a regatta, and I knew Liz would love the atmosphere and the fact our accommodation was right on the seafront.

There would be lots of time to explore the shops and beaches and, despite the fact she would moan the whole way, I knew Liz would love clambering the 199 steps to Whitby Abbey. All in all, I felt sure she was going to have a great time. And as it turns out, she did.

But I'm still banned from booking holidays, even to this day.

11. Keeping an eye on ewe

Today, Paul took me on a tour of the farm which made me feel like a royal visitor. We walked about the pens and fields arm in arm, waving at the ewes who gathered at the fences to have a good look at the new member of staff (I'm sure that's how they see us!)

They always surge forward to greet Paul anyway, but this was the first time I'd met them as First Lady!

'Can you understand her?' I imagine one saying to the other.

'No, I cannot, indeed.'

'Sure, she sounds funny.'

'Aye. I think she's from England.'

'And you know rightly, that lot are a funny old breed.'

12. Lambs, lambs everywhere...

I f it were possible to go mining for sheep, then Paul and I would be very rich right now.

The reason I say this is because lambs are springing forth everywhere. So much so that it feels like we have hit a sheep seam!

Lambs are landing in fields, dropping into piles of straw and appearing in barns quicker than I can count. I'm almost scared to lift the toilet seat lid in case a lamb pops out, and I've taken to checking under the bed to make sure we haven't got any stowaways.

The honeymoon is well and truly over. No, I mean it literally is over; the end of our holiday coincided with the start of lambing and so it's all handson deck. Anyone would've thought Paul planned it that way.

I don't know if I'm coming or going and have no idea where to run first, especially as I'm still getting used to living on the farm.

Now I know how my dad felt all those years ago when my mum was in hospital and I arrived early. He didn't know which way to run, either. Mind you, there was only one child in that scenario. We've got sixty and counting. Oh, hang on, wait...make that sixty-one.

13. Ewe, me and them

I'm in awe at how quickly lambs are up on their feet after being born. But then again, I suppose if they didn't, they'd end up inside a fox.

I wouldn't mind having children if they grew as fast as lambs or calves. Heck, we could have a few minutes of cooing over them as babies, then they'd be toddlers, into everything and stumbling about in that cute way they have. Then, about three months later, they'd finish school and be ready to join the working world, at which point they could start bringing in some rent. Lovely!

14. Order, order

I feel like a waitress in a sheep café.

'One bucket of silage, one bucket of water, four scoops of nuts and a special,' I shout from the middle of the sheep shed. Paul, who is stationed at the far end where the food bags are piled high, counts out scoops of food using a silver dish, the contents of which is poured into an assortment of buckets set at his feet.

The special is for the cute ewe in the far pen who can't eat the big nuts due to teeth issues, and so has a serving of smaller pellets which she finds easier to chew.

I'm having to bellow to be heard over sheep who are bleating very loudly.

Honestly, the way they perform, you'd think they were poor, starved creatures who never get anything to eat, when in fact, they're spoilt rotten.

During lambing season, most of the sheep shed is divided up into individual pens made of wooden or metal hurdles. These little units, equipped with straw, food and water, provide a safe space for ewes and their new lambs to rest and bond in relative peace. Temporarily separating them from the rest of the flock also reduces the risk of the lamb getting accidentally clattered (a Northern Irish terms meaning to fall or be knocked over) by the older sheep.

We build the pens around the perimeter of the shed and leave enough room in the middle for a big straw bed which expectant ewes can lounge on.

With a bucket in one hand and a scoop in the other, I set off on my rounds.

The bleating gets louder and more incessant as I approach the ewes. 'Yes, my loves, I'm going as quickly as I can,' I soothe. They eye me suspiciously as I lean over and pour their supper out, as if it's a trap, but as soon as I retreat, they dash forward and tuck in.

The more pens I visit, the quieter the shed becomes until there is relative quiet, save for the sound of munching.

I love being in the sheep shed, especially when it's piled high with lambs. The air is thick with the sweet smell of silage (dried hay) sheep nuts, straw and wool. The lambs, some of whom are only a few hours old, have already found their voices and are giving a few experimental bleats which float up to the rafters, creating a joyful cacophony of sound.

Twins and triplets will often pile on top of each other to sleep, while singles snuggle up to their mums. But, just like human children, they will do their best to fight sleep, even when they're clearly exhausted. I watch in wonder as their eyelids grow heavy with sleep and their little heads dip as they try to try to stay awake, their warm breath making pretty patterns in the frosty air.

With everyone tucked in, Paul and I bid the sheep sweet dreams, turn out the light and go home.

15. Thermometers

It's the height of the Covid-19 pandemic and people are buying thermometers as if they're going out of fashion. So much so that thus far, I've failed to lay my hands on one.

This morning I awoke with a cracking headache and, ever the drama queen, am worried I've caught the virus.

'Should we try and buy a thermometer today?' I ask Paul over breakfast as I write out our shopping list.

'No, I've got one you can use.'

'Oh, great. Where is it?'

'In the shed.'

'Why isn't it in the first aid box?'

He looks up. 'I keep them out there so I can get to them quickly.'

'Hang on, are those the ones you use to take the lambs' temperatures?' I ask, suspiciously.

'Yes.'

'And don't you take their temperature by sticking the thermometer up their ars...'

'In their rectum, yes,' he says, unblinking.

'Um, I'm OK thanks,' I say, pushing my breakfast away and pulling the shopping list towards me, on which I hastily write 'thermometer.'

16. Whatcha doing?

I find Paul's job as a vet and farmer fascinating. So much so that I keep asking questions, which I'm sure isn't annoying at all.

'What are you doing?' I ask, appearing by his side in the sheep shed. 'Feeding the lambs,' he says, dipping into a bag of milk mix and whisking up a storm.

'And now?' I say, popping my head around his shoulder to peer into the field. 'Feeding the sheep,' he replies at the same time as surveying his flock.

'How about now?' I enquire, peering over the fence in the small barn. 'Inspecting the ewe's hooves to make sure they're clean.'

'Whatcha doing now?' I ask on entering the big barn later that day.

'Helping Margaret to perform a vasectomy on this ram.'

'Hi, Margaret.' I smile and wave, although I'm not sure why, as it's abundantly clear that she's in no position to wave back, her hands being somewhat full, but she smiles, nonetheless.

Margaret is a friend of ours and a veterinarian who is an expert in her field. As such, she often comes to the farm to perform such procedures.

The ram looks spaced out (not a technical term). He's sedated and under local anaesthetic, so can't feel any pain. ('I should bloody hope he has been sedated too,' my dad exclaims when I tell him about the op. 'I'd want more than a shot of anaesthetic if someone was messing about with my gonads too, the poor *sod*.')

Back in the barn, and in a bid to make conversation, I ask Paul, 'So, are you having a good day?'

'Yes,' he replies, as Margaret casually places a suture in the ram's scrotum as if it's the most normal thing in the world. Paul looks at the ram and blinks. Then after a few seconds, adds, 'Well, I'm having a better day than this guy, anyway.'

A good point well made.

'Why were you castrating that ram-lamb?' I ask later as I help Paul clear away his instruments (or tools, as I incorrectly call them.)

'Vasectomising him, dear, because I'm going to keep him as a teaser.'

'A what?'

'A teaser. He's a nice enough ram-lamb, but I don't want to breed from him, so we give him the snip so he can't reproduce, and it will be his job to help get the ewes in season, but obviously he won't be able to get them pregnant.'

'He'll be exhausted,' I gasp, thinking of the number of ewes we have.

'Yes, but happy,' Paul smiles. 'Then we take him out and put the ram in, who will mate with the ewes and hopefully produce good stock.'

I nod, but don't really understand.

'And that's called a teaser?'

'Yes.'

'In that case, can his first name be Malt?'

17. Have you treated one of those?

I love animals, which is good, as I used to write for a magazine for veterinarians, and Paul is a farmer and a vet, so we get to talk about them a lot.

One of my favourite lines of questioning is asking Paul about all the animals he's treated over the years. I love hearing about his jobs, from working in high street practices to operating theatres in universities across the UK and abroad.

So, whether we're careering around the Hertfordshire countryside of my childhood, or exploring country roads in Northern Ireland and I spot animals, I press on with my questions.

If, for example, we pass a field full of Belted Galloway (Scottish cattle), I will ask: 'Ever treated one of those?'

'No, I don't think so. I do love them, though.' I make a mental note to find a Belted Galloway print for his Christmas present.

Today, we zipped past a field packed with pigs. I give it a second and try to resist the temptation to ask, but fail. 'Ever treated pigs?'

He blinks. 'A few. Though not as many as farm vets, obviously.'

As we flicked through the television channels later on, we found a programme on ferrets.

'Ever had to make one of those better?'

'The odd one.'

'How about the even ones?' I ask, innocently.

Then, as I was flipping through a magazine, I saw an article about cheetahs. Aha! He can't possibly have seen any of these in high street practice!

'I have, actually,' Paul says, rather proudly.

'How and when?'

'I was working in London as an anaesthetist when we were called to treat one.'

Amazing.

While we are driving in the car later on, a woman on the radio is talking about the joy of keeping chickens. I turn to look at Paul and before I can even ask, he says, 'Yup. Many of them. They're popular companion animals on account of being able to provide eggs and companionship.'

I consider this, then after a while ask, 'Have you ever treated the male equivalents? I bet that was difficult. I've heard they're a right load of cocks.' I laugh at my own joke and then watch the tumbleweed slowly drift by.

'How about werewolves?' I ask, keen to fill the silence, 'Ever treated one of those?'

'Oh yes,' Paul replies and then, without missing a beat, 'but only during night shifts, obviously.'

He's getting good, ain't he?

18. Come in, Number Six

'**N**umber six, is that you?'

I'm looking at the rams in the field near our house. They are big, strong, strapping lads. But it's the one in the middle that I can't stop staring at. He's stocky with lovely, thick creamy wool and a handsome face with a strong nose and deep-set eyes.

Yes, I admit it, I'm besotted with Number Six, but not just because he's a lovely-looking ram. The main reason is because he was the first lamb I ever delivered. The gorgeous woolly wonder landed in our lives (and in my arms) last year.

Somehow, I managed to help bring him into the world and for that reason, he'll always be special to me.

Have you ever seen a film where one of the characters has a flashback, and the screen goes wobbly to indicate the fact the timeline is changing? Right, well, we haven't got the budget for that, so you're just going to have to use your imagination for the next bit (wobble, wobble) here we go...

I'm with Paul for a post-Christmas visit and we are having a lovely time. We've had our pseudo-Christmas lunch and have swapped gifts, although I did tell Paul not to worry about presents because, as I conveyed during one of our phone conversations, 'all I want for Christmas is ewe.' Anyway, moving on...

Dorset sheep are unique in the fact that they can lamb at pretty much any time during the farming calendar, which explains why Paul was up to his ears in lambs at the time of my visit.

Incidentally, if I had a pound for every time one of my friends exclaimed, 'I didn't know that,' when I shared this fact, I could buy a mansion in the Bahamas. (Although to be fair, I didn't know sheep could lamb outside of spring either, until Paul told me. But I know now, so am claiming full smug points. Thank you.)

Anyway, as I was saying, Paul and I were on sheep patrol on this particular night and it was freezing. I was wrapped up well against the elements, with a hat rammed down to my eyebrows and a scarf pulled up over my nose, meaning only me eyes were visible.

As we neared the end of our inspection, I made the silly mistake of thinking we'd gotten away with it, and that we could return to the house without having to help any ewes give birth. After all, everyone seemed calm and content. But as we approached the last pen my heart sank, as it became quite clear that the ewe was very much in the throes of labour and would, indeed, need assistance.

Now, I'm the sort of person who can't help but shout '*sheep*' when I see them in a field, especially on car journeys, much to the annoyance and surprise of anyone unfortunate enough to be travelling with me.

But stating the obvious while happily hurtling past them in the car was about as far as my involvement went. Indeed, I could've written everything I knew about sheep and lambs on the heels of a caterpillar's boot. And in case you were wondering, the list would have looked something like this:

- They have four legs
- They go 'baa'
- They are cute
- I want some as pets

And, as a desk-dwelling journalist, I was of the firm opinion that I'd never have cause to acquire any more knowledge than that.

When I met Paul, my life changed for the better in a host of ways, and I soon discovered a range of sheep skills I never knew I had. Learning opportunities seemed to present themselves with rather frightening regularity, and that night was no exception.

I looked on in bemused amazement as Paul swung into action. He clambered into the pen and approached the ewe slowly and quietly, 'I just want to have a little look and see how far along you are, pet,' he explained.

The ewe knew Paul of old, and as such was easy to handle and didn't take much persuading to lay down, at which point he went about examining her. His face was etched with concentration as he tried to ascertain the position of the lamb.

'Could you get me some gloves, please?'

'Of course,' I replied, my heart thumping in my chest as I dashed off to get them. I returned a few minutes later and handed them over.

While he put them on, I turned my attention back to the ewe and noticed she'd been marked with a blue spot, meaning she was expecting a single lamb. Ewes with red spots were expecting twins, while those with two red spots were carrying triplets – good luck with that, then!

'Right,' Paul said, 'I've found a foot.'

'Just a foot? That doesn't sound good.'

'No,' he said, trying not to smile. 'The foot's attached to the lamb.'

'Oh good.'

Patience has never been my strong suit, which is unfortunate, as there's often no telling how long these things will take.

'What's happening now?'

'Well, the lamb's facing the right way, which is good.'

'And which way is that?'

'Front feet first.'

I nodded and started pacing up and down, as if I were an expectant parent who'd been banished to the corridor for getting under the feet of the midwife.

'Go and have a chat with her,' Paul said, nodding to the ewe, 'it will help keep her calm.'

'OK,' I said, happy to be given something constructive to do, even though the ewe was as cool as the proverbial cucumber. But I sat next to her anyway and stroked her nose while offering words of comfort. She looked up at me and let out the occasional bleat, which was perfectly under-standable in the circumstances, but very reserved.

Then she started panting and I found myself panting with her. I clutched her hoof and gave it a little squeeze. As her bleats got louder and longer, I gritted my teeth and shut my eyes. She was being brave. I, on the other hand, was being a complete wuss. After a few minutes, I turned to see what was happening down at the other end, hoping against hope that I wouldn't faint.

Ever so gently, Paul eased out a set of hooves, which looked like a tricky and slippery task, as they were covered in a thin film of red slime. The hooves were followed by a spindly pair of legs. There was a pause and then the ridge of a little nose appeared. I cringed as the head and neck slowly emerged, but as soon as they were out, the rest of the lamb quickly followed. It's shoulders, body and back-legs shot past me in a blur of blood and liquid.

The lamb landed on the straw and was still. My heart plummeted.

Paul ran his hand along its mouth and nose, to get rid of the gunk (I think 'clearing the airways' is the proper term) but there was still no movement. Next, he grabbed a piece of straw which he rubbed along its nose. I held my breath.

The lamb gave a sudden jolt, shook its head vehemently

and let out the loudest and cutest sneeze I'd ever heard. The movement caused its ears, which had been flat against its head, to 'pop out' like flaps in a picture book.

'Well done,' I said, giving the ewe a kiss on the nose. 'You're a clever girl.'

'There you are,' Paul said as he scooped the lamb up, 'go and see Mum.' Before he nestled it next to her, he had a quick look underneath and smiled. 'It's a girl.'

'A girl,' I echoed as I turned to address the new mother. 'Congratulations.'

The ewe sniffed her lamb excitedly and started licking her clean.

'And congratulations to you,' I said, looking at Paul. 'You're amazing.'

'Thanks,' he grinned, cheeks pinking. 'I'm not a bad midwife.'

'Not bad? You're blooming fantastic,' I said, putting my arm around him.

We looked down at the new arrival and her mum.

'I can't believe that lamb fitted inside that ewe.'

'Well, she would've been curled up for most of the gestation,' Paul explained.

'So, she only uncurled when it was time to be born?'

'Exactly.'

'It's magical.'

Suddenly, I felt exhausted and emotionally drained, and all I did was *watch*. I reached for Paul's hand and turned to the door.

'Er, where are you going?'

'Back to the house.'

'Oh no you don't.'

'Why not?'

Fear snaked down my spine. I turned to see Paul pointing to a pen and *then* I knew why not. Ah.

Apparently, witnessing the miracle of birth had inspired the ewe on the other side of the shed to 'give it a go,' and now she was in labour.

'Excellent,' Paul said as he washed his hands under the tap and made his way to his next patient. After a quick examination, he exited the pen and started walking away.

'Where are you going?'

'To get more gloves.'

'Oh, good,' I said, pleased to see he had everything in hand. Except, a few minutes later, he was handing them to me.

'What are you doing?'

'Giving you gloves. You'll need them to lamb.'

'To what?'

'Well, you just watched your first delivery, so now it's your turn.'

'Are you mad? I can't deliver a lamb.'

'Of course, you can.'

'Of course, I *can't*. In case you've forgotten, I'm not a vet. Which is a blessing for everyone, animals and humans included.'

'You don't have to be. You don't think farmers call out vets every time a sheep lambs, do you?'

'Er, yes.'

'No.'

'Ah, but I'm not a farmer, either,' I said triumphantly.

'So…'

'Come back. You can do this. You can do anything you want to.'

'Not true,' I pointed out. 'I couldn't be a brain surgeon. Can't do maths.'

'Stop stalling for time.'

Getting the gloves on was difficult enough, mainly because my hands were shaking so much. I knew Paul wouldn't do anything to put me, the sheep or the lambs at risk and I trusted him one hundred percent. I just didn't trust myself.

'What do I do first?'

'Put your hand inside her and let me know what you feel.'

It seemed like an odd time to be asking about the inner workings of my mind, let alone be having a heart-to-heart, but I went along with it.

'Well, I'm a bit worried. My palms are sweaty…'

'Not what *you* feel emotionally, what you can physically feel inside *her*.'

'Oh, I see.'

The ewe was already straining. 'I'm sorry,' I whispered as I gently pushed my hand inside her. 'I'm sorry, I'm – oh, it's lovely and warm in here,' I added, a note of surprise in my trembling voice. 'No wonder the lamb's reluctant to come out, it's obviously nice and snug in there.'

At that moment, and to my great surprise, a wave of brown liquid gushed out of the ewe and landed all over me. As I looked forlornly down at my stained clothes and wondered if there was a setting on the washing machine for the removal of amniotic fluid, I considered how surreal the situation was, which could only happen in the animal sphere.

I mean, you wouldn't be able to stroll onto a maternity ward, having had zero medical training, push the staff out of the way and say to the expectant mother, 'Mind if I have a go, love? I'm not a clinician, but I've always fancied having a crack at this, and don't worry, I'm a big *Call the Midwife* fan, so it'll be fine.'

My train of thought was derailed by the realisation that my fingers had found something spongy, which I immediately reported to Paul. 'Could be soft tissue. Or organs. To be honest, it could be anything, really,' I blabbered, aware that I was quickly losing my grip on reality.

This is madness, I thought to myself. I can't even get to the end of the lane without a map, and that's a straight road. So, what chance do I have of finding a lamb inside a ewe, when I have no idea what is meant to be where?

I showed willing for a few more minutes and then gave up.

'Nope, I can't feel anything, sorry. You'll just have to take over.'

'You've got to go in further than that.'

I shot Paul a look and reluctantly pushed in up to my wrist. 'Nothing.'

'Further than that.'

'Surely not?'

'Yes.'

'Sorry, sorry,' I whispered again as I plunged deeper. I had no idea what I was doing. I closed my eyes to try and envisage where my hand was in relation to the ewe's body. I splayed my fingers but could feel nothing apart from liquid. Then, to my utter bemusement, I felt something solid and circular. I moved a little more and felt another circle. Eventually, after flailing around in my mind for the right words and taking a few deep breaths, I managed to speak.

'I've found hooves. I think.'

'Good,' Paul said, calmly. 'What else?'

'Erm,' I pushed past the hooves and felt something else. 'Nose?'

'Great.'

Not for the first time, the surrealness of the situation washed over me. I was sat in a shed in Northern Ireland with my hand wedged firmly inside a sheep, who had a lamb firmly wedged inside *her*. As far as first date activities went, it was a showstopper.

Personally, I think *Blind Date* should stop packing contestants off to far-flung destinations and instead, send them to farms in the middle of nowhere to deliver lambs in the pouring rain at midnight. It would be much more entertaining and I for one, would love it. I'd rather do that than lounge on a beach or go shopping, but then, I've always been a bit different.

Back inside the sheep shed, I'd received instructions to pull the legs straight and then pull them *out*. I was so bemused that I didn't even question it.

'It's just dawned on me,' I said as I struggled to get a firm grip, 'that I'm the first person to have ever touched this lamb.' Paul didn't reply, so I rambled on.

'It must be strange for the lambs, though, mustn't it? I mean, there they are, minding their own business, tucked up all safe and snug and warm inside their mum, when suddenly, a strange thing invades their space, pokes them in the face and drags them out.'

I finally managed to grab hold and, after a few more moments of pulling, the hoof popped out. I gasped at my own strength and tugged a little bit more until the leg was straight.

'Good. Now do the same to the other leg.'

The second time I went in, I was a little bolder and managed to grab the hoof on my first attempt, but before I could get a firm grip, it disappeared.

'Er, where did it go?'

Apparently, the lamb had taken a dim view of being prodded and poked and, to exemplify its point, pulled its hoof out of my hand, as if to say, 'Leave me alone!'

Undeterred, I went back in and tried again, but it was like playing tug of war with a live piece of rope, which is to say, exhausting and almost impossible.

Having eased the second hoof out, I wrapped my fingers around both and gently pulled. Then, very slowly and inch by beautiful inch, the lamb emerged; head, neck, body and – woosh – the rest!

I lowered the lamb onto the straw to check everything was accounted for: one head, two ears, two eyes, one nose, a mouth, four legs and a tail. We were in business!

'Hello, baby,' I whispered as I cleaned its nose and mouth.

It shook its head, as if it objected to such interference in the strongest of terms, but the movement only served to make its ears 'ping' out, which made it look even cuter.

The lamb slowly blinked and looked about, as if to say, 'What just happened?'

I was wondering the same thing.

I reached out and wrapped my hands around its little body, marvelling at the feel of its ribs under my fingers. Its wool was soggy and saggy, which made it look as if it was wearing a baby-grow that was ten sizes too big.

'Is it OK?' I asked, petrified I'd broken it or something.

Paul gave it the once-over and assured me it was fine.

'Can I just have a few more minutes of cuddles?' I asked when he went to take the lamb.

He smiled sadly, 'That's not very fair on its mum, is it?'

I buried my nose into the lamb's wool to inhale its lovely newborn smell, before begrudgingly handing it over.

Paul laid the new arrival next to its mum, who bleated happily and licked her freshly minted lamb.

'Well done,' Paul said, sweeping me into a hug.

I went to wipe away a happy tear but stopped, realising my gloves were covered in blood. As I whipped them off, I couldn't stop smiling. 'I did it,' I whispered. 'I delivered a lamb!'

'Yes, you did,' Paul said, proudly. 'We'll call him Number six, because he's the sixth lamb to be born in this group.'

'Oh, I was going to call him Tristan,' I said, failing to hide the note of disappointment in my voice.

'Well, that can be his unofficial name.'

'Can we keep him as a pet?' I asked, brightening. 'He was my first delivery after all.'

'We'll see.'

We sat in the straw and watched Number Six being fussed over by his mum. Then, after a few minutes of looking about, he began to rock back and forth.

'What's he doing? Is he unwell?' I asked, suddenly worried.

'No, he's just trying to get up.'

'Surely, he's too young to…' but before I could finish, Number Six had hauled himself onto his knees and, with one more almighty push, was on his feet and swaying dangerously from side to side.

After a few more moments of this, he tentatively put one foot forward and then the other and just like that, he'd taken his first, very wobbly, steps. But still, for something so tiny who had literally just crashed into the world, it was impressive.

'That's astounding,' I uttered, my eyes as wide as saucers. I was so impressed that I gave Number Six a round of applause.

'It is impressive, Paul agreed, 'but it's also instinct. In the wild, lambs must be up and about quickly, otherwise they'd end up inside a fox.'

'Good point. I reckon even I could get on my feet in record time, if it meant I avoided becoming a carnivore's dinner.'

I gazed lovingly at the little lamb and hugged Paul.

'I'm on my way to becoming a lamb midwife,' I squeaked.

'Indeed, you are,' he smiled.

But just like a real student midwife, I'd need to deliver

many more lambs before I would feel confident enough to be left to it. Fortunately, there were fifty more ewes waiting to lamb, meaning there would be plenty of opportunity to practice.

19. Hedging my bets

I t's pouring down; the kind of angry rain that stings your face and bites your fingers. My hands are shaking and stinging with the cold and my feet throb, but I won't stop walking. I can't.

Today, one of the ewes caught us off guard by having her twins early. But that isn't the issue. Let me explain.

When the ewes are approaching their due date, we either put them into one of the fields in our lane or pop them in the sheep shed opposite the house so we can get to them quickly if they need us.

But, as I said, this ewe lambed unexpectedly early, meaning she was still in the outer field when her lambs arrived in the early hours.

Thus, when we went out to check on them this morning, we were greeted by the beautiful, if surprising sight, of two little lambs snuggled up with their mum.

Their coats were sparkling white, and they were bone dry, meaning Mum had done a great job in getting them washed and cleaned up before we were on the scene.

She clearly didn't need human intervention at all and was quite content to crack on, which was great to see and just as well, seeing as she went into labour so early! A quick check confirmed she had a boy and a girl: one of each flavour!

We returned to the field a short time later with the trailer. The idea being that we would pack up the trio and take them to one of the fields nearer our house to keep an eye on them. The closer they are to our house, with its regular human activity, the less likely it is that a fox will be tempted to try and snap up the lambs for supper. Of course, there's never any guarantee that a predator won't try its luck in the fields around our house, but they do tend to be more wary.

Paul and I were chatting away as we opened the gate to the field and sauntered in, excited at the prospect of taking the new arrivals home. Suddenly, Paul stopped in his tracks, and I followed his gaze. When I saw what he was looking at, my heart plummeted to my boots.

The new mum was standing in the middle of the field with one lamb by her side. *One?* My blood ran cold. Where was the other one? I quickly scanned the field from left to right in case she'd wandered off, but there was no sign. 'Maybe she's standing behind her mum?' I suggested as I broke into a run, although I knew I was clutching at straws.

'Not a fox, please don't let it be a fox,' I whispered under my breath as I tried to get near the ewe and her lamb. She looked at me nervously as I approached and protectively stepped in front of her lamb, blocking it from view.

In the main, Dorset ewes make brilliant mums because

the instinct to protect their young is very strong, which is beautiful, see. But, despite being pleased that she was looking out for her remaining lamb, (her little boy) in that moment, I was also filled with sadness because her other baby was missing.

'You walk around the field in a clockwise direction and check under all the hedges. I'll do the same in an anti-clockwise direction and we'll meet in the middle,' Paul instructed, his voice calm and measured.

So that's why I'm now trudging through the wet, long grass, my heart hammering so loudly that I can hear it in my ears, while the rain soaks me to the skin.

The idea of her being lost and frightened is bad enough, but the thought of her freezing cold and sopping wet as well makes it even worse, somehow. What if she's slipped down a bank and hurt herself? And if that's the case, we may never find her; she's too small to make a big noise and besides, it's blowing a gale, so even if she does bleat, we may not be able to hear her.

I stop to get my breath back and close my eyes, straining to hear something, *anything*, over the screaming wind. After a few seconds, I *do* hear something else, so open my eyes and rush towards the sound, hoping it's the lamb making her way out of the bracken, but I grind to a halt and feel foolish when I see that it's just loose branches being battered by the rain.

I can feel myself falling deeper and deeper into despair and my mind is playing tricks; every twig that snaps under-foot, I mistake for a pathetic bleat. Every stone I see in the distance, I think is her little body.

Wiping the rain from my glasses only serves to steam up even more, so I take them off and squint into the bushes, praying I'll spot the forlorn little mite sitting in between some branches or disguised as a shrub, but nothing.

As my resolve sinks like a lead balloon, I remind myself of 'The Parable of the Lost Sheep' in the Bible, which tells the story of a shepherd who leaves his flock of ninety-nine in order to find one that's lost. Rather wonderfully, he didn't give up until he found the lamb. Mind you, he didn't have the Northern Irish weather to contend with.

Slipping on mud and leaves as I scramble up the hill, I pull up my hood, although I don't know why as I'm already drenched, but at least it's something constructive to do. As I reach the top of the field, I slow down because I'm puffed out. Hands on hips, I scan the hedgerow from left to right in one last-ditch, desperate attempt to find the baby.

In my head, I list what I can see: Twigs. Gap. Bushes. Gap. Something jagged. Bush. Gap. Tree. *Hang on.* I stop and scan the scene from right to left, this time, until my gaze again falls on the jagged shape.

As I struggle to focus, my heart leaps for joy, but my head tells me to calm down. I haven't got my glasses on, after all, and could be seeing things.

I break into a run. As I get nearer, the fuzzy shape becomes clearer and, yes, it looks like a bedraggled, dirty, damp but very much alive lamb. I practically throw myself into the bush, skidding in the mud and catching my hands on the branches, but I don't care. Yet I don't let myself believe it's really happening until my fingers slide over her coat that's slippery with rain. Thank God.

I scoop her up and hug her little woolly body close to me to warm her up. I'm almost scared to look at her face, petrified she might have been dragged and dropped by a predator. What if she's had an eye gouged out by birds? I've heard that happens.

Taking a deep breath, I force myself to look and thankfully she's in one piece. Her ears are plastered down on the sides of her head, and she blinks intermittently to get the raindrops out of her eyes, but apart from looking thoroughly miserable, she's OK. I hold her tight and breathe in her newborn lamb smell.

Relief washes over me as I stumble to my feet and shout to Paul, who is scouring the other side of the field. I scamper to meet him, going as fast as I can but taking care not to slip. We meet in the middle and hug, keeping the little one nestled between us. She looks up and stares at me, then Paul and gives a pathetic bleat as if to say, 'You aren't sheep!'

'Well done,' Paul beams. 'Good spot. She was well hidden. Must have tottered off and got lost.'

He checks her over and confirms she is fine, which is a huge relief. We load the ewe into the trailer and I sit in the passenger seat of the car with the lambs on my lap, which will save them from skidding about in the back. They'll be reunited with their mum when we get home.

I feel like that person who found the World Cup in a bush, except this is a million times more exciting than that. I'm almost in tears, I'm that relieved.

I stroke the lamb's ears as we make our way down the country lanes. They're warming up nicely. 'Soon be home and back with Mum,' I soothe, as I glance at Paul and smile.

What a lovely end to the morning. Now, what will the afternoon bring? I hope it includes a cup of tea. And maybe a celebratory biscuit, or three.

20. We love sheep

Sometimes I get so nervous and tongue-tied that I can't communicate properly.

The words seem to get tangled and when they do emerge, they don't float like the butterflies I'd envisage in my mind, but thud like stones falling from my pockets.

Of course, being able to articulate is a key requirement of being a journalist, which is why I'm somewhat relieved to have left that field in order to look after sheep in theirs.

Sheep know the rattle of a bucket means food is coming, and that if they're quick, they can be at the front of the queue, snaffle a nut and when the human's not looking, run around the back and join the queue again! The clunk of a gate means they'll soon be on the move to a new field and fresh grass, while the splash of water means that, somewhere, a bucket it being filled for a refreshing drink.

I've watched quite a few ewes give birth now, and every time I ask myself, 'does she know she's having a lamb?' To some extent, she must do. After all, she's carried it around for nearly 150 days! And sometimes, my mind wanders, as I imagine what their thought process might be…

Pain. Sudden. Unexplained. Comes and goes like sharp, cold thing. I know something special is happening cos the hoomans are all soft hands and whispers. I bleat. See eyes that don't belong to sheep but seem kind. Something soft on my nose. Gentle.

Then the pain has gone! Oh, but so has the silence. Bleats bounce on the air. A soft, wet, struggling, snuggling thing is suddenly next to me. Something I've never seen before, but I've felt it. I know its smell, its voice. I know it is part of me. Something runs through my wool and into my skin. Feels like rain, but it's warm and seeps in and stays. It's what hoomans call *love*.

From where I'm sitting, which is on the grass, now that the birth is all over, it's clear to see the ewe adores the scrap of a thing that's lolloping beside her. She drizzles him with licks, kisses and love. Her warm breath thaws him.

He already knows the sound of her bleat; he'll have heard it from inside the womb and now, he'll follow it anywhere. It is an invisible cord which will always bring him back to her side.

He looks like a half-baked sheep at the moment, all loose skin and patchy wool, but his mum will keep him tucked in the folds of her body at night, let him suckle when he wants, and gradually, day after day, he'll grow in stature and confidence. She'll teach him sheepy ways.

The ewe blinks at us and gives a little bleat, which perhaps is sheep for 'thank you?' We are part of her flock now. After all, we helped deliver her baby.

Sheep will keep secrets, if you ask them to. They're good at it. Your words simply wash over them. Occasionally, they'll stop and stare at you, as if to say, 'Is that so?' before returning to the matter in hand – lunch!

If they feel the occasion really calls for it, they'll call to their friends who'll move closer until you feel their soft breath on your face. They can't do anything to help, other than listen and put their warm bodies next to yours. But sometimes, that's enough.

People think sheep all sound the same, but that's not the case. They have individual and beautiful voices, just like humans. Lie in a field and let their 'baas' float over your head, like invisible balloons filled with hope and joy, and *then* tell me they all sound the same.

Do you remember the colourful parachutes you used to play with as a child? Standing in a circle with your friends, you would each grasp a bit of the material and, on the teacher's instruction, flap wildly, shooting a rainbow of colour into the sky. And then, just as you began to fear it would never come back, the magical material would slowly but surely float down, its silky softness slipping through your fingers, comforting and familiar.

Well, listening to sheep is like that, comforting, reassuring, familiar and true.

Watching them swirl around the field as if they're heavy clouds being blown about by a cotton wind, always makes me smile.

New pastures are ahead as winter lets the summer pass.

21. Gloves

Recently, I received a beautiful pair of pink gloves from one of my new in-laws, and I was really touched by their thoughtfulness. Unfortunately, I didn't read the instructions before bunging them in the washing machine.

Still, it's an ill wind that blows no one any good. On the plus side, I now have a lovely set of gloves which will fit a sheep.

All I have to do is shrink another pair, and one lucky ewe will look like a true *fashionista*. She'll be the envy of the flock and then they'll all want a set. What have I started?

22. Frazzled

Something's wrong.

The ewe has been struggling to deliver the first of her twins for a while, and Paul decides it's time to intervene.

As he pulls the lamb out a few minutes later, I gasp. I've never seen anything like it. The poor thing is almost completely covered in a dark brown sludge which is so thick, it looks like he's been in an oil slick. The few bits of skin that aren't covered in the gloop are patchy and red raw, making it look as if he's been burnt.

'What on earth?'

Paul gives the sickly lamb to the ewe and then goes back to try and work out what's happening with the lamb still inside her. I hold my breath and wait as he carries out an examination.

After what feels like hours, but can only be minutes, Paul shakes his head. 'It's not developed properly. I'd say the lamb's been dead a long time.'

My eyes fill with tears as he goes about delivering the dead lamb, which, when it appears, is still inside its sack and is nothing more than bones and skin, poor thing.

'That's why the first lamb is that colour,' Paul says. 'He has been laid next to the dead one all this time while toxins were seeping out. The sack provided him some protection, but it's a miracle he's alive at all.'

I look at the poor scrap of a lamb and sigh. His mum's brilliant and has already licked him dry, but the sludge has stained his wool. His little eyes are crusted shut with dirt and he's very quiet. Not wanting to startle him, but unable to stop myself, I gently reach out and give him a pat. He feels like a dry flannel.

As Paul says, it's a miracle he's alive and time will tell if he will survive. Nonetheless, the ewe's besotted with her new baby and so are we.

'That poor second lamb,' I weep. 'He didn't even get a few seconds of life.'

'Let's focus on the one we have, shall we?' Paul says, hugging me. I nod and watch as the ewe nuzzles her baby.

Our lamb creche and labour ward has suddenly become a Special Care Baby Unit. Paul puts a heat lamp in the pen to keep the bubba warm and I add straw for extra comfort.

I've never seen such a small lamb. I thought he was premature but apparently, he was fully cooked and so had to come out of the oven. The reason he's so tiny is because there wasn't much space in the womb, what with their being two lambs.

Paul milks the ewe to get her colostrum (the first draw of milk is a highly nutritious source of energy which helps the lamb maintain body temperature and is key to survival), which he pours into a bottle attached to a long feeding tube. Then, with gentle hands, he lifts the lamb up and inserts the tube into his mouth and into his tummy.

This is a quick way of ensuring the lamb gets that essential first feed, and a much-needed energy boost after such a traumatic entrance. Usually, healthy lambs quickly learn how to suckle from their mum, but this little one is far too small for that, so swift action is needed. He struggles when the tube first goes in, but soon calms down. After dinner, the lamb returns to his mum and snuggles up, but it isn't long before his eyes start to close.

'Sleepy time,' Paul says.

'Good idea.'

'Not you, the lamb.'

'Oh, right.'

Soon, the lamb is making little snoring noises.

'Sweet dreams, little one,' I whisper.

As we walk home, I have a thought. 'If humans count sheep to fall asleep, do you think sheep count humans?'

Paul smiles and puts an arm around me. 'And that's why I married you.'

'Why?'

'Because no other woman on earth would ask me a question like that. And yes, I think they do.'

I nod triumphantly. 'Thought so.'

23. Keeping strong

On entering the sheep shed this morning, I'm relieved to see the lamb's a bit livelier, though not yet on his feet. He still looks bemused, but that's not surprising, given the traumatic start he's had. His coat is still stained and looks about ten sizes too big. But for all that, he is gorgeous.

When he sees me, he lets out a few pathetic bleats and yawns. Despite his apparent tiredness, he continues trying to stand, which he does by rocking back and forth. But all this seems to do is make his ears flap, which gets him maximum cute points, but not much further forward in the standing stakes.

His mum is very chilled and seems happy to let me pick up her lamb. But as I do, I gasp because his wool is so rough.

Do you remember those 'magic flannels' you used to be able to buy in the 1990s? They looked like little cubes and would expand when placed in water. I think I had about ten at one point. I didn't want the flannel, you see, I just enjoyed watching it transform.

Well, this lamb looks and feels like one of those flannels, because he has seemingly unfurled overnight. I can now see that he has long legs and a lovely, fluffy tail. His wool is still brown and damp in places, but other areas have dried, revealing white patches and giving him a stripey appearance.

'He looks like a Frazzle,' I tell Paul as he joins us.

'Hello, Frazzle,' Paul says, stroking him gently. The lamb looks up at us and gives a loud bleat. 'Yes, I think he likes his name.'

I lean over and kiss on the head. 'Welcome to the fold, little one.'

'Look at us,' Paul smiles, pointing at the calves and sheep. 'Now we've got flock, stock and Frazzle.'

I love it.

24. Hay, good lookin'

'Do you think Frazzle's warm enough?' I ask Paul as I clamber out of the pen one afternoon. 'Has he got enough bedding?'

Paul looks over my shoulder, 'Erm, where is he?'

'What do you mean?' I turn around and realise that Frazzle has disappeared after being buried under a mound of straw.

'Woops.' I leap over the fence and pull a very confused, but mostly annoyed-looking lamb from the bedding mountain. I then set about removing bits of straw from his ears while blowing the dust off his nose. 'Sorry mate.'

Is there enough bedding in his pen? That would be a yes.

25. Baa codes

It seems a strange thing to ask a stranger when you're standing in the middle of a field, but hey-ho.

'Well,' I say, 'I can't wait to see how many ewes are in lamb, but I suppose time *wool* tell,' I grin and resist the temptation to add jazz hands.

The woman who has come to scan our sheep (we'll call her Scanning Lady because I'm creative like that) stares at me blankly. Well, that went down like a lead balloon. To fill the awkward silence, I start laughing at my own joke, in the hope that it will help. It doesn't.

To be honest, I'm struggling to understand why she isn't laughing too. After all, she *did* ask me for a pun, and I provided one.

As usual, I look to Paul for help and an explanation. 'A pin, dear,' he whispers. 'She said, "do you have a pin?"'

Ah, that makes more sense, seeing as how we're joining gates together using long pins.

As I said, Scanning Lady is here to tell us how many lambs we can hope to expect come spring. (And yes, you are right, we *are* lambing now, but our sheep are split into two groups. This means that one set of ewes have been busy shelling lambs like peas, while the others have been enjoying some 'Netflix and Chill' time, or whatever the sheep equivalent is, with the ram. Thus, they should now be pregnant.)

I've quickly learned that Northern Irish people are very hospitable, friendly and always willing to lend a hand. To this end, Scanning Lady has come over to help us build the holding pens which we're fashioning out of an assortment of silver hurdles and gates. Her help would have been greatly appreciated in normal circumstances, but today it is pouring down and freezing cold, meaning we are even more grateful.

I was struggling to link my hurdles together when Scanning Lady appeared and asked (or so I thought), 'if I had a pun.' And that was when I came up, quite frankly, a corker of a pun. Well, it *would* have been a corker, if she had indeed actually been *asking me* for a pun.

As the penny drops so loudly it could wake the dead, I nod to show I've understood the request. 'I do have a pin, yes I do,' I ramble, 'And I would love to give my pin to you.' I can't seem to stop talking but am desperate to move away from 'pungate' as quickly as possible.

Having passed on my pin, I go back to fighting with my hurdles and wonder if I'll ever learn to understand the local dialect. Maybe I will. But then again, there's a high probability that I won't, and will be required forevermore to say 'pardon' every time someone asks me a question.

On a different note, I absolutely love the fact that it's someone's job to scan for sheep. Life must be an utter joy.

I mean, it's basically getting paid to participate in the best treasure hunt ever! (When scanning, do they look for 'baaa' codes, I wonder?)

I don't recall being told, during my careers meeting at school, that one could earn a living by scanning sheep. If I'd known, I would've given it serious consideration.

In terms of equipment, Scanning Lady has a van with a trailer on the back. She opens the gates of the trailer and unfolds a ramp and a holding pen which she assembles in about two seconds. It's like watching a magician at work.

The truck houses a computer, the scanning machine and a chair. (I wonder what computer package sheep scanners use. Do you think they spend a lot of money buying extra RAM? Sorry, couldn't resist.)

The sheep have been rounded up and are waiting patiently in their holding pen. Paul opens the gate and feeds the first five ewes into the gated area Scanning Lady has provided. Then he encourages them, one at a time, to walk up the ramp and into the scanning machine.

The first ewe disappears for a few seconds, there's the sound of something being sprayed and then she appears at the door at the other end of the trailer. Cautiously, she looks about and then, seeing no danger, trots down the ramp and into the holding pen for scanned sheep, where she sets to work munching grass.

I look at her and clap my hands with joy because a red spot has been sprayed on her back. Red dots denote twins, blue mean they're expecting a single and green means they're not pregnant.

The sheep queuing up to be scanned look like they're

waiting to see the fortune teller at the fair, which I suppose they are.

Do you think sheep would enjoy going to a fair? I think they would. Perhaps we should've hired a helter-skelter to keep them entertained? Or at the very least, had candy floss to hand out afterwards, in much the same way as children are given stickers after visiting the dentist.

My eyes widen to the size of saucers as the ewes emerge from the trailer. It's a veritable feast of colour as they troop out: Red, blue, blue, red, red, red. There are so many that in the end, I lose count. On the plus side, our sheep now look like huge M&M's.

Are you hedging your bets with that one?' Paul asks, as a sheep walks past sporting red and blue spots.

'No,' Scanning Lady chuckles: 'Blue and red spots. One and two. She's having triplets.'

I jump up and down with excitement and rush over to congratulate the ewe, thinking, as I do, that I should make booties for the new arrivals. Mind you, with four feet per-lamb, I'd have to get started very soon. And learn to *knit*, of course.

As this is the first sheep scanning session I've ever seen, Scanning Lady kindly gives me a demonstration of how the machinery works. As the ewe enters the trailer, Scanning Lady runs the probe just in front of the udder and a grainy picture appears on screen.

At first, all I can see is a vast black empty space with murky white lines pulsating over the top. But then everything slows down, the mist clears, and I can make out two, tiny kidney bean shapes.

'There they are,' she says triumphantly, pointing them out. 'One lamb's laying over the top of the other, see?'

I can.

'They're the size of small rats at the moment,' Scanning Lady smiles. 'But they'll soon grow.'

I can't believe lambs are tucked up inside that ewe right now, their little hooves, legs, eyes and ears already formed. It's amazing and beautiful and for once, I'm speechless. I also can't stop looking at the image. This must be how humans feel when they see their baby on screen for the first time. A miracle. I wipe a tear from my eye as I leave the trailer.

'Are you OK?' Paul asks, putting his arm around me.

'Oh yes,' I nod. 'I'm just thinking about the amount of work coming our way. All those night patrols and early starts. It's enough to make you weep.'

26. The sheep who came in from the cold

Three rams are standing in the yard, and I didn't put them there.

'Where did they come from?' I ask Paul as I clatter out of the kitchen.

'I thought you bought them down?'

'How? They're a bit big to juggle and I haven't got my trailer licence yet.'

'Well, in that case, they found their own way home.'

'But that means they've traversed through at least two fields, crossed a lane and walked down the driveway.'

'Yup.'

'That's amazing.'

I put my buckets down and stare at the sheep superheroes. They look calm and collected, not like they've just completed a massive trek at all.

'Sure, they were born here, it's little surprise they found their way home.'

'And I was born in Essex, but I don't think I'd be able to find my way back to the hospital without a Satnav.'

As we chat, the rams walk to the sheep shed and stand expectantly, waiting to be let in. When neither of us move, the ringleader wanders over and taps me on the leg with his hoof, as if I'm a waitress in a café and he's trying to get my attention. I can almost hear him saying, 'Three portions of silage and your best water, when you're ready, luv.'

I look at Paul, who smiles. 'Well, they have come all this way. They can have a scoop of food for their troubles and another for their cheek.'

I nod. 'Come on then, you troublesome trio. But once you've eaten, it's back to your field. And I daresay we'll give you a lift in the trailer.'

I know, our sheep are spoilt rotten.

27. What's that you say?

I can't understand a word anyone's saying. Mind you, I think the feelings mutual.

The kindly man in front of me clearly has no idea what I've just said. But judging by the look on his face, he either thinks I've invited him on a mission to Mars or proposed.

I'm equally embarrassed. I absolutely love the Northern Irish accent, but I'm struggling to understand anyone at the moment.

When I first went to the local shop on my own and was waiting in the queue to pay, I jumped at the sound of two men arguing. It took me a moment to realise that they were actually friends just having a laugh and a joke (or enjoying the craic, as they say around here.) But they were speaking so quickly and enthusiastically that, to my untrained ear, it sounded aggressive.

Back in the bakery, I'm consulting my list and wondering if fairy cakes are a 'thing' around here.

The fact that I'm like a child in a sweet shop isn't really helping my concentration. The shelves are crammed with all kinds of goodies which smell amazing. Quiches sit next to huge sausage rolls while freshly baked bread rolls jostle for space next to pies. There's also a cake counter heaving with all sorts of delights, from tarts and iced buns to rocky road slices.

'Do you have any fairy cakes?' I ask, speaking slowly and loudly, just like people do when they're abroad and trying to talk to the locals.

On reflection, trying to mime being a fairy was probably a mistake.

In the end, the baker decided that the only way to get the crazy English girl out of his shop, was to throw one of everything at me while shouting 'free of charge' (I think) and booting me out the door. I was, however, extremely happy with my spoils and staggered home with my own bodyweight in baked goods.

Later on, Paul is agog at the amount of items I have acquired.

'Erm, have you invited a lot of people round for supper or are you expecting us to eat all of this?'

'Apparently,' I say, ignoring his question, 'this is soda bread and *this*,' I continue, holding something aloft as if it's long-lost treasure, 'is potato bread.'

'I know,' he laughs

'Oh.' I forget that he's probably been devouring these things all his life.

'Well, I've never heard of or tasted them. So, whack on the pan and let's have lunch!'

Later, I sneak a paper bag out of my pocket. It contains something I spotted in the bakery and was curious to try. It's called a Fifteen. I take a bite and it's heavenly; all marshmallow goo held together with digestive biscuits and cherries. It's a Northern Irish traybake and possibly the best thing I've ever tasted. I'm not surprised to hear that a friend of a friend put on a stone in weight after moving to these parts. The food is delicious and the cakes out of this world!

When dishing up the sweet treats to Paul, I find myself

pondering, not for the first time, how wonderful it is to shop locally. The local high street boasts a butcher's shop and a bakery, but alas, no candlestick maker.

When Paul took me to show the high street for the first time, I was amazed by such a selection of shops.

'But don't you use supermarkets?'

'Sometimes, but we like to support independent traders and shop locally when we can.'

I remember walking up the quaint street with its enchanting individual shops, each with beautiful signage, striped awnings and eye-catching displays.

The sun was shining as I watched people mill up and down the street; some carrying brown paper bags bulging with fresh fruit and vegetables, others swinging pints of locally produced milk. Young mums pushed prams with excited toddlers in tow, heading to the library or the park.

Older gents leaned on their cars as they chatted to acquaintances. Ladies popped into the butcher's shop to buy bones for their dogs. Boys ditched their bikes outside the bakery, disappeared inside and emerged a few minutes later with their after-school spoils and big, sugary smiles.

It's as alien as it is beautiful to me. In London, people are always in a hurry. They don't even exchange smiles, let alone pleasantries. But here, the pace of life is different. Shopkeepers know customers' names and greet them on arrival with a smile.

It felt as if I'd stepped back in time to a better, calmer era. I smiled as I swung my shopping bags. Welcome to the 1950s.

28. Giving out and giving in

As previously mentioned, I adore the cadence of the Northern Irish and Irish accents but am still trying to get my head around sayings, turns of phrase and colloquialisms.

'She was giving out to him in the car park,' Paul tells me over dinner.

I almost choke on my chop. 'Is that legal?'

'What?'

'Well, you know, doing that… in public.'

Paul laughs. 'No. Giving out to someone means shouting at them. Like if we were having an argument about me not putting the washing out or something, you'd be giving out to me about it.'

I stare.

'Like telling someone off.'

I nod as if I understand, but I don't. With all these new things to learn, every day is a school day.

29. Special delivery

'**K**eep an eye out for the courier, they could arrive any time,' Paul says as we prepare breakfast for the animals.

'How exciting.'

I'm walking back from the top field when I see a local farmer pulling into the yard with a trailer. As I get nearer, I see five very excitable calves inside. 'They're huge,' I exclaim.

'Aye, and they're only three weeks old,' the farmer grins.

'They're almost as tall as me.'

'Ah,' Paul says, appearing by my side, 'Your delivery has arrived.'

'I'm sorry, what?'

'This is the courier,' he says, pointing to the farmer. 'And these are your calves.'

I almost fall over in shock. *My* calves? But I don't know anything about them.'

'Sure, you will once you've bought this lot up,' the farmer grins. 'Now, where do you want 'em?'

I fight the urge to say, 'in our house'. They're so adorable, I just want to cuddle them on the sofa and maybe watch a moo-vie.

Fortunately, Paul is the brains of the operation and, unbeknownst to me, has spent the morning getting ready for the delivery. As such, the shed is now a fully-fledged calf nursery with various pens generously filled with straw.

I marvel at how Paul can make these things happen right under my nose and I never notice. Possibly because I have the observational skills of a twig. Not sure how I ever made it as a journalist? No, me either.

Paul has decided that I need to be kept busy until I find a job. I did assure him that I was more than happy to be the official 'sofa inspector' and 'television show reviewer,' but it didn't wash.

Instead, and in order to keep me out of mischief, he has made me a mother, as it were.

It turned out that his farmer friend was rapidly running out of room on his farm and needed to recruit some 'calf foster parents' until he got sorted. And Paul put our names down.

I peep into the trailer and five little black and white faces peer back at me. 'Hello, girls,' I coo, already smitten. You can keep your chocolates and flowers; *this* is the kind of surprise gift I love!

The farmer smiles at my enthusiasm and opens the trailer. Hesitantly, the first, bravest mini moo makes her way down the ramp, tentatively puts one hoof onto the concrete and looks about her. Then she spots the open gateway to the big pen and speeds up. Buoyed by her confidence, the others follow and soon, they're all safely installed in their new home, their nerves dissipated.

'Now for the hard bit,' Paul says. 'Teaching them how to drink milk.' He smiles knowingly. 'It could be a long night.'

I stare at him; my eyes narrow with suspicion. '*Could* or *will*?'

The first job is to hang the trough onto the gate of the pen, then it's up to the house with a churn to mix hot water with powdered calf milk.

I pick up the churn, which holds twenty litres of water, and almost put my back out.

'Want me to carry that?' Paul asks.

'No,' I say, resolutely. 'I'll be fine.'

I try again, this time gripping the silver handle with both hands. I heave and eventually, it moves. Yes, it's only an inch or so off the ground, but it's a start.

I triumphantly shuffle off down the hill, gritting my teeth all the way, Relief washes over me as I make it to nursery and put the churn down with a bump. The sweat is pouring off me and it takes a good ten minutes to get my breath back, but I did it! But my joy doesn't last long as it dawns on me that I'm going to have to lift the churn again to pour the milk into the feeders.

It isn't pretty, but I eventually work out how to get a good grip on the handle at the same time as getting the churn high enough to pour the liquid into the five feeding compartments. It's a shaky start and I end up wearing some of the milk, but it isn't a total disaster.

I hope the calves might give me a round of applause, but they don't and are clearly unimpressed. Tough crowd.

'Come on,' I call, tapping the feeder. 'Your milk is served.' But they just back further into the corner of the pen and stare at me.

I decide to kick it up a gear. 'Come and get your dinner. Hmm, yummy milk,' I sing, tapping the compartments in turn.

The calves are unmoved by my performance and simply look at each other as if to say, 'She's weird.'

'We'll have to go in,' Paul concludes.

'Really?' I look at the calves and then down at their huge feet and immediately regret not buying steel toe boots.

Ten minutes later, I am still regretting it.

'Oh… f…udge.' I stop and ease my boot off to massage my poor, bruised toes.

The smallest calf and I have been dancing around the pen for a while now, but while she's showing no signs of fatigue, I am.

'Come on. Don't you want any dinner?'

Every time I approach her to guide her to the feeder, she backs away like I'm brandishing a bottle of burger sauce. 'I only want you to have a nice full tummy.'

I push from behind; she puts on the brakes.

I dip my hands in the milk and let her lick it off, in the hope it will entice her to the feeder, but she's having none of it.

In the end, it's her contemporaries who show her the way. One of the braver ones approaches the feeder, tentatively licks the teat, realises that is where the good stuff is, and sucks some more. One by one, the others follow, as does my little madam, who obviously doesn't want to miss out.

Another lesson for me: nature knows best.

30. First feeds

I f you've ever seen a Newton's cradle swinging back and forth, you'll have some idea of what hungry calves look like when they're vying to get to milk.

I can hear the calves calling for their breakfast when I am halfway down the lane and the noise intensifies as I open the door. As the sunlight leaks in, they surge forward and try to clamber over one another to get to the front.

The calves try and suck the teats before I've even got the feeder on the gate, which doesn't help. And it doesn't matter how quickly I pour the milk, there's always one bright spark who cannot wait and simply sticks her head into the flow, resulting in her and her friends getting a good soaking. But they are not put off by this and simply set about licking milk off one another.

As soon as the first finishes her milk, she wastes no time in headbutting her neighbour out of the way to nick hers. The ejected calf will either retaliate and muscle her way back in or proceed to push *her* neighbour (the calf on her left) out of the way to get her helping.

This pantomime goes all the way down the line until the poor calf on end is pushed out, but of course there's nobody left for her to steal from, so she headbutts her neighbour (on the right) and the whole pantomime starts again, like a massive game of dominoes. Happy days!

31. Text me

I 'm doing paperwork indoors when my phone beeps. It's a text message:

Your Husband lent me his phone as my battery is flat. I'm hungry. Can I have some milk, please? Moo. Love from number 2423.

Two minutes later my phone buzzes again.
Mooooo. Brekkie please. Moo-moo. Love 2423 and 2420.
'OK, OK, I get the hint. I'll go and feed the babies,' I laugh.

Paul looks up from his paperwork. 'Nothing to do with me. It's the calves. Technologically savvy,' he says innocently.

I knew it. I knew it all along.

32. Toddlers and teachers

P aul and I now understand what it must feel like to be parents.

Our lambs are toddler age, by which I mean they are inquisitive and cheeky. They follow us around the pen as we refill their water buckets or give them more straw, getting under our feet and tripping us up, all the while looking at us with their big eyes as if to say, 'Whatcha' doing?'

If they could speak, they would be at the '*but why?*' stage which so many human children go through, asking a million questions a minute and never being satisfied with the answers. But they're cute, so I'll let them off.

The calves are the same, except they're huge. At just four weeks old they're almost at eye level with me, and I'm five foot three. Their limbs are long and slender, while their eyes shine with intelligence and interest. They watch you intently when you visit them in the morning, no doubt wondering if breakfast is on its way.

I used to dream of being a teacher and am obsessed with documentaries about teaching. Looking after the calves has given me some idea of what it must be like trying to control a classroom of unruly children. Challenging is the word that springs to mind.

Just getting the feeder hooked onto the gate involves a lot of hoopla, as the calves rush forward and stick their heads in it, even though it's still empty. 'Geroff!' I shout, almost dropping it on the floor.

In case you're wondering, calves are heavy (about eighty pounds) and they grow rapidly month on month, so when there are five of them all sucking at the teats of the feeder, it's difficult to keep a firm grasp.

I'm sweating by the time I have the feeder in place but at least I've done it. Wiping the sweat from my brow, I lift the churn and start to pour the milk. As usual, one of the babies hasn't got the patience to wait until her portion is in her bowl and instead puts her legs on the bottom bar, making her taller than the others, and sticks her head into the stream of milk, thus getting soaked. Again.

I manage to persuade her that she'll get a better deal if she drinks from her bowl, which she eventually does, but her head is still covered in milk, meaning she can't act all innocent when Paul visits them.

I think the older sheep may have been meeting up with the calves at night and swapping notes on the best ways to get extra food.

The next afternoon when I go to collect something from the meal store, the rattle of the key in the lock causes pandemonium and I see that the usual sheepy suspects have formed a queue at the front gate in the hope of getting a snack.

It started out as a sporadic event, when one or two sheep would wander over to the gate to try their luck whenever someone entered the shed, but it's quickly progressed into a daily group activity, and if I'm not careful, we'll have obese sheep and no food.

However, I'm a big softie and decide that giving them one nut each will be OK and go to the store to get some. On returning to the gate, I am shocked to see a sheep sailing past me at eye level. Yes, she has learned to crowd surf.

Having found herself at the back of the crowd, it appears she decided to climb onto the shoulders of her mates and travel down the line until she was close enough to disembark right in front of the feeder.

She peers up me with a smug look on her face, which is fair enough. Full marks for tenacity.

And yes, I did give her a nut. But I'm not sure if it was for being clever or for her cheek.

33. Glasses

I've been confounding opticians for years.

My eyesight's never been great. I have a lazy left eye which may have been a result of being born prematurely. As a toddler, I had to wear a patch over one eye when reading in a bid to strengthen the weak one, and wore glasses throughout primary school. (Pink Minnie Mouse frames, if memory serves, because I'm the epitome of cool.)

When I was about seven years old, I had an operation to tighten the muscle which meant I no longer needed glasses.

As I got into my mid-thirties, I began to struggle at work and found myself squinting at the screen. Then, a few months before our wedding, the optician finally got me. I needed glasses not only for driving, but for reading, writing, computer work and close-up tasks. So, for pretty much everything, then.

Sadly, Minnie Mouse frames weren't an option and I was reduced to choosing two pairs of boring, grown-up frames.

Unfortunately, I'm also very forgetful, meaning Paul and

I end up playing the 'hunt the glasses game' at least once every ten seconds.

Because I keep one pair in the car so I can't possibly go out without them, the other pair could end up in a range of exciting and increasingly bizarre places including, but no limited to: the sheep feed bag, the calf milk carton, the washing machine, the washing basket, the peg box, the fridge and the car boot.

The other day, we turned the house upside down looking for my glasses, which I'd had at milking but removed when they got covered in poo.

'Have you checked the coat you were wearing in the parlour?' Paul asked.

'Already looked,' I said, my head in the washing machine, just in case.

'Are you sure?'

'Yessss.'

'Because I've just found them in the pocket of the coat you were wearing in the parlour.'

'Well done,' I said, straightening up. 'You passed the test. I was just making sure you were paying attention.'

34. Moving cows is a community event

Today we're helping a farmer move cattle from one end of a village to the other.

As we make our way along the country lanes, I see people coming out of their houses and there are several tractors and other farm vehicles wending their way through the village.

'Is something else going on as well?' I ask, winding down my window. 'Did I miss the memo about a country fair or something?'

'No, they're coming out for the cattle move.'

'Like a spectator sport?'

'No. To help out.'

I'm confused. 'Why on earth does it require so many people?'

'Oh, you'd be surprised. There's a lot to do when it comes to moving cattle. Human gateposts are much in demand. In fact, that's what you're going to be today.'

I'd been called worse.

Ten minutes later, I'm standing in a driveway, so the cows don't make their way down there as they move from one field to the other.

Opposite me, Paul is blocking a pathway and there are people doing similar things all along the route. The cows will make their way out of the old field, which is severely lacking in grass, mooch through the village and walk up the hill to a new field full of lush grass. It'll be like their birthday and Christmas all rolled into one.

The hum of a quad bike and the farmer's voice is carried on the gentle breeze.

Listening intently, I can just about hear the clip-clop of the cows' hooves on the concrete as they make their way up the road. It sounds as if they're wearing high heels and preparing for a night out on the town.

Suddenly, the farmer appears from around the bend with a string of enthusiastic cows behind him. The girls are two abreast and going at quite a pace, kicking up stones and bits of mud with their big hooves as they trip-trap up the road.

I feel like a mayor watching a village parade as the girls process past me, turning their eyes to the right in some sort of agricultural salute. It's fascinating seeing them up close.

Each cow has her own individual and beautiful markings in a variety of colours: black with white patches or white with black specks. Others are completely brown, black or white and a couple are a gorgeous shade of auburn, like they've rolled in autumn leaves.

Their breath frosts the early morning air, making swirling patterns, as if Jack Frost has been employed to do a bit of freelance.

The cows keep coming, and I'm just about to get my lunch box out for a quick snack when the pace slackens off a bit. There are a few seconds of silence and then three stragglers scoot around the bend in a bid to catch up with their mates. The shiny red quad bike isn't far behind, acting as mechanical sheep dog. The driver waves as he trundles by and then disappears into the distance.

Silence descends again, save for some birds in the nearby trees. It feels almost as if the cows were never there in the first place. Perhaps I've just had one of the most surreal, but brilliant hallucinations ever.

Paul assures me that they were indeed real, and we jump into our cars and negotiate a number of thin, twisty country roads in order to get ahead of the cows and once again position ourselves in gateways and driveways.

It feels like we're taking part in some bizarre rural paperchase, with the farmer taking on the role of the hare, joyously scattering cows in abundance across the countryside for us to follow.

People pile out of their cottages and wave as we pass, from parents and children to grandparents, grandchildren and elderly villagers. I even see a few families sitting on picnic blankets and tucking into sandwiches while enjoying the free entertainment. As we pass fields and yards, farmers put down their forks, rest their wheelbarrows or jump out of their tractors to lend a hand. It's wonderful to see such community spirit and I can't help but smile.

I'm at my next post when I spot a car coming down the road. There's no way they'll be able to drive around the moos now. Will they be angry at having to stop and wait?

The vehicle slows, the driver winds their down window and I prepare for an earful of abuse from this person whose journey is about to be waylaid. But to my astonishment, they're smiling. 'Can we do anything to help?'

'Sure, if you could just drive into that gateway over there

to stop the beasts from wandering down the lane, that would be grand,' Paul says.

'No bother,' they grin. 'It's nice to be of use.' And off they go. Nobody seems to be in a rush around here.

Paul and I wave to the farmer and the cattle as they march by. The cows are panting heavily, after all, they've had quite a walk and it's a sunny day, so they'll be glad of some water and fresh grass when they get to their new home. It feels like we're standing at the finish line of a massive event, which I suppose we are, and I cheer them on with gusto.

The farmer suddenly chucks a right into a field and the cows follow, filing in calmly and quickly. But when they think they're out of sight, they let their guard down and start galloping and lolloping across the field, enjoying the grass under their hooves and the new smells. They're clearly overjoyed at being outside in the sunshine and in a new home. I know the feeling.

35. Bullies

'Number seventy-six is being bullied,' I tell Paul as I come in from feeding the calves.

'Why do you think that?'

'Well, the calves all came over for their milk, including number seventy-six, but then, once the calf next to her had finished her milk, she pushed number seventy-six out the way and had her milk too.'

'And what did number seventy-six do?'

'Just backed away and went and stood in the corner. She looked so sad. She's definitely being bullied, and I won't have it in our calf house, I won't!'

Paul cleans his glasses contemplatively. 'No, she's not being bullied. When did you ever see her not defend herself and finish her drink?'

I think about this. Now he has mentioned it, never.

'The only reason calves don't feed is when there's something wrong,' he explains.

'Yes,' I nod in agreement. 'Like when they're being bullied.'

'No. Like when they aren't feeling well. I'll pop down and take her temperature.'

Sure enough, when he comes back, Paul has news for me.

'Yes, she's quite dull and has a very high temperature. I've given her some anti-inflammatories and I should imagine she'll be fine, but then tomorrow one of her pen pals will be ill.'

'How come?'

'It's a bit like when children start school for the first time. If one of them has even a *hint* of a cough or a cold, it goes around the class in no time. Or when students get Freshers' Flu during their first term at university. But they get over it, as will our calves.'

'I'm a failure as a calf mother,' I cry, 'I can't even feed my own children without one of them getting sick.' (Yes, living with me really *is* this exhausting. Think yourself lucky, you can close this book to get away from me, Paul has no such luck.)

'Them getting sick is nothing to do with you, or the way you make milk or the way you feed them,' Paul says before hugging me. 'Calves get sick, but they generally get better, too. Trust me, I'm a vet.'

I love the fact I automatically assumed the calf was being bullied. I suppose it's because I think of the calves as children in a playground who needed looking after. I also love *Eastenders* and as such, everything in my life has to have a 'doof-doof' moment.

But Paul, being scientific, calm, rational and of course, a vet, knew that certain behaviours in particular animals indicate illness.

And there you have it: the reason I'll never be a vet and why I got an A-Level in theatre studies. Because everything is a drama, drama, drama!

36. Pigeons

Yesterday, I was defending pigeons against those who describe them as flying rats and vermin.

I pointed out that they were very resourceful, what with making nests in rafters. And of course, that they were very cute, with their little bobbing heads.

Today, as I was tidying the barn, I felt something on my hat. I took it off and inspected it and sure enough, one of them had shat all over it. I glared up at them. They looked down at me, blinking, heads bobbing, as if butter wouldn't melt.

Well, that's gratitude for you.

37. Don't count on me

Trying to explain maths to me is a bit like trying to juggle jelly; messy, pointless and an utter waste of time. Many have tried to teach me, and many have failed.

When I got an E in my maths GCSE (and ten other GCSEs, from A* to C, I might add) there was much rejoicing that I'd somehow managed to avoid getting 'unclassified'.

The closest I got to pi was having it with gravy for my lunch, while counting to twenty involved removing my shoes *and* socks.

When I tried to retake the exam, the maths teacher ran from the room, screaming. Once their colleagues had dragged them back in, it was decided it was best for all concerned if I abandoned all hope of ever getting the grade.

Somehow, I managed to get into university and have a career without encountering too many problems, despite the blip on my CV.

Another knock-on effect of Covid-19 (which disrupted and ruined many lives) was the fact that many GCSE and A-Level students didn't take their exams. Instead, they were awarded marks based on the predictions of their teachers.

I sent up a silent prayer that I was no longer a student, because if I was, my E grade would have been revoked on account of it being too generous.

So, this year, I'm taking the bull by the horns and resitting my maths GCSE, spurred on by *Educating Essex,* with which I'm currently obsessed.

The poor teachers have no idea what they're letting themselves in for. After all, I think that zero minus five equals nothing. I wish I was making this up, but sadly, I'm not.

I have images of turning on the television to watch the local news and hearing the newscaster say, 'Mathematics teachers across Northern Ireland are resigning in their thousands. The cause of this mass exodus from the profession is yet to be identified.'

Er, that would be me.

38. Farce food

The sheep aren't happy. We've changed the brand of meal they get and it's not gone down well.

We usually have to fight to get to the trough, on account

of our path being blocked by a stack of sheep.

Today, it was business as usual, until that is, the sheep at the front of the queue took her first mouthful. She didn't go as far as spitting it out, but by the time I got to the gate and turned around, she and her mates were standing behind me, bleating, as if to say, 'Excuse me, you seem to have given us the wrong food, hooman.'

I explained that I hadn't made a mistake and that was their lunch. 'If you've got any complaints, please speak to the manager. His name is Paul. Dealing with disgruntled sheep is above my pay grade.'

39. Sheep and me

The sheep and I are locked in a battle of wills, and the sheep are winning.

I've been given a new job on account of the fact I've not killed anything. Yet.

The ewes have lambs with them now and so in addition to grass, they get a daily helping of nuts. This boosts their nutrition, which in turn helps them provide their babies with vital milk. The ewe nuts are also mixed with lamb food which gives the youngsters a vitamin boost. So, delivering this daily ration is an important role and one I take very seriously.

The sheep have the run of two huge fields. The first is on

the slope of a hill, the second on flat ground above it. When I get to the first field, the sheep are nowhere to be seen. They must be right at the back of the next one and haven't heard me, because if they had, they'd be here.

I decide to sneak up on them, and so drop my bag of sheep swag (nuts) as gently as I can on the other side of the gate and squeeze through the bars.

I throw my bag onto my back and, like an anachronistic Santa, slowly climb the hill, bent as low to the ground as I can, chuckling to myself as I go. I really want to surprise them today. If they rumble me early doors, I'm going to invest in some camouflage gear and crawl up the hill on my stomach, army-style. Anything to get the better of them.

To save my poor knees, I decided to take the least steep route (I've had two operations on them because I suffer from chondromalacia patellae – creaky knees to you and me. A condition usually sustained by doing an obscene amount of exercise. I started to suffer from this when I did precisely no exercise. Typical.)

The path brings me up to a gate in the corner of the first field which leads directly into the second. I've never entered via this way, so the sheep won't be expecting me. I manage to get over the gate silently and pop my head around the hedge.

As predicted, the sheep are stationed at their usual lookout posts facing the other direction. I chortle to myself like a cartoon villain.

But as I step into the clearing, one of the eagle-eyed (or should that be sheepy-eyed) residents spots me and raises the alarm with an almighty baaa! The others quickly turn their heads, take a second to focus on me, register the bag, and start to run. Within seconds I'm surrounded and being pushed towards the troughs.

'Alright, alright,' I laugh. (As an aside, if you ever need cheering up, go and see some sheep, I guarantee you'll feel better immediately. Their cheeky faces, excited bleats and the feel of their warm breath on your face can hardly fail to raise the spirits.)

On reaching the first trough, I lean forward to tip the food inside. In their excitement, the sheep surge forward which throws me off balance and before I know it, I'm falling headfirst into the trough.

Somehow, I manage to turn on the ball of my foot and spin around, having quickly decided that landing on my backside is preferable to taking all my teeth out on the rock-hard ground, which I would have done, had I not managed to turn. The outcome was indeed preferable, but not ideal.

I am laying longways, my legs sticking up in the air at one end, my arms flailing out the other and my torso in the body of the trough, while eight sheep attempt to climb over me to get to the food. The others who aren't so fussy, start nibbling my hair, my coat and my fingers.

I immediately regret having had a shower and changing into freshly laundered clothes when I got back from milking this morning. My once black trousers are now covered in dust and my bottom covered in mud. That will teach me.

'Gerrof,' I harrumph, trying to get a grip (literally and metaphorically) on anything to give me leverage. Eventually, I manage to push myself up with the help of two conveniently placed sheep.

I turn and look at them all contentedly eating their lunch. It's a lovely sight and makes all the hard work, mostly of my own making, worth it.

I definitely won that round of 'sneakuponasheep.'

Score: Sheep: 25,000. Holly: one (Yessss!)

40. Watchmen

T he hill sheep have gotten wise to me after I crept up on them yesterday.

They had obviously regrouped and refined their strategy overnight, because when I went to feed them this morning, they were sitting in a group in the middle of the top field, with sheep stationed at either end, acting as lookouts, so there would be no way I could creep up on them.

I told you before, they're cunning, are sheep.

41. Poorly lamb

One of the ewes is having problems giving birth naturally. She's been brave, but the time has come to intervene to stop her from getting stressed. I hold my breath as I watch Paul conduct an internal examination, his face full of concentration.

After what seems like hours, but is probably only a few minutes, he starts to pull, and slowly, a pair of hooves emerge, signalling the lamb's entrance to the world.

He slips out relatively easily and is soon snuggled up next to his mum, who goes about licking him enthusiastically. But her work isn't over yet, she's another lamb to deliver. Thankfully, it's right behind its brother and practically slides out on its own accord, which is a relief, and it's another boy!

Lamb number two is laid next to his mum, who stops sniffing her firstborn and turns her attention to the new arrival. This is often the way with twins, as the ewe naturally knows how to split her time and attention equally between them. But after a few seconds, she turns her back on lamb number two and goes back to lavishing all her love on the first one.

'Don't they only tend to neglect their lamb if they think something's wrong?'

Paul nods as he gently lifts lamb number two. 'Hello, little one,' he whispers. The newborn looks even smaller in his hands and my heart melts at the sight.

He goes about examining the lamb with soft, gentle

fingers, runs a hand over his head and looks at his little body, before shaking his head sadly. 'He's not formed properly,' he says softly. 'Look, his head's misshapen.'

I force myself to look and through my tears, can see that his skull is dome-shaped. I turn my attention to the rest of his body and realise he hasn't really got enough skin to cover his confusion of badly developed bones. In fact, he's almost translucent.

His poor little face looks squashed and misshapen, and his tongue is lolling from the side of his mouth. He's shaking and quiet, but, for all that, one of the most beautiful lambs I've ever seen. His wool, such as it is, is slippery, soft and shiny white.

'I'll go and get some milk to see if we can get him to drink, at least,' Paul says. 'Will you cuddle him until I get back?' I don't need asking twice.

I snuggle him into my woolly jumper in the hope that he thinks I'm his mummy. I can feel his heart beating erratically inside his chest as I run a hand over his little head, feel his floppy ears and stroke his nose. I can't believe it took me so long to realise he was so unwell. But maybe I didn't want to see.

I start to walk up and down, back and forth, jiggling him like a baby and cooing in his ears. Then I notice that his eyes are still shut.

By the time Paul gets back, realisation has dawned.

'He hasn't got any eyes,' I sob, my whole body shaking with sorrow. I hold him out to Paul, as if he can do anything about it. But even his veterinary expertise won't help us this time.

Paul nods, his eyes full of sadness. 'The poor thing isn't fully developed.' As he speaks, he runs a hand gently over the lamb's head and tucks him under the chin. He doesn't have to tell me he won't live long. I roughly wipe my face, so my tears don't land on the lamb and startle him.

Paul lets me cuddle him for a while longer before giving him a feed of warm, comforting milk.

'You're so beautiful,' I whisper softly, hoping he can hear me. Paul hands him back to me and I rock him from side to side, as I've seen human mums do with their babies. Then I sing him a lullaby and when I can't sing anymore because of the lump in my throat, Paul puts his arms around me, so the lamb is between us, and we wrap him in warmth and love.

The lamb snuggles into my chest and lets out a contented sigh. Then, less than half an hour after he arrived in our world, he is gone.

'He had more love lavished on him in thirty minutes than many animals get in their lifetime,' Paul says. 'I don't think he could've been any more loved and I'm sure he felt it.'

I nod and sob softly. Deep down, I know that if he'd been born in the wild, the ewe would've abandoned him long ago. Not out of cruelty, but because she would just naturally want to plough all her energy into looking after the healthy lamb. They know when something is sick or dying, and so pay it no heed. That's nature for you; brutal but practical.

I hope he felt loved during his short time with us, because he was, very much. I hope that, right now, he's running about in long grass and bleating happily with his lamb friends in a huge, sunny, heavenly field. I hope he is full of mischief and joy. As it should have been and should be.

42. Sheep SOS to the rescue

It looks like there's been an explosion in a cotton wool factory.

Paul and I are standing at the entrance of a field which is full of Mule sheep (so not ours, obviously). Most of them are happily milling around and getting on with the business of being sheep. That is, eating, bleating, ruminating, staring off into space etc. Nothing out of the ordinary.

But there's always one, isn't there? Or in this case, three. From my viewpoint, I can just about make out the fence which divides this field from the next. I can see a lot of shrubs, some trees and, yes, three woolly bottoms sticking out of a hedge. But they aren't grazing, they're stuck.

As we approach, it becomes clear what's happened. Not content with the acres of grass directly under their feet, the three amigos wandered off from the rest of the flock to try and get to the grass on the other side of the fence. And the first part of their cunning plan went very well. Indeed, they would have had no trouble getting their sleek heads through the mesh. But they wouldn't have been so smug once they finished their little snack and tried to get *out* again.

The first sheep we encounter has her head wedged about three mesh squares down, which means she's kneeling, but her bottom's pointing to sky. She's thrashing about in a desperate bid to free herself, but to no avail. Then, to make matters worse, she spots us, which winds her up even more until she's just a writhing black and white blur. (Mule sheep have white bodies and black legs and faces.)

Paul approaches and gently but firmly grabs hold of her. He waits until she reduces her wriggles-per-second and proceeds to work her backwards. The key, apparently, is to get their ears back through the fence first, and the rest will follow. Usually.

Happily, this ewe, who looks like she's been there all-night, judging by her sogginess and the amount of wool stuck to the fence, is keen to get out.

Once the ears are free, her head follows and, after one final heave, she's out. She blinks a few times, moves her head gingerly from side to side (her neck must be sore) shakes her legs out as if she's a dancer limbering up for a performance and then she's off, galloping across the field to her mates, letting out joyful bleats as she goes.

We trudge on, taking careful steps as the mud is thick beneath our feet. The next sheep is partially hidden by a tree, and we can just about see her leaf-covered bottom sticking out from the hedge behind it. She sees us as we round the trunk but is clearly too exhausted to put up a fight.

within minutes, Paul has got her free. She bleats, gathers

110

her strength and makes her way across the field to her friends, while we move onto contestant number three in the Great Sheep Escape Game.

The final contender is, naturally, the furthest away and I'm out of breath by the time we get within touching distance of the casualty. But before we can do anything, she manages to wriggle free and shoots off as if she's got a rocket up her backside.

'Typical,' Paul smiles.

Personally, I'd say something a bit more colourful, if I wasn't gasping for air.

Job done, we make our way out of the field, glad that we've managed to help.

Paul and I had been on our way to check our own flock when a walker waved us down to tell us about the sheep in distress.

All the farmers around here know each other and as such, are always happy to help one another out. Today, it was our turn to be the local Sheep SOS Service, and I couldn't be prouder.

It feels good to be part of the community and part of a team. Perhaps we should get some logoed T-shirts and a little van with a phone number emblazoned on the side. A future business opportunity, methinks.

Legend has it that St Bernard dogs used to carry barrels of whiskey around their necks to aid stranded travellers. Perhaps we could have a similar setup for our rescue operations, but instead of a dog, we could have a goat (no kidding) with a packet of silage around its neck, which we could feed to sheep in need.

I articulate this idea to Paul who just gives me *the look* which means 'as if!'

'I like the Mule sheep,' I say, taking Paul's hand, as I attempt to reverse out of this particular conversational *cul-de-sac.*

'Oh yes, they're handsome beasts,' he agrees. Then, after a second of contemplation, adds, 'but not as pretty as Dorsets.'

'Oh no,' I concur. 'Not as pretty as Dorsets, obviously.'

43. A big welcome and a helping hand

'You are most welcome.' Those were the first words I heard when I arrived at Paul's farm on my inaugural visit to Northern Ireland, and I've felt 'most welcome' ever since. Indeed, everyone I've met has been friendly, welcoming and always willing to lend a hand.

When Paul got his trailer stuck in thick mud in a field one afternoon, for example, he called a friend who was on the scene in ten minutes with a big truck ready to pull the stricken vehicle out.

Similarly, there have been many occasions when, just seconds after answering his phone, Paul has been dashing out the door to help someone in need, be it helping get a friend's car out of a ditch, lending a hand when there's cattle to be moved or loaning a piece of equipment. But there's not always an emergency.

Friends will flag him down when we're driving around the country roads, clearly pleased to see him and eager for a chat. The car will slow to a halt, Paul will wind down his window and his friend will lean against the door while they merrily exchange views on the weather.

'Forecast says rain,' one will utter, while the other shakes their head, sorrowfully. 'Aye, it's a bad job. No good for working in the fields.'

The first time I witnessed one of these encounters was when I was visiting from the mainland, and I distinctly remember thinking that everyone had gone stark-raving mad.

When Paul started to slow down unexpectedly, I assumed there was something wrong with the car, maybe a puncture or something? We came to a halt outside a farm, where a man, whom I presumed was the farmer, was leaning leisurely against the gate. Had I missed something? Had he been flagging us down? Maybe he needed Paul's help with a poorly pig or a sick sheep?

Safe to say, my nerves were in shreds, mainly because I didn't know what was happening. (It doesn't help that I can't remember who anyone is and don't recognise people, even those I've met them before.)

So, my first thought was, 'This person is a stranger' and my second thought, because I'm from a city, was, 'Are we about to be car-jacked?'

And, because my brain can conjure up a host of

devastating, calamitous and nightmarish situations faster than a cheetah on speed, my third thought was that we were going to have to attend to some kind of emergency, because that was the only other reason I could think of as to why someone would suddenly stop in the middle of a road.

Having ascertained that we were *not* about to be a) robbed or b) dragged into a tragic event, I calmed down. A bit.

'What's happening?' I asked, craning my neck to see if smoke was billowing from the back of the car and I'd failed to notice.

'Sure, I've not seen Colm in a brave while,' Paul said, gesturing to the man leaning in the window, who smiled and nodded. 'How's you?'

Fighting the urge to say, 'Petrified we're all going to die in a variety of new and exciting ways,' I uttered something about 'being fine thank you,' while keeping an eye on the road.

'What if someone comes flying up behind us and wants us to move?' I whispered, twisting uneasily in my seat, concluding that if we were about to be squashed by an oncoming vehicle, I at least wanted to see what type and make it was.

If you just suddenly stopped your car like that in London, you'd be lucky to have any tyres left after ten seconds, let alone hubcaps. But here, even when another car *does* come down the road, which it did, there was no problem.

In fact, on recognizing Paul, the driver smiled, waved, pulled up, abandoned their car and mooched over to join the conversation. 'It's a bad job about the weather,' they said, right on cue.

The relaxed attitude seemed a bit surreal and unnatural to me, a former city dweller, but I liked it. I liked the fact that the pace of life is different. That you can literally take time to smell the flowers or have a catch up with a pal, seemingly paying no heed to the rest of the busy, manic, panicking world. And it's brilliant. I share my thoughts with Paul and his friends.

'Sure, everyone has time for each other out here,' Colm beams. 'Welcome to the countryside.'

'Aye,' another friend says with a smile. 'Everything's better here. The pace of life, the people, the scenery.' He turns and gestures to the green rolling hills and the crashing waves of the sea which can be viewed from almost every house in the village. 'Life's grand here.'

I nod. It certainly is. And this kindness and willingness to do good turns is not just shared among friends, but given freely and gladly to total strangers, too.

For example, before lockdown kicked in, Paul and I popped to a retail park to do some shopping. As we made our way towards the shops, he spotted a young couple having car trouble. Their vehicle had clapped out right in the middle of the car park, and the young woman was getting flustered as a queue formed behind them.

Her partner got out and started pushing the stricken vehicle to get it to a safe spot.

Quick as a flash, Paul dashed across the road to help and within minutes, others had joined in, so that in no time at all, they were all out of harm's way.

I watched as people offered them use of mobile phones so they could call for assistance, while others handed over bottles of water and snacks, on the assumption that they could be waiting a while for the breakdown services to arrive.

On another occasion, I was reversing into a space in a busy car park when a passing gentleman stopped and waved. I decided I didn't know, but wound my window down anyway.

He ambled over and proceeded to tell me he thought the space I was trying to get into was 'a wee bit small,' but with a bit of manoeuvring, I should manage it.

Not that anyone would ever actually stop to talk to you in London anyway, but even if they did, the exchange would probably have ended there. But not here.

To my amazement, bemusement and delight, the man put his shopping down and guided me into the space with an exciting array of hand signals and lots of 'lefts,' 'rights' and 'that'll do you, nows.'

I was touched by his kindness and for sparing the time for me, a stranger. I thought perhaps he'd helped me because he was worried that his own car would get crunched, but he didn't even have one, he was simply walking past and decided to help.

'Thanks,' I beamed.

'No bother,' he smiled. Everything here is 'no bother.'

But these acts of kindness, although 'no bother' means so much to the recipients. People are so time poor nowadays, rushing hither and thither, wanting everything done yesterday and seemingly never having enough time, that often, they forget to carry out acts of kindness when the opportunity presents itself. So, it's nice to see that such selfless acts haven't been completely forgotten.

It seems that everyone has a smile and a kind word. I used to smile at people when I headed into London for work, but soon gave up as I got bored of being glared at. Alternatively, they would look away or take twenty-five steps backwards (which is an interesting manoeuvre to attempt on the packed 6.45am to Baker Street) because they assume you've just broken out of prison or are about to try and sell them something.

Now, I'm learning to smile at strangers again and wave to people I see in the shops or in the street. Human interaction is so important, as the lockdowns demonstrated.

The other thing I can't get used to in the countryside, and tight-knit communities, is the beeping of horns.

The first time it happened, Paul and I were out for a drive and I was just dozing off, when the car behind us pipped its horn and I almost jumped out of my skin.

'What's wrong?' I said, frantically turning in my seat, expecting the driver to be so close they could come in for a cup of tea. 'Did you do something wrong?'

'No,' he laughed. 'Why?'

'That person pipped their horn at us.'

'Yes.'

'Well, in London, that means they either want you to speed up, or stop so they can punch you in the face for, and I quote, "being a shit driver."'

'Weird,' he says. 'No, that's just one of my mates saying hello.'

'Right. Can't he just… pick up the phone to say that?'

'He could. But we don't always get time for that, so beeping is a nice way of acknowledging each other as we go about our day-to-day business.'

I nod. 'That makes sense.'

It still makes me jump, though. Paul has a lot of mates which equates to a lot of pips. But now, despite my nerves, when I hear a honk, I smile. It's nice to have friends and be acknowledged.

But being as my interest in cars, on a scale of one to ten, is less than zero, it still hurts my brain to think that people can recognise each other based solely on the car they drive. Skills. These people have serious skills.

44. Coated in love

paul has made a coat rack and says it is a present, which is lovely.

But I suspect the *real* reason he got creative was because our hallway floor had disappeared under a carpet of coats. This is my fault, as I tend to shed my many layers when I get back from milking.

I go about gathering the coats and ceremoniously place them on the rack.

It turns out that the coats had been covering a range of exciting objects, including hairbands, magazines, jackets (various), wind cheetahs (or wind leopards as I call them), body warmers, buckets, feed bags and a few disgruntled spiders who scuttle off to find shelter elsewhere.

Standing back to admire his handiwork and the plethora of coats, I congratulate Paul on a job well done. Although now it looks as though there's about thirty people living here, when in reality, it's just the two of us. (Sing along, children of the 1990s!)

45. A horny issue

The calves are having their horn buds removed today.

This is a quick process and a necessary one. By removing their ability to grow horns, the farmers are removing the risk of a cow catching itself and causing long-lasting damage. It also eliminates the risk of the farmer being impaled on the end of the horns, which would inevitably be attached to a tonne of muscle. So, it is a win-win-situation.

There are various ways of disbudding, but the one the local farmer uses involves the application of a disbudding iron (which to me looks like a massive curling tong) to cauterise the horn bud (which is presumably where the phrase, 'nip it in the bud' comes from. Or that could be something to do with flowers.) Each calf receives adequate amounts of anaesthetic (which blocks the nerve to the horn) and painkillers, so they don't feel anything.

'Holly can draw up the anaesthetic for you,' Paul tells the farmer, with a smile.

'Can she?' I say, aghast. Does he not know how bad I am at numbers? Does he want dead calf carcasses all over the barn?

After all, my inability to do maths was one of the many reasons why I didn't go into nursing. Can you imagine? 'Oh, I'm sorry, doctor, did you say five mills of morphine? Oh well. It's an ill wind that doesn't blow anyone any good. At least the undertaker will have some more business this week.'

'Am I allowed to do that?' I say, as I snap back to reality.

'Yes.'

'But I don't have a license. And I'm not, in case you've forgotten, a vet.'

'Farmers administer drugs too.'

'I'm not a farmer, either. What if I get it wrong and the calf feels pain?' I babble. 'Or I give it too much and it dies?'

'You'll be fine. Now stop making excuses and draw up what he needs,' Paul smiles, handing me the medicine bottle and syringe.

It never occurred to me that farmers can administer some drugs without the presence of a veterinarian. I suppose this makes sense, as it means they don't have to haul their vet out of bed every time there's a minor ailment to deal with.

Still, my hands are shaking as I draw up the first dose. 'Is that right?' I ask, holding the syringe aloft.

'Yes.'

To aid me in my job, Paul has written the amount on

each bottle and stays by my side throughout. Still, I appreciate his kindness and efforts to boost my confidence.

The farmer and I get a rhythm going. I fill one syringe and pass it to him, which he administers to the calf while I draw up the other syringe. He takes the new dose and sets down the empty syringe next to the relevant bottle, which I get ready for the next calf.

'Horlicks,' says the farmer.

'What, now?' I say, always ready to serve hot beverages when they're required.

'No, he's saying that so as not to swear,' Paul explains. 'The men try to curb their language when you're around because you're a lady.'

My eyebrows shoot up so much I need to climb a ladder to get them down again.

Wow. That's so sweet and gentlemanly. I don't burst their bubble by saying that when I worked in newsrooms, I used to swear so much that I could've made a sailor blush. I know it isn't ladylike and I shouldn't have done it, but you sort of just get caught up in the culture and urgency. Not that is an excuse for having a mouth like a sewer, but there you go.

I did once ask a fellow journalist if they thought they could ever give up swearing.

'I've got more chance of shitting in the Queen's handbag,' was the bold reply. Fair enough.

I turned my attention back to the non-swearing farmer. 'Why did he say Horlicks? What's he done?'

'Stabbed himself with the needle. I'll get the accident book.'

His colleagues found it hilarious, but thankfully he didn't skewer himself too badly and besides, the needle was empty.

The job is soon done, and I can't stop smiling. I did it! I'm basically the animal nursing equivalent of Florence Nightingale. Someone fetch me a uniform and a lamp.

Medicine administered, the calves are put into a tiny crush (a pen which holds them secure so they can't hurt themselves or the farmer) and the cauterisation is carried out. The calves are so calm and well behaved, *I'm* the one with my hands over my eyes.

Once done, the little buds are covered in silver spray which prevents infection, so now they look like they're going to a naff 1980s fancy dress party. Or auditioning for Barbarella. But still, they look cute.

It's while packing away the equipment that Paul notices something is amiss.

'Erm, do you have any bull calves?' he asks the farmer.

'I hope not.'

'Well, I think you do.' He nods to one of the calves in the corner.

'How do you know?' I ask before my brain has a chance to catch up with my mouth.

'It's got a willy.'

We turn as one to gaze at the calf and the tell-tale area.

'Unbelievable,' the farmer mutters, taking a closer look. 'It is as well.'

'How did that happen?' I ask. 'Well, not *how* did it happen, I mean how did he sneak in here?'

'The farmer committed the cardinal sin of assuming they were all girls.'

I nod knowingly. As a journalist, you're told never to assume. That way evil lies. And prison.

'Can we keep him?' I ask, batting my eyelashes.

'Nope.'

Darn.

So, all these weeks we've been referring to the calves as 'our girls' and there has been a boy in the mix all along! Paul and I are slightly embarrassed that neither of us spotted this when we were wrapping the calves in their coats.

The thing is, now I know he's a boy, I cannot *un*know it. He's very handsome and well built, but has the most awesome eyelashes I've ever seen.

'I'll house-train him and everything,' I continue, determined to keep him as a pet.

'He can sleep in a basket in the living room and I'll take him for walks every day, I promise.'

'Nope.'

Darn.

Thankfully, the farmer doesn't have the capacity to take 'our boy' away today, so he can frolic with the girls a bit longer. Then he'll go and learn how to be a bull in one of the farmer's fields. He's such a handsome boy, I bet the girls won't be able to resist him and he will father many calves.

When the farmer has gone, I return to the calf house to bed up (put fresh straw into the pens) and give them milk. They seem to have forgotten about their ordeal and are soon merrily drinking.

I'm so proud of my brave little soldiers. If I could, I'd give them a treat, just like mothers do when their children come out of the dentist with a clean bill of health, no fillings and a sticker declaring 'I'm a clever boy/girl.' Maybe I could stretch to some stickers for our calves. Or at least a star chart, because in my eyes, they are all stars.

46. Shopping habits

Apparently, social media shows adverts based on your browsing history. The idea presumably being that you'll be inspired to purchase a selection of similar items to make life easier.

Therefore, Paul often gets adverts for books about science and veterinary medicine, in addition to sheep paraphernalia and material for PhD students (which makes sense, as he is one.)

Intrigued, I decide to take a look at the adverts offered on my computer, expecting to see suggestions for books on Jane Austen and Shakespeare.

I boot my laptop, go online and am promptly offered a selection of cuddly giraffes and aardvarks, a soup ladle shaped like the Loch Ness Monster, a first aid kit, a book entitled *Cooking if you are an idiot* and a maths textbook for three-year-olds. Fair enough.

47. Stamping it out

I 've been robbed. Well, not actually robbed (sorry, I'm a journalist, sometimes I can't help but spin a story.) Let me explain.

I'd popped to the post office to buy some stamps, as I'm getting through them rather quickly nowadays. I've taken to sending my parents and friends cards and letters as an alternative to texting.

If I'm being totally honest, the main reason for doing this is because I like to play the 'how long will my letter take to get to England this time' game.

It never fails to amaze me that I can post something from Northern Ireland on a Monday, and it will be with the recipient on the mainland on the Tuesday. Just to be clear, that means a postman (or woman) has to collect my letter and take it to the sorting office so it can be transported to an airport, whizzed to England, sorted again and taken to its destination.

The organisational and logistical skills required to pull this off on a daily basis makes my eyes water. I can just about manage to get myself out of bed in the morning with a month's notice, let alone anything else.

'One book of twelve first class stamps, please.'

The cashier nodded. 'That's ten pounds and twenty pence please, love.'

'I'm sorry, you must have misheard me. I only wanted to buy a book of stamps, not the actual *post office*.'

'That's how much they are now, I'm afraid.'

My eyes nearly popped out of my head. It would be more cost effective to invest in a carrier pigeon or send smoke signals. In the end, I yield, but not before making a mental note that maybe texting is the way forward after all. Yes, I know I'm contrary, it's one of the traits that I hate about myself. But I love it, too.

Sadly, I misplaced my eye-wateringly expensive stamps and turned the house upside down looking for them, but to no avail. Some weeks later, I was out checking the sheep when I got caught in an almighty downpour. I put my hand in my pocket to retrieve my hat but instead pulled out a waterlogged book of stamps.

I must have stuffed them in there on the day of purchase and promptly forgot all about them. And by the looks of them, they aren't salvageable. I might as well have taken a £10 note out of my purse and thrown it down the drain.

On a side note, if you ever find yourself wanting to send something from, or to Northern Ireland, you can use UK stamps, on account of the fact that it is part of the United Kingdom. But, if you want to send something to The Republic of Ireland, you will have to buy a completely different type of stamp, because not only is it a different *county*, it's also part of Europe.

Obviously, I didn't know this when I first came out here, and was merrily sending wedding invitations to Paul's family in the Republic using stamps I already had. It was only when I started moaning about the fact that we hadn't received any replies that Paul realised what had happened, and we had to quickly replicate everything *tout suite*.

The *stampgate* episode reminds me of the time my parents and I went on a daytrip to Southend in Essex. Mum loves it because she spent a good chunk of her childhood there.

Many a weekend, my nan would bundle herself and her offspring onto a bus and make the trip from north London to Southend in order to visit *her* aunt who lived by the sea. In fact, my mum spent so much time there that she was actually christened in a local church.

One day, Dad and I decided to make it our mission to locate the church and take Mum there as a surprise, which we did. We even managed to find her name listed in the church log, which was a very special moment for all of us, but for Mum in particular.

Hers was a difficult childhood to say the least; money was always tight and there was nothing in the way of treats, which was why she looked forward to the Southend trips so much; they seemed to be one of the few bright spots on the horizon of her youth. I tell a lie, there *was* another bright spot ahead, which was when she met my dad. But that is a different story for another time.

Southend is a place of faded charm and grandeur, but it appeals for that very reason. If you ever find yourself in the area, I'd highly recommend a visit.

It's crammed full of cafés, quirky gift shops and amusement arcades that draw you in with exciting, hypnotic flashing lights and happy, robotic, repetitive music.

The high street, packed with a selection of shops, is a real treat for anyone interested in architecture, history or indeed, both. Take the time to look up, past the window displays and beyond the modern awnings and you'll see aspects and elements of the original buildings; from bricks which were once bright red but have faded with the passing of time, to stonework etched with the names of shops which have long since been forgotten. In this respect, Southend High Street is a palimpsest of the taste of successive shoppers over the decades.

As far as I know, Southend gained its High Street during the Edwardian era. It all began with the opening of Garon's Market Store in 1885, which proved so popular with consumers that other shops soon sprang up around it.

Whenever my parents and I visit, we always walk along the seafront, regardless of the weather. We enjoy seeing dogs dashing excitedly up and down and circling their owners, before scooting off to jump in the surf or sniff the seaweed. And whatever the time of year, the smell of fish and chips is always too good to resist, and we eat our fill inside one of the lovely seafront cafés.

As we stuff our faces, we watch as adults and children wander past with big, happy ice-cream-stained smiles.

In its heyday, Southend was *the* place to go on high days and holidays, and the destination of choice for many Londoners who could easily get there on the train.

Indeed, it remains popular to this day. It seems that most people, regardless of their age, love paddling in the sea, eating candy floss, walking along the longest pier in the country and generally forgetting their cares for a while.

In the early days of my parent's courtship, they would often go to a dance or to the pictures. On one such evening, as the credits rolled on the latest Hollywood epic, they both came to the same conclusion, which was that they didn't want the date to end. And so, on a whim, and presumably, on Dad's last drop of petrol, they drove to Southend for a moonlit seaside stroll and a late-night serving of fish and chips. Anyway, I digress. Now, where was I? Oh yes, I was telling you about one of our family outings. It was a chilly Saturday afternoon in December, and Mum had popped into a shop to buy her weekly quota of stamps. (She enters a vast number of competitions and is single-handedly keeping the post office afloat with the number of stamps she buys for various entries.)

The assistant greeted my mum with a smile and gave her the stamps.

'Oh,' Mum said as she inspected them, 'Do you have any Christmas-themed stamps I could have instead of these plain ones, please?'

The assistant looked through her stock book. 'No, sorry, madam, we've only got these ones,' she said apologetically, handing over a set of stamps depicting The Virgin Mary and The Messiah – in technicolour. Mum tried to hide her smile. 'These will do nicely, thank you.'

My mum is one of the nicest people I know, and as such, wouldn't have dreamed of telling the assistant that she couldn't have given her a more Christmassy set of stamps if she'd wrapped them in tinsel and presented them with an accompanying Fir tree.

On hearing this woeful tale of misunderstanding as to the true meaning of Christmas, I tutted. Dad shook his head in disbelief and whispered, 'Jesus Christ.'

Well, exactly.

48. Genius

I call Liz to share a cleaning tip which I think will revolutionise housework and make me a household name like Mrs Beeton.

'I have a new cleaning method and it's going to change your life,' I say breathlessly before she can get a word in edgeways. 'So, go into the room you want tidy and take a good look at the mountain of detritus that would usually take about four thousand hours of manpower to clear. Do you have that horrendous image in your head? Good. Now for the genius bit. Lean into the room, grab the door handle, pull it slowly towards you and click it shut. Mess instantly gone.'

'So just to clarify,' Liz says slowly, 'you're suggesting I simply shut the door on the mess?'

'Yes! Go, enjoy the rest of your life. Frolic naked around the house, if you want. Eat yoghurt without a spoon. Learn to knit. Have a rave (actually, don't do that, we're in lockdown.) You can thank me later. Don't be jealous that I thought of it first. I know, I'm a genius.'

49. Gissa job

'**A**nything I can do to help?'
   'Buckets.'
'I only asked.'

But Paul isn't being disparaging, he's giving me a job, which is to make sure that the ewes have enough food and water in their buckets.

'Oh, OK,' I say, putting on my gloves and coat, happy to assist.

As I walk out into the chilly, early morning sunshine, I can't help but smile at the fact this is part of my daily routine now. I stop to watch Paul as he leans on a fence to count sheep. As he does, I think how lucky I am to have found him (and his flock, of course.) Then, I haul myself over the fence to do my rounds.

The sun yawns from behind a cloud as I move down the field, my boots wet with early morning dew. I take a moment to listen to the sheep calling for their breakfast and feel the wind on my face. I can see fields stretching down to the sea and smell salt on the breeze.

I turn and wave to Paul as joy rushes over me like a wave. 'Welcome to my new office,' I shout, throwing my arms out. I know, it's a hard life.

While I'm working with the animals, my thoughts turn to other matters, chief of which is the fact that I need a job. I know this but am not relishing the prospect.

I ask Paul if I can be a full-time housewife and lamb

foster mum.

'No,' is the swift reply.

That isn't the answer I was hoping for, and so will just keep asking the question until he changes his mind. And if that sounds like the response of a spoiled child, it's because it is. I am a *very* spoiled child inside a grown woman's body.

The thing is, I may be a qualified journalist and former press officer, but I have zero self-confidence. The global crisis of coronavirus and the fact that England and Northern Ireland are in lockdown, with many businesses subsequently folding like deckchairs, also isn't helping the situation. Thus, my job prospects aren't looking particularly rosy.

But I do need a means of income, and fast. But what? What would the Land Army girls do?

Answer: Get on with it. Keep calm and carry on. And stop moaning.

I always find myself asking 'what would the Land Army girls do?' when I find myself in a pickle.

These remarkable women worked their fingers to the bone during World War One and Two to keep the nation fed and the animals cared for. We owe them, and all the women who stepped up to take over a host of jobs when the poor men were called up to fight, a great deal.

All over Great Britain, women were taking on jobs they'd never done before, working as dispatch drivers, farmers, forestry workers (the beautifully and colloquially named Lumberjills) pilots, mechanics, nurses and many other roles besides. Not to mention those who worked in the munitions factories or as wardens and fire watchers.

I look around me and ask, what's the biggest local industry? **Answer:** farming.

So, I could try and get a job milking cows. After all, I do have experience. Just. Let me explain.

When Paul and I were dating (or courting, to use that lovely old-fashioned phrase) he would visit me in England and then I would fly to see him in Northern Ireland. Conducting a long-distance relationship is hard, and so we took it in turns to do the journey.

It's a bittersweet thing, when the love of your life lives so far away. You spend half your time looking forward to a long weekend together, which is over in the blink of an eye, and the other half pining and counting the weeks until you're reunited.

As such, I feel so lucky that we are now husband and wife and don't have to plan visits weeks in advance. It's wonderful spending every day together.

Anyway, I digress. Where was I? Oh yes, telling you about my first milking experience. What follows is my diary from that time.

Now, as I said, the budget doesn't stretch to special effects and so you're going to have to use your imagination again. Back in time we go. Hold on tight...

50. Land Girl

I 'm going to go milking with Paul today. I'm excited and nervous in equal measure, having heard so much about the herd.

As well as being a vet and having his own animals, Paul does milking shifts at a local farm. When I was over in England, I'd regularly get messages saying, *going milking*, then, two hours later, *cleaning up* and finally, *home*.

I'd often imagined him milking, but now I'm going to see him doing this important activity first-hand and I can't wait.

After lunch, I emerge from the house with my hair pinned up and tied with a spotty blue headband, channelling my inner Land Girl. In addition, I'm wearing waterproof trousers and new Wellington boots. I grin at Paul, feeling enthusiastic and smart. Hands on hips, I proudly declare, 'I'm ready.'

Two seconds into my first shift, and presumably as part of some bizarre welcome ritual, one of the cows looks at me, turns around, lifts her tail and proceeds to liberally spray me in shite. But instead of being horrified, I'm delighted. It's great being able to get this mucky at work!

I leave the parlour three hours later covered from head to toe in poo, pee, water, straw and mud. Everything aches and the least said about the state of my hair, the better. I run my forearm across my forehead to wipe the perspiration away, but this only makes things worse, as my arms are also covered in poo. Catching sight of my reflection in the car door, I turn, stony-faced, to Paul.

'That,' I say slowly, picking bits of straw out of my hair, 'was the hardest work I've ever done. I ache in places I didn't even know I had. It was physically and mentally draining and frankly, I loved it.' He smiles with relief as we remove our gloves and hold hands.

That night, I was asleep as soon as my head hit the pillow and for once, I didn't have bad dreams, only cow-filled ones, which was lovely. So much so that I spent most of the next day mulling over my first milking experience.

Being allowed into the milking parlour felt a bit like going behind the scenes of a show; somewhere you wouldn't normally have access to, but where the magic happens.

The noise was the first thing that hit me as I entered the milking parlour, on account of the machinery being so loud. There was the sound of the clusters being put on the cows, the milk being pumped through various pipes to the tank and gates opening and closing. Combined, these noises took on a rhythmic quality, like a steam engine in motion.

I could also hear the cows calling, the farmers chatting and the hum of machinery far off in the fields.

The smell also took some getting used to. It was a combination of silage, hay, straw, cows and their excrement, to put it politely. It made my eyes water, but now, I don't even notice it.

You enter the parlour on the ground level but the pit, where staff stand to milk the cows, is accessed by a few shallow steps, and is therefore at basement level. This is also where the clusters live; machines which are attached to the cow's teats so that they can be milked out. The milk is then whizzed along the pipes to the milk tank, where it is stored ready for the milk tanker to collect and take to the factory.

The first time I went into the parlour, someone has already bought the cows (the stars of the show) in from their houses and they were standing in the holding bay, patiently waiting to be let into the milking area.

Because they were standing behind a gate, they looked like excited Christmas shoppers queuing outside a super-market, eagerly waiting for the doors to open so they could grab bargains. Sure enough, no sooner had the gate started to move than they were surging forward, each one keen to get to the font to get their dinner, which is served as they are milked

We were standing in the pit as they came in, which meant we were literally looking up at them, and I can confirm that cows are beautiful close up. And I was as fas-cinated by them, as they were of me.

I approached one of the black and white cows tentat-ively, gently putting my hand out so as not to startle her. She sniffed my hand and moved her nose up my arm to my shoulder. Then, she sniffed my ear and nose, snuffling closer all the time until all I could see was her pink nose and feel her warm breath on my face, which made me giggle. Suddenly, she snapped her head back, nodded, as if in welcome and trotted back to the other girls standing behind her, as if to share the gossip.

On further inspection, I noticed that all the cows were chewing.

'What are they eating?' I asked, not sure where they could've got any food from, unless one of them had snuck off to the tuck shop while we weren't looking.

'They're ruminants,' Paul smiles. 'They ruminate.'

'Of course, they do,' I say, nodding wisely. 'Good. What does that mean?'

Here's the summary: When cows eat, they swallow their food, quite quickly without really chewing. It ends up in their rumen, which is their first stomach, where it sits, fermenting in lots of liquid.

Once they've finished eating, they bring the grass back up to their mouth and chew it properly: this is 'chewing the cud' which breaks the tough grass stems up before returning to the rumen. Then the rumen liquid and finely chewed bits of grass slowly pass to the next compartment, the reticulum.

The result is that they constantly look like they're munching on large bits of chewing gum. (This is my observation. obviously. Just thought I'd clarify in case you thought you'd picked up a veterinary textbook by mistake. Easily done.)

'That's amazing,' I coo. 'I mean, that's like me eating a chocolate bar and then being able to savour it all over again, while burning calories with all the chewing. Why can't humans have rumens? Oh, and I'm a poet and I don't know it,'

On top of the crushing realisation that it's unlikely humans will ever develop a rumen, I also discovered it's a myth that cows have four stomachs. Apparently, they have one stomach and four chambers. Disappointing.

51. Making friends

I look forward to going back to the milking parlour.

Initially, my main job is to simply put the cleaning bubbles on the cows' teats, which is wiped off before the clusters go on.

Therefore, the piece of equipment which dispenses the suds soon becomes known as 'my' magic bubble wand. I love it because when you press the 'trigger' a plethora of beautiful bubbles pour forth from the nozzle, making it look like we are at a child's birthday party.

There's a rhythm to milking; The clusters make a sucking noise as they are put on the teats (which sounds like someone drinking the dregs of a milkshake through a straw) and there's a gentle whooshing noise as the milk travels from the cluster up the pipe towards the tank.

The way in which the staff milk has its own rhythm, too. Everyone has their own job to do. Sometimes, they will mix and match but often, they adopt one key role throughout the session.

I begin by distributing my bubbles and work my way down the line. The next person gets their paper towels ready and follows me, wiping the bubbles off as they go. When we're about halfway down, the next person begins putting the clusters on, and we get a rhythm going.

As the first line of cows are milked, we bring in the second line, who enter on the opposite side, and the process begins again.

The clusters, which fall off once each cow has been milked, are then cleaned and put on the cows opposite. Once all the girls are milked out, they're cleaned and released. We continue in this fashion until all 200 cows are milked and settled in their houses, where they either chill out in their beds or socialise.

The cows can often be found standing under the huge, yellow scratching brushes which are at their disposal in their 'lounge area'. The brushes are essentially big rollers, like those you would find in a car wash, which are attached to the walls by long metal arms. When a cow stands under one of these, the roller rotates thanks to an electric motor, which enables the cow to have a good scratch/massage, and it's clear to see how much they love it. They almost smile.

As the end of milking, it is hugely satisfying to know that all the cows have had their dinner, have been milked and are back in their houses and having a rest. But our work is far from over. The clean-up operation requires all hands on deck and can take the guts of an hour.

All the floors and surfaces must be cleaned by hand (scraped and then hosed down), while the machinery is cleaned via a three-rinse cycle. It was while waiting for this to finish during my first shift, that I was introduced to another key member of staff.

'You've not met Bob yet, have you?' Paul asks.

I shake my head.

'Come on then,' he grins, and with that, he grabs my hand and we run out of the parlour, around the side of the building and down a corridor. I feel as if I'm a contestant on *The Crystal Maze* and am about to be asked if I want a mental, physical, mystery or skill game.

We career around the corner and come to a clattering halt. 'This is Bob.'

'I can't see anyone.'

Paul walks towards what looks like a motorised skip. 'This is Bob.'

I grin, vacantly, not sure what is happening.

'He's a vital member of the team who cleans the holding yard beautifully.'

'Oh, so he's computerised?'

'No, you have to drive him.'

'You mean *you* have to drive him?'

'No, you.'

'Erm, no. I can't.'

'You can.'

A few seconds later, and despite my protests, I am astride the machine and turning a key, which kicks it into life. It sounds like a sports car firing up and I struggle to hear over the noise as Paul gives me a crash course in driving Bob.

My steering is all over the place and keeping him on course is difficult. 'I have been driving for about twelve years,' I insist as I swerve all over the parlour.

'You'll get the hang of it.'

As he says that, some of his colleagues appear in the doorway, which makes me shudder with horror. I don't want them to see my bad driving!

'Can I stop now?' I call over the sound of the engine. 'I look like a twat who can't drive.'

'Well, you'll just have to un-twat yourself,' he laughs, 'my nephew has no problem driving Bob.'

'And how ol hew?'

'Ten.'

'Great.'

'And don't f your cleaning brush down,' he said, gesturing

He steers me onto into the passage and lets go, as if I am a child who had just had the stabilizers removed from their first bike. I screech all the way, gripping the steering wheel for all I am worth in a bid to keep the darn thing in a straight line.

Somehow, I manage to get the machine around the corner and into the holding yard, where I drive up and down so slowly that I'm overtaken by a tortoise.

'Put your foot down,' Paul shouts. I shake my head, too scared to go any faster. But at least I'm learning a new skill. Perhaps I'll make a good parlour maid after all.

I'm reminiscing about my stint with the cows as I make dinner.

'Do you think I could get some milking shifts?' I ask Paul.

'I don't see why not,' he smiles. 'Why, is that something you'd like to do?'

I nod. 'I'd like to do something worthwhile. And if I did the morning shift, I'd have enough time during the day to help you look after the animals and for us to spend time together. So, an ad-hoc role would be perfect.'

'Sounds grand. Let's have a chat to some farmers and see if there's anything going.'

I smile, despite the thousands of butterflies whirring in my stomach. The thought of stepping outside of our little home, this haven, makes me nervous, but it has to be done. Think of the Land Girls, I tell myself. Think of them.

52. While the boss is away...

I 'm having a nightmare that Paul has gone out and all the sheep have escaped.

Except I'm not dreaming. Paul *has* gone out and the sheep have indeed, escaped.

I was just making the milk for the calves when I spotted something out the corner of my eye. It was white and woolly and shouldn't have been there. I looked around and to my horror, saw not one sheep but an assortment, all filing out of the shed as if they were going on a school trip.

One of the older ewes is leading the charge, followed by some of her friends and their lambs, who are skipping behind. Loitering at the back, with their heads down as if sulking, are the teenagers. I can almost hear them saying, 'Mum, I don't want to hang out with you, it's so embarrassing.'

I drop what I'm doing (literally, the churn goes flying) and run outside to try and get in front of them but seeing at they have four legs each and I only have two, they soon outpace me and are in the lane in no time.

I run to the shed for a bucket of meal, which invariably sets off the sheep in the other half of the house, who are thankfully, still penned in.

As I feverishly pour meal into the bucket, I spot the open gate through which the sheep made their escape. It's blowing and creaking in the breeze, taunting me. As I stare at it, fear snakes down my spine; I must've forgotten to put the chain on properly and it wouldn't have taken much for an inquisitive sheep to push the gate open with her nose and bingo – freedom!

I run back outside and call the sheep, desperation dripping from my voice. Some of them turn to look at the mad woman violently shaking a bucket, but the majority ignore me and continue munching on the free buffet of grass and hedges.

My brain's whirring as I try to think of a Plan B. What would Paul do? Oh, that's right, he wouldn't be in this situation in the first place, because he wouldn't have been so absentminded.

Anyway, I decide the best bet is to cut across the lower field and head them off at the pass. What I categorically *don't* want to happen, is for them to make it to the end of the lane, because if they get that far, all hell will break loose, because they could go one of four ways and I'll never get them back.

I approach the gate, decide to leap over it heroically, misjudge it spectacularly, catch my boot on the top bar and go careering headfirst into the field. Winded but not hurt, I get up and jog across the field. As I do, I can see them on the other side of the hedge, the little blighters.

My plan is to creep to the gate without being spotted, climb over and shoo them back.

But then I realise I don't have to climb over, because, by some miracle, I'm small enough to fit through the bottom bars of the gate. This is good, as it means I won't risk rattling it and potentially spooking the sheep.

I emerge triumphantly on the other side of the gate and stand on the path to block the lane. The sheep see me, blink, turn and casually make their way towards home.

'Yes,' I whisper.

Unfortunately, I'm premature in my celebrations as the ringleader chucks a right at the last minute, and the whole gang follows. I curse under my breath. At least the gate leading to the next field is closed. When I catch up, I see that they've bundled themselves into a corner and have nowhere else to go, which causes me to cackle like a cartoon villain. 'Now what are you doing to do?' I ask, then immediately wish I hadn't.

By way of an answer, the ringleader looks about her, spots a gap in the hedge and leads the troops through, as if she's starring in the sheep version of *The Great Escape*. Now, if a human tried to do that, they'd get shredded to pieces on the thorns and brambles, but sheep are made of sterner stuff and pass through without any problems whatsoever.

'Oh, you have no idea how close you lot are to becoming kebabs.'

I chase them around the field once or twice, with *The Benny Hill Show* theme playing in my head as they dodge me with ease.

In the end, I decide I need help (in more ways than one) and seek the assistance of Mummy-In-Law. However, when we return, the sheep have made their own way into the little shed in the middle of the field. I run over and slam the door shut.

'Hurrah,' I say triumphantly, as if that had been my plan all along, when in fact, the sheep had sorted it for me. 'Right, you can stay there until Paul gets home and then you'll be in trouble for being so naughty.'

Of course, I don't mean it. It was my fault for not checking the gate was closed in the first place. Sheep are inquisitive and will follow each other. It's what they do.

I go back to the sheep shed to check on the others and find that one of the toddlers has decided to shove her head into the bars of the silage feeder and get wedged.

'Really?' I say, hands on hips. 'This isn't helpful behaviour.' She looks at me with sad eyes, but this doesn't stop her from chewing on the silage in front of her as she does so. There's always time for food when you are a sheep, whatever the circumstances.

I try my best to get her out; I cajole, I plead, I push her ears back in a bid to fit her smoothly through the bars, but to no avail. We talk about how it would be better for her to reverse, as opposed to continuously stepping forward, as she'll never get out that way, but she pays me no heed.

Such is my desperation that I briefly consider using butter to slide her out, but with one more triumphant pull, I manage to get her head through the bars and we both fall onto the floor, panting and exhausted. After a second, she stands, shakes her head, gives me a dirty look and runs off, bleatingly angrily all the way back to her mother. 'You're welcome,' I sigh.

As soon as Paul gets home, we go to the little sheep house in the field to look at the escapees. Because Paul is effectively their boss, the sheep generally do as he says, which means he doesn't need a bucket of food to convince them to move. So when he opens the door, they all file out obediently, as if butter wouldn't melt.

'Unbelievable,' I say. 'They only play up when you aren't here.'

Back in the shed, they gather around Paul's legs, look up at him with sad eyes and let out long, mournful bleats as if to say, 'Your wife was mean to us, she locked us in the shed while you were gone and didn't feed us. We're poor, mistreated, starved sheep. Don't you feel sorry for us?'

In response, Paul pats each of them on the head and gives them treats. Treats!

'Should you give naughty sheep treats?' I ask. 'You're rewarding bad behaviour.'

'Or should that be baaa-d behaviour?' he grins.

I shake my head indignantly, but smile, nonetheless.

53. Sheepy concerns

'I'm worried about you being over there,' my friend Gemma tells me one day when we speak on phone.

'I know what you're going to say,' I interrupt, aware of the fact she loves history. 'But The Troubles were a long time ago, and...'

'Oh, not *that.*'

'What then?'

'It's the sheep.'

'Eh?'

'The sheep. I don't trust them. Always look like they're plotting something. You just watch your back.'

'Right.'

After our conversation, I go for a walk around the fields to check the sheep. As I turn, one of them gives me the evil eye and I'm just in time to spot another disappearing into a hedge.

Was it my imagination, or did she have a notebook and pencil in her hoof? Gemma was right. They are sneaky. Very sneaky. I shall have to keep my eye on them. Just in case.

54. New girl

I feel a bit sick. Tomorrow, I start my new job and I'm concerned I'm in danger of letting people down. Again.

After graduating and spending a couple of years working as a journalist, I got tired of being called 'a hack' and other unsavoury terms (according to popular belief, journalists are the spawn of the devil who'd sell their own grand-mother for a story.) I longed to be part of a profession which was admired and trusted – like nursing, for example.

One of my dear friends is a nurse and she's wonderful at it; compassionate, kind and hard-working with nerves of steel and a strong stomach. She often talks about how rewarding her job is and I am in awe of her.

As you know, I'm a fan of the television drama *Heartbeat* and its hospital spinoff *The Royal*. The groovy 1960s soundtrack and stunning Yorkshire scenery did nothing to dissuade me of the notion that nursing was a wonderful profession, which I'm sure it was and still is. But the main thing I forgot to take into consideration, and this is the crucial bit, is that *The Royal* is *fictitious*.

Back in the real world and in modern times, many people still regard nursing as a calling. I never really had one of those, but I sure as heck wanted one. So, I decided to get a job in a hospital and work my way up.

Safe to say, Florence Nightingale I was not. It's worrying at the best of times, to discover that you have no hand-eye coordination whatsoever, but it's even more disconcerting when you learn this while working on a ward with actual patients.

I found manoeuvring wheelchairs terribly difficult and kept apologising to patients as I bumped them into walls. I spent most of my time crying in the toilets and feeling sorry for the patients, whose happiness I was doing nothing to improve. Most had either had a stroke or were suffering from dementia, and I felt utterly useless. The frustration and fear on their faces was heart-breaking and I just wanted to wave a magic wand and make them better.

My stint on the wards reinforced the idea that everyone in the healthcare system is a true superhero; from the cleaners and porters to surgeons, paramedics, pharmacists, physiotherapists, caterers, telephonists, receptionists and everyone else.

I also have every respect for nurses and healthcare assistants, who are special and outstanding. To be able to go into that challenging environment every day with a smile on your face and lift the spirits of those in need requires grit and determination, which are qualities I certainly do not possess.

They provide intimate care as if each person is a member of their own family, with all the respect, kindness and gentleness that goes with that.

But I knew straight away that I had made a mistake. For someone who had supposedly worked in the field of communication, I often found myself tongue-tied when trying to talk to patients and unable to help at all.

I felt awful, not only for this reason, but because the interview panel had given me a chance to change careers. But I just couldn't do it. I was meant to be there to assist the senior staff in a non-medical role, but if anything, I just made things worse.

I'd been in the job for three months when I spotted the advert for a press officer in the administration department. Well, I've never completed an application form so fast in my life and there was relief all round when I landed the role.

I think they gave me the job to protect the patients by getting me off the wards and out of harm's way. The move also meant another, much better candidate, could apply for the practical ward job and start their career in healthcare.

Having been hauled off the ward and into the relative safety of the press office, I swore never to swerve off of my chosen career path again. Journalism may be perceived as an immoral and unkind profession, but at least I knew what I was doing. Sort of.

I worked in PR for a while, which was more up my street, but still lacked the human-interest angle I craved. You see, I adore writing good news stories, not only because they shine a light on the kind people of this world, but because simply reading about them can make people feel happier. At least, that's my experience.

Then I began to think about the transformative power of words and language; how they can make people happy or transport them to different worlds, even if just for a little while.

One day, I was watching TV when I came across Channel 4's *Educating* documentary series, which charts what life is like in the UK's senior schools.

Cameras filmed in Essex, Yorkshire, the East End, Cardiff and Greater Manchester and showed inspiring teachers going to any lengths to help their students. And from that moment on, yes, you've guessed it, I wanted to be a teacher.

Do you remember Toad from Winston Graham's wonderful *Wind in The Willows* book? The lively little amphibian (well, big amphibian actually, seeing as he was the same size as his mates Badger, Rat and Mole), who had huge enthusiasm for life but a tiny brain? He was into a different fad every five minutes, from caravans and cars to hot-air balloons and planes. Well, I'm the human equivalent of him when it comes to careers.

Unfortunately, or fortunately depending on your viewpoint, my teaching aspirations were thwarted early on due to a number of factors.

As previously mentioned, I don't have a 'C' grade in GCSE maths, and therefore, wouldn't have been offered a place on the postgraduate course in the first place. In addition, and as one of my friends helpfully pointed out, I would have, and I quote, 'lasted approximately ten seconds in a classroom because children can smell fear.'

I'm also a very nervous person, I don't react well to stressful situations and vitally, children hate me.

Despite this, I still love the idea of teaching and really admire the profession. I adore the thought of enthusing people with a love of storytelling and creative writing. So much so that I have enrolled on a creative writing Master's degree and would like to become a creative writing teacher. Lesson one will be: Always have a book in your bag for emergencies.

All these grand plans whizz through my head as I lay in bed. Perhaps my problem is that I often fall in love with the *idea* of a profession but have no idea as to the realities of the job.

But, thanks to some farming friends, I will soon discover the realities of milking cows. *Very* soon in fact, as my alarm is due to go off in seven hours and my first official shift will begin soon after.

Our friends assure me that this arrangement will help them out as much as it will help me, and while I think they are just being kind, I am very grateful.

My stomach lurches with nerves and excitement. I want to be a good cow milker and I don't want to let my new bosses, or the cows, down.

55. This is not a drill

I didn't know there were two six o'clock in a day.

When my alarm goes off at 5.30am, I hit the ceiling and bounce off every wall. Groaning, I reach over and turn it off, sighing with relief as the incessant noise stops.

'Time to go and see your friends,' Paul says. I try to get the duvet back over my head but he's having none of it.

Reluctantly, I slouch to the bathroom. 'I can't believe I'm up at this hour,' I mutter, hopping around on the cold tiles while trying to get my socks on and brush my teeth at the same time.

As I stumble into the kitchen, I see that Paul has put my flask and a breakfast bar on the table. I smile at his kindness and then blink in disbelief at the clock. It's not even 6am and I'm up. There never were such time! I ram my woolly hat on and look at my reflection in the kitchen window.

Clad in a thermal vest, three jumpers, a padded shirt, two pairs of trousers, two pairs of socks, Wellington boots and gloves, I bid Paul a good day and quietly close the door behind me, not wanting to disturb him further or wake the sheep.

Once I'm safely in the car, I risk a look in the direction of the sheep shed and can just make out their fluffy forms stretched out in the straw, hopefully having lovely sheepy dreams.

The news is being announced on the radio as I set off,

the headlights brushing back the darkness and turning menacing jagged shapes into friendly-looking hedges and trees. As I swing out onto the main road, a rabbit dashes in front of me and bounds through the beams of light before disappearing into the safety of a hedge. I'm glad I'm going slowly.

I pass some houses and hope my headlights don't disturb those slumbering inside. Then the houses stop, and I'm surrounded by fields once again. I know the inky sea is beyond, and I wonder if it too, is calm, as if asleep.

I'm still shaking my head at the fact I'm up so early. The pitch-black surroundings send a shiver down my spine. It feels clandestine, being out at this hour, as if I'm a spy on a top-secret mission. Or perhaps it's because it feels like nature is sharing some of her secrets with me.

I turn the radio up and listen to a bubbly presenter who is clearly attuned to being up with the lark.

I'm so busy listening to upbeat tunes that I completely overshoot my turning. Everything looks so different in the dark and I continue for a good five minutes before I realise what I've done.

Luckily, I know this road because I've accidentally taken it before, so I don't panic. 'By my calculations,' I mutter, confidently turning to the left, 'this should take me back to the main road.' Or not.

With gradual horror, I realise that I am in fact, sitting in someone's front garden. My full beams are on and shining directly into what I think could be their bedroom. I'm sure they appreciate being rudely awoken at this unearthly hour. One up all up, that's what I say.

I quickly flip the full-beams off and try to do a three-point turn, which turns into a ten-point-turn as I try to make as little noise as possible, not easy on a pebble-dashed driveway. Somehow, I manage to snake out of the front garden without someone flinging open the window and throwing something at me and, with a sigh of relief, am soon heading in the right direction.

I've reported on council meetings and court cases, attended conferences at The Palace of Westminster, interviewed politicians and professors, given speeches at prominent events and quizzed key decision makers during press briefings.

With my reporter's kit (notebook, pen, Dictaphone and press pass in hand), I could handle anything, or at least *look* like I could, which is key.

As I said, I'm a shy, nervous person with more issues than *Vogue*, but for some reason, I love reporting. Every journalist will tell you about the rush of endorphins you feel when you break a news story and see your name on the front page of a newspaper. It's not humble and it ain't pretty. But it feels darn good.

I travelled the length and breadth of the county in pursuit of news stories, and so going on adventures doesn't faze me. And yet, on the first day on a new job, I'm petrified.

Turning into the farmyard, I'm comforted to hear the hum of the milking machines and see a wedge of yellow light shining onto the cobbles where the parlour door has been left ajar. Somehow, it feels welcoming.

I jump out of the car and stride towards the entrance, pulling my hat down over my frozen ears as I go. Stopping,

I take a deep breath, grasp the handle, slide the door across and step inside.

The first line of cows is already being milked and the second are making their way in. The rest are huddled together at the back, looking over each other's shoulders as if trying to see all the action down at the front.

'Morning, girls,' I smile as they file past. 'How are you this morning?' They don't say much in reply, but they are my colleagues, after all, and I think it's nice to ask.

Some of them are the bovine equivalents of those humans who are 'morning people', all skippy and keen for breakfast. Others look how I feel: knackered. They slouch in, ears down, eyes heavy with sleep. These are *not* morning bovines, and I am certainly *not* a morning person and so instantly relate to them.

The cows that don't do mornings glare at me, as if to say, 'Why on earth have we been kicked out of bed at this hour?' They practically slump into their troughs, but soon perk up when they hear the food coming down the shoot. I have a similar reaction when food is involved and it always cheers me up.

That cows are milked twice a day, every day when they are 'in milk' astounds me. They work so hard, getting up early so that the tanker has produce to take back to the factory for processing.

At the height of their production, a cow can give more than twenty-five litres of milk per session, which takes them about ten hours to produce. I watch, mesmerised, as the milk flows out of their teats and through the pipes towards the milk tank.

I then blush with embarrassment as I think of all the times I've stood in a shop and thrown a bottle of milk or a block of cheese into my basket without thinking where it comes from, or the work that goes into getting it there.

Three hours later, I stagger into the watery sunlight and shield my eyes, shocked by the brightness, like a mole who has broken ground after sleeping all winter. I check my watch: 9.15am. In my previous career, I'd just be starting my working day, having got my first cup of tea from the staff kitchen and settled at my desk before doing a seven-hour keyboard workout. Then it would be off to the gym and home for a microwave meal for one in front of the TV before bed.

Now, my working day is over, and my gorgeous Paul is waiting for me at home, as are eighty sheep who want their breakfast. But that isn't work, that's a privilege.

Plus, I've done my daily exercise already, what with walking up and down the parlour, so there's no need for a gym membership. And the rest of the day is mine to do with as I wish. Amazing.

56. A drop of tea

The first shift seems to have gone OK and I didn't make any major mistakes, which is a relief. As I make my way to the car, the farmer comes over.

'Thanks Holly. We're all just going to have a drop o' tea. Would you like some?'

'That's very kind of you but I've bought my own,' I say, waving my flask.

He looks a bit confused but nods. 'Oh, OK then. See you tomorrow.'

I relay this exchange to Paul when I get home.

'Why didn't you say yes?'

'Because I had my own flask. Seemed silly to take from their tea pot.'

'But you love breakfast.'

'Yes.'

'That's what he was offering. That's what a drop o' tea means'

Excuse me?

'You know, cereal, toast, orange juice.'

'I missed out on breakfast?'

'Well, he did offer.'

'No, he didn't. He said, "a drop o' tea!"'

Paul laughs. 'Well sure, what else would you call it?'

'Breakfast!'

'That *is* breakfast, at least it's what we say in these parts. Well, you'll know for next time.'

Too right. I'll have my napkin tied round my neck quicker than Winnie the Pooh at the mention of honey.

57. Text message

Heard you did your first milking shift this morning. Just checking you're still alive. Charlie x

I smile. Charlie runs a local dairy farm with her dad and has been milking for years. But not only is she up at all hours seeing to the cows, she has children, a husband, various pets and a host of voluntary jobs. I've long suspect that she is, in fact, Superwoman, whose cape is perpetually in the wash.

58. Cheesy sentiments

'What are you at?' Paul asks. 'And before you say it, I know you're looking at a bottle of milk, but why?'

'It's amazing,' I say, staring all misty-eyed as if it's a newborn. 'I'm just thinking of all the hard work and effort that goes into producing the contents in that bottle. From the cows in the fields who give us their milk, to the farmers who work around the clock to gather it up, the drivers take it to the factories, the drivers who take it to the shops and the people who stack the shelves so we can go and buy it. I just find it astounding.'

And it's true, isn't it? Because if the farmers and those in the wider agricultural field, the drivers and the factory workers etc. suddenly said, 'Sod this for a game of soldiers, I'm off to have an easier life,' then everyone would suffer.

59. Worker bee

As we get into the parlour today, Paul is immediately called upon to assist the visiting vet with a caesarean. I'm so proud of him, he's so clever and knowledgeable.

But it's at times like this that I'm pleased to be a worker bee. Tell me what you need me to do, and if it's in my capability, I'll do it. If it's producing a press release, writing an article, filling buckets for thirsty sheep, loading up hay racks for excitable calves or, unbelievably, milking cows, I'm your woman. I am not a leader. But I am happy and proud to be able to keep the basics going, while experts do their thing.

Sadly, the calf delivered by caesarean was long dead, but thanks to Paul and his colleague, the cow will hopefully be OK.

'I'm sorry about the calf,' I say when I see the farmer.

'Aye, 'tis sad, but that's farming,' he says, stoically.

I nod. Yes, I'm beginning to understand it's not all rainbows, birdsong and unicorn droppings.

60. Cows and effect

You've got to have good reflexes to work in a milking parlour if you want to avoid getting mucky. I do not and therefore, get liberally covered in shite every time I do a shift.

At first, I thought it was a weird greeting ritual the cows carried out every time a new member of staff joined the team. Now, I think they just do it out of badness.

On my first official shift, the cows were standing together as they waited for the gate to be opened. As they peered down at me, I had to resist the urge to put them in hair nets and rollers, as they looked like little old ladies gossiping over the fence.

They sniffed me cautiously, putting their big, wet noses against me and breathing warm air all over my face.

I opened the gate and the first cow walked in, looked down at me, turned, raised her tail and pooed all over me. Nice. I like to think it's a sign of affection.

I was standing in the wrong place at the wrong time in the parlour again today, when a cow decided it was the opportune moment to empty her bowels. Safe to say, I got absolutely covered in liquid poo precisely ten seconds after starting. It was everywhere, over my hat, in my hair and over my coat. Some even went down my facemask, which wasn't really the aroma I wanted in my nostrils after just having had my breakfast.

Quick as a flash, I dashed to the sink in the tank room, washed and dried my glasses so I could see where I was going, then ran to the car, deposited the hat, mask and gloves, wiped my raincoat, grabbed a new mask and pulled the hood of my thick blue cardigan up over my head to keep my ears warm. Thus, I was back with my colleagues in less than five minutes. 'Sorted?' my boss asked. 'Sorted,' I smiled, feeling warm, fresh and ready to work.

Such incidents may make you cringe, feel ill or put you off of such work completely, but I love it.

The wearing of masks is necessary during the Covid-19 outbreak, but it isn't half difficult to milk with them on. I walked into a gate the other day because my glasses were that steamed up and I didn't see it until it was too late. Lucky, I didn't take all my teeth out. But I digress...

The cows are individually numbered so the farmer can keep track of them, both in their houses and on computer system, which tells him when they last calved and if they are on any medication or treatment plans. Each cow wears a set of numbered ear tags which correspond to the number painted on their hind quarters. They also have collars which tells the computer when they've entered the milking parlour and determines how much meal they get.

I love looking at the numbers and imagining the stories each cow could tell if they could talk. For example, numbers 1914 and 1939 would have memories of the war, 330 would have to pick the children up from school and 404 would always have some kind of computer problem!

Farming never stops. I'm exhausted and I only milk six times a week. Farmers, on the other hand, milk twice a day, every day throughout the year. I think everyone who buys milk should do a shift in a dairy. It's a real eye-opener.

61. Communication stations

'**P**ardon?'
   One of the farm assistants is trying to make conversation while we wait for the cows to come in, but the machinery is so loud and his accent so thick, in addition to the fact everyone is wearing masks, that I'm struggling to understand him. I've asked him to repeat himself three times and I think we're both a bit embarrassed.

He chuckles kindly before speaking slowly and loudly: 'Have you had any more lambs?'

'Not personally,' I grin. 'But the ewes have, yes.'

I'm not sure if he understands my sense of humour, but I think he smiles. It's hard to tell with masks on, but his eyes crinkle up at the edges, so I think it's positive.

Before I can embarrass myself further, the cows come in and we walk off, relieved, I think, to have a task to be getting on with.

The speed at which the experienced milkers can move is incredible. Within seconds of having grabbed a cluster, they've attached all four vacuum cups to the cow's teats and are moving on to the next. It reminds me of watching old footage of factory workers putting chocolates into boxes as they whizz down the production line, their hands a blur as they deftly fill them.

I'm so busy admiring the speed of my fellow workers that when a cluster falls off the cow, it makes me jump. Suddenly, another clatters to the floor, followed by another, and I watch in horror as this continues all the way down the line until all the clusters are hanging limply on the floor. I pick one up and press it to my hand. No suction.

'Power failure' someone shouts.

I look up and, sure enough, the computer screens have all turned themselves off.

Paul disappears and returns a few minutes later carrying a three-legged stool and a milking pail. 'Right then,' he says, handing me the equipment, 'we'll just have to revert to the old-fashioned way of milking each cow individually. Come on, only 150 to go.'

Thankfully, he was joking. But while we're waiting for the engineer to arrive to bring us back to the twenty-first century, Paul shows me how to milk by hand, having selected one of the more chilled-out cows for me to practice on.

'You grip the teat like this and squeeze,' he says, demonstrating. I watch in awe as milk squirts from her teat. 'Your turn.'

I gingerly take the cow's teat in my hand and am surprised at how warm and soft it is. I squeeze gently, but nothing happens. I try again, all the while worried that I'll hurt her. Moving my fingers up, I replicate the movement but am firmer this time, and a little bit of milk comes stuttering out. 'It's still warm!' I declare, as if I've just discovered something new.

'Yes,' Paul says, calmly.

'That's amazing.'

'Of course, it's warm, it's coming out of her. Sure, they don't teach anything in schools anymore, do they?'

By the time I've milked out the teat, which seems to take an age, my hand is throbbing with the effort. I peer into the bucket, thinking it must be close to overflowing, but am disappointed to see there's hardly enough for a cup of tea.

'And farmers used to milk all cows like this? It must have taken ages. Thank goodness for modern technology,' I sigh, waving at the engineer as he walks in. Just in time.

62. Tracking progress

T he cows were keen to clear their bowels this morning, meaning I had to keep reaching for the long-handled scraper to push their poo off the walkway and into the drain. While doing this, I imagined myself as an operation assistant in the RAF during war time.

'Stools are on the moo-ve, sir. north by northwest. But it's OK, sir, all clear now.'

I know. It's fun in my head.

63. Choosing sides

The dairy cows are split into three houses which each consist of around one hundred ruminants. That's a lot of moos to milk!

We had houses when I was in senior school. Ours was a Church of England institution and so they were named after cathedrals, York, Durham and Canterbury.

Every year, we'd compete in inter-house competitions in everything from music to sport and it was great fun.

As such, I can't help thinking that we should start having house competitions for the cows. There could be points for different activities; such as the house which yields the most milk in a month or which generates the most poo etc. We could even give out medals!

The dairy houses are just named 'one,' 'two' and 'three,' but I think it would be fun to give them names.

And yes, I know I sound like a typical 'townie,' trying to inject cute names and fun games into serious agricultural activities. Indeed, there would be no prizes for picking me out as the former city-dweller in a 'spot the townie' competition in the milking parlour.

Indeed, it was all Paul could do to stop me taking my sparkly Wellington boots with the fake *diamanté* studs to the parlour. He did this on the pretext that they weren't practical and that he 'didn't want them to get ruined on the first day'. To be fair, he did supply me with some lovely green boots instead, which he insisted would keep me warm *and* dry (he's kind and thoughtful like that) but I also think he did it because he didn't want his colleagues laughing at his wife, which is understandable.

Anyway, back to naming the houses.

The next day, while waiting for the cows to come into the parlour, I think about *Romeo and Juliet*, who belonged to The House of Montague and Capulet, respectively, which gives me an idea. Perhaps we could name house one, The House of Moo-ntague and the other, The House of Cow-pulet. (You can have those suggestions for free, Mr Shakespeare.)

However, that would leave one house without a name, so it's back to the drawing board. Suggestions on postcards, if you please.

64. Tail tales

One of the cow's tails was bleeding today. Paul concluded that one of the other heifers must have accidentally stepped on it. (The cows have beds which they sit on when they want to relax, but sometimes they leave their tails sticking out the end, which means that they occasionally get trodden by passing cows. That said, most of them tuck their tails in, as they are sensible like that.)

Paul did a marvellous job of patching her up by putting a pink bandage on her tail, and she now looks very pretty, but I suspect all the girls will want one now.

65. Cow with horns

Yesterday, I was admiring one of the cows who has a lovely set of horns. Today, another cow who also sports horns, walked past me and dipped her head as if to say, 'Look, I have pretty horns too.' I smiled as I gave her a pat. Seemingly satisfied, she bobbed her head in acknowledgement and carried on walking. I tell you; these cows are such *prima donnas*.

66. Lost on me

We are watching a Northern Irish comedy panel show. It's a bit like *Have I Got News for You*, so is very political. Someone says something and the audience crack up, as does Paul.

I have no idea who the joke was about but am informed that it's something to do with a minister in the Northern Irish government. The next time someone on the panel cracks a joke, I laugh too, as it seems like the polite thing to do.

This reminds me of when I used to report on lectures at veterinary conferences in my capacity as a journalist. Sometimes, the speaker would make a science joke and the audience would dissolve into laughter, while I would just stare, blankly. Nope, far too intelligent for me.

67. What I love about cows is their geography

Maps. That's what cows look like to me. Black and white maps. I could stare at their markings all day, they're so pretty. Each cow has a unique set of markings, just as each human has a unique set of fingerprints.

Paul tells me to take it easy as I drive into work, as it's been pouring down all night and the roads will be slippery.

Excitingly, I have to employ the windscreen wipers when I get into the car after work, too, but not because of precipitation. Instead, I need them to clear the windscreen of straw which is billowing out from the huge diet-feeder opposite (a piece of machinery used to prepare the cows' breakfast – a mixture of silage, straw and meal. Yum.)

The straw is being carried on a gale which is screaming off the coast. You don't encounter that problem too often in multi-storey car parks in London.

When I drive to work in the mornings (at 5.56am, just in case I hadn't mentioned it before), the roads are pitch black and so I take it very slowly indeed. I've learnt to be on the lookout for foxes, hares, cyclists and, based on one terrifying experience, joggers who seemingly have a suicide wish, since they opt to go out into the dark wearing black clothing with no reflective gear whatsoever.

I used to drive in silence as I navigated unfamiliar roads, but I've built up my confidence enough to now be able to have the radio on. It feels like being part of a special club, where the joys of the early morning are our shared secret: from seeing the pale moon hanging in the sky and hearing birds singing to watching the light levels slowly change from blacks and greys to purples and blues. I often gasp as shades of green, brown and yellow slowly seep back into trees and fields, as if Mother Nature is colouring by numbers.

Out of habit, my ears prick up when the traffic report comes on. As usual, the M25 kicks off proceedings and we are told it is blocked solid in both directions. I suck air between my teeth and shake my head.

Years of commuting from Hertfordshire to Peterborough (a glorious three-hour round trip if you were lucky), has turned me into a traffic update fiend.

I undertook that journey, from my home to the office and back again, every day for six months. Then, and apparently because I looked like death, a kind colleague offered me use of her spare room during the week, which I immediately accepted.

To be honest, I was so tired, I would've happily had someone put me on a coat hanger in their wardrobe and I would've slept soundly. But happily, the room was lovely and I also made a great friend.

Anway, that experience, followed by six months of

working in North London, just about put me off commuting for life.

I took the North London job because I wanted to further my career, but it also meant I could live with my parents for a while before relocating to Northern Ireland.

The fact that the office was just fifteen miles from my parents' house also sweetened the deal. I calculated that I could do the journey in about twenty minutes, which would make my jaunt to Peterborough look like a walk in the park. But I was wrong on all counts, which became painfully clear on my first day.

Driving the route on a Saturday when the roads were empty was one thing. It was quite another trying to replicate the trip on a Monday morning, when the world and their dog wanted access to the same strip of tarmac at the same time. Therefore, it *still* took me about two hours to get to work and the same amount of time to get home again, meaning I was almost crying with frustration after the first week.

One particularly notorious set of lights are so bad that you could be waiting for up to an hour before you get a go. After a month of this, I took to packing a picnic and reading *War and Peace* while I waited.

Thus, I vowed (again), never to take a job which involves a massive commute. Not even if it was the role of head nose scratcher for the anteaters at London Zoo. (Well, for them I might make an exception.)

So, when the milking job came up, which is just a fourteen-minute drive from our house, it was a dream come true and an answer to a prayer.

The thing is, though, I still listen out for the English traffic reports, particularly those for London, as, sometimes, I forget that I've moved. Because, while I'm on that little ribbon of road in the darkness, my internal navigation system resets, meaning I still cringe whenever I hear mention of that bloody set of traffic lights far away, in North London.

68. Sheep SOS hit the road again

P aul and I were driving down a country lane today, when we saw two lambs happily gambolling along the roadside and nibbling on hedgerow, apparently helping themselves to an afternoon snack.

Paul identified them as one of his friend's lambs and thankfully, they're right outside the field where their mums and mates are, so haven't wandered far. Being inquisitive animals, they probably found a lamb-sized gap in a bit of wire mesh and squeezed through.

We pulled over and scooted across the road. As we got nearer, I could see the hedgerow was in a little verge, meaning the lambs weren't about to tumble into the road and get squished by oncoming vehicles. But we certainly weren't going to risk leaving them there. Instead, we watched them for a while, hoping they'd go back to where they'd scarpered from in the first place. Alas, they were having none of it, and for some bizarre reason, suddenly decided that the best course of action was to turn around and stick their heads straight through the wire mesh, meaning they were stuck fast. Brilliant.

'Are you having a laugh?'

Good job the squares of mesh were big, and their heads were small, otherwise they would have nigh on shredded themselves. As it was, all this did was momentarily halt and confuse them. While they were busy figuring out their options (none, by my calculations), Paul and I snatched our opportunity, stepped forward and each scooped up an escapee.

'He-he, I've got a lamb,' I crowed. Whenever I see a lamb, I can't help but want a hug. I suppose it's a bit like when other women see human babies and want a cuddle and to squeeze their chubby cheeks.

After a few more moments of cuddles, I reluctantly said goodbye and placed the lamb back in the field with her pal. They both stood for a second, seemingly confused as to how they'd gotten from one side of the fence to the other without moving their legs. Suddenly, they found their feet and galloped off to find their mums, and presumably, grass us up. I imagined them saying, 'The big bad hoomans picked us up, Mum!'

Or else, they'd be boasting of their adventures to their friends, 'I flew! I swear to you, I just pushed off the ground and woosh, I was up in the air, over the fence and back on the ground. And look, I ain't even got wings!'

On the way home, we discussed what we thought sheep wings would look like. Possibly like those of Pegasus but fashioned out of cotton wool balls instead of feathers. If you have any other suggestions, please send them in on a postcard.

'What would it be like if sheep could fly?' I asked, warming to my theme.

'Impossible,' Paul said.

I shot him a look. Strange, he normally joins in with my flights of fancy.

'Impossible to work with,' he continued.

'I suppose so,' I laughed. 'Yes, they're hard enough to control when on solid ground, let alone if they could take to the sky at any moment, which they would, as we couldn't bring ourselves to clip their wings.'

Still, it would be worth the chaos just to see the sky full of sheep and to hear their blissful, beautiful bleats, which would float to ground as softly, gently and as welcome as snow on Christmas morning.

I marvel at how exciting my weekdays are in this, my new life. No more being stuck behind a desk and nipping to the shop for a sandwich, which was the only time I got any fresh air.

In my new life, I'm outside most days in all weathers, and apart from conducting sheep patrols, feeding calves and milking, there is no rigid plan, we just play it by ear and see what the day has in store. It's unpredictable and fun, like today, when Paul and I acted as unofficial sheep SOS rescuers.

I didn't think I would cope without a routine or a regular

job, but I can, and I love it. It's amazing what you can do when you try.

Caring for the animals is an honour. I love my life and I know I'm a very lucky lady.

69. What the cluck?

'**E**xcuse me, what's your cock like?'

I almost drop my shopping in shock.

I'm even *more* shocked when I turned to see that the person asking the question is a little old lady, who is standing at the counter and addressing the shopkeeper.

'Aye, it's a grand specimen,' he said, proudly. 'It's huge too. Will need some carin' for, I can tell you.'

Not knowing where to look and feeling embarrassed, I frantically look about for something, *anything* to distract me and my gaze falls upon a poster which proudly states, 'Cock for sale!'. Not only that, but there are *photographs*.

The little old lady sees my looking and nods appreciatively. 'It's a fine cock, isn't it? I had them all the time in my youth,' she says with a sad smile, 'but I just don't have the energy to give them the care they need, nowadays. It happens, as you get older.'

I fish about in my bag for my glasses and pop them on, at which point the image of the cock floats into view.

'It's certainly.. .big,' I say, trying to contain my laughter as relief washes over me.

There was indeed a cock for sale; The type that will happily scratch about in the garden and hang out with hens.

I giggled at my silliness. I often forget that I'm living in the countryside now, and things are different. This is a community where people look out for each other and where shopkeepers will happily put adverts in their windows when customers have things to sell, including, in this instance, a cock.

I took another look and must admit, it is impressive.

70. On the fence (literally)

I slipped while climbing over a fence this morning. Let's just say I'm glad I'm not a boy, otherwise, I'd have a high-pitched voice for weeks. And yes, it did make my eyes water.

71. Whether the weather is fine

Everyone is obsessed with the weather, but I'm not. At least, I *wasn't*.

'Seen the weather forecast?' friends will ask on a Sunday morning as we emerge from church.

'Nope.'

They then suck their breath in, frown and shake their heads, as if they've just looked at my car and are about to give me a very large estimate for work that needs done.

'You should. Sure, it's going to rain very heavily this week.'

When I worked in an office, it didn't matter to me one way or the other what the weather was doing.

But having worked outside for a while, now, I can understand why it's so important; mainly so you don't drown or catch hypothermia. People around here, and particularly those who work in agriculture, are wise and always dress for the weather. But it took me a while to learn this important lesson.

The first time I left future Mummy in Law's house to go for a romantic stroll with Paul, I almost got swept off my feet. So much so that I had to put stones in my pockets to stop me from being blown over the fields and far away.

Later, when we were lambing and I had to stagger off to check the sheep at silly o'clock in the morning, the cold air took my breath away and chilled me to the bone, making it abundantly clear that my giraffe onesie and slipper socks just weren't going to cut it.

'Girl, you must've been freezing your tits off,' Liz said when I told her about my attire. She's observant, my oldest friend, I'll give her that.

If it wasn't for Paul, who always thinks ahead, I probably would have frozen to death in the first few weeks of living here.

On my arrival, he very sweetly and kindly presented me with a new pair of Wellington boots, a raincoat, body-warmer, hat and woolly gloves.

I have since obtained a snazzy set of thermal vests (sexy and practical) and extra thick socks. Thus, when I go out now, I look like a female Michelin man, but I don't care. As Paul says, this isn't a fashion show. Just as well.

I don't mind hard graft or putting in the hours, but I can't work at my best if I'm cold. But if I'm warm, it's all systems go.

For this reason, I too have now become obsessed with the weather. I've even got an app on my phone which sends me updates at all times of day and night, so much so that Paul must think I'm having an affair with a weather fore-caster. I grab my mobile as the message alert bleeps. 'It's a weather update,' I say, with a silly smile on my face. 'Looks like it'll be sunny tomorrow.'

However, as always, it's a case of one step forwards and two steps back. Being ready for all weather eventualities is great, but it does mean I'm constantly washing and prepar-ing. I seem to have spare socks, gloves, hats, sunglasses and bottles of sun lotion everywhere: in cupboards, in cars and in sheep sheds. But rather that, than be found in a block of ice or burnt to a crisp.

72. A bit about me

Here I am, having chewed your ears off for pages, and I've not really told you much about my past life, have I? If you're interested, please do carry on. If not, jump ahead, I won't be offended. But just in case you wanted to know, I was born on a sunny September morning in 1985...

No, stop. Sorry, this isn't going to work. Look, I'm thirty-six years old and frankly, we don't have the time, space or indeed, the budget, to include information about every year of my existence thus far. Plus, I'm a journalist, so let's just cut to the chase and then get back to the animals, shall we? Sound good? Good.

So, here are the headlines:

I wasn't so much born on Friday 20 September 1985, as evicted. My mum was suffering from preeclampsia and the medical staff had to get me out and fast.

Having driven my mum to the hospital and delivered her to the appropriate ward, Dad was heartily thanked by the staff and then unceremoniously booted out, having been told by an assertive midwife that 'they would manage from here,' while muttering something about it 'being women's work.'

My dad had just got back home and slumped into bed when the phone rang. He almost took his teeth out as he stumbled down the stairs in the dark and tried to locate the receiver. Being the 1980s meant most people kept their phones on a little table in their hall or front room. (Just though I would mention in case younger readers wondered why Dad didn't just keep his mobile by his bedside.)

'Hello?' Dad squeaked when he finally got the receiver to his ear.

The doctor told him to get back to the hospital quick-sharp because, in short, things had developed quickly which meant Mum required a caesarean and dad needed to sign the paperwork.

Having thrown on some clothes and shot up the road in record time, Dad clattered back through the doors of the hospital to be met by a stony-faced medic who greeted him with the words, 'And where have you been?'

Before Dad could decide whether to

a. Answer him or,
b. punch him in the face,

the doctor, who looked about twelve, continued, 'As you didn't get here in time we had to proceed without your permission. But Mum and baby are doing well.'

Indeed, we were, just in different parts of the hospital, meaning poor Dad didn't know which way to run first. To his wife, who had just come out of surgery, or to his new baby

179

who had been taken to the Special Care Baby Unit (SCBU).

Seeing the fear and indecision etched on his face, the doctor thawed slightly. 'Your wife is just waking up now, so why don't you go and see your daughter, and then you can see your wife and tell her the good news.'

Dad nodded and followed him silently down the corridor. After a few moments, he stopped in his tracks. 'Did you say daughter?' he asked, slowly. 'We have a daughter?' The doctor nodded and smiled for the first time. 'Yes. Congratulations.' Then it was Dad's turn to smile.

'She's lovely,' Dad told Mum as she opened her eyes a while later. Mum nodded and smiled, exhausted but relieved.

'What do you want to call her? Dad asked. 'Holly or April?'

Dad always liked the name April (as do I, because it's Dad's birthday month), but Mum preferred Holly.

People often think I'm called Holly because I was meant to be born near Christmas, but that's not the case. Nor is it because my dad likes Buddy Holly. Well, he *does* like him, but again, that wasn't why I was given my name.

Indeed, when I asked Mum why she chose it, she couldn't really give a reason, other than that she thought it was pretty. If they'd had a second daughter, I'd like to think my parents would have called her Ivy.)

When I was born (evicted) I weighed two pounds and two ounces. Apparently, I was so small and undercooked that my bottom wasn't developed properly and was as flat as pancake. In fact, I was so small that Dad could fit me in his outstretched hand.

SCBU had nappies for premature babies but none of them fitted me as I was so tiny. And when it came to clothes, Dad was advised to go to the local toy shop and buy dresses meant for dolls. Safe to say he got a funny look from the shopkeeper when he dashed in, picked up a doll and said he wasn't bothered about taking her home, he just needed the pretty dress she was wearing.

Incidentally, Dad ended up purchasing both the dress and the doll, and she's been the fairy on our Christmas tree every year since.

Back at the hospital, Dad was well pleased with his purchase; the dress was still huge, but it was a start. My auntie, who would also become my godmother, came to the rescue by knitting sets of booties and matching dresses.

My early days were spent in an incubator which looked suspiciously like a transparent seed box. One day, a kindly nurse asked my somewhat bewildered dad if he'd like to give me a wash. 'But surely she's too tiny to bath?' he uttered. You could understand his confusion, as my poor parents hadn't even been able to hold me up until that point.

The nurse smiled. 'You don't have to move her. We can wash her where she is.' And with that, she produced a cotton bud which she dipped into a bowl of warm water. Then she reached through the opening in my seed box and began to clean me with soft, gentle movements.

My dad, who must have been hanging onto his sanity by the thinnest of threads by this point, grinned manically and mirrored her. (Fast-forward thirty-six years and I'm living and working with what are essentially giant, living, breathing, bleating cotton buds – I love the serendipity of this.)

To ensure I was kept snug and warm in my seed box, I was often swathed in bubble wrap. My first teddy bear, a rather sad-looking grey dog with big blue eyes and pink ribbons, was placed in my incubator to keep me company and was named Squeak. Thus, we were commonly referred to as Bubble and Squeak. (Incidentally, one of Paul's favourite sheep is called Squeak, another quirk I love.)

The midwives and doctors were amazing, and I received the most wonderful care. Over the next few months, I contracted and overcame pneumonia and a host of other illnesses. I was born with red hair (think of a carrot), but the medics had to shave it off to insert a tube in my head for a blood transfusion. When it grew back, it was dark brown. And I was one of three babies on the SCBU who was named Holly.

Sadly, not all of them survived, while others suffered brain damage. After all these years, I always think of those poor babies and their families who didn't have the happy outcome I did.

I hope those who lost their babies were able to get the help they needed, and went on to have another baby. And I hope the babies with additional needs received everything they required and have a good quality of life. I know, from the stories my parents told me, that all the parents adored their babies and loved them unconditionally.

My parents were able to take me home on Christmas Eve, exactly one hundred days since I was born. On receiving this news, my dad went home, threw up a tree and decorations in ten seconds and took me home to the best Santa's grotto ever.

Apparently, I was fascinated by the lights on the tree and would stare at them for hours. One of my favourite photos shows me atop the Christmas tree, as if I'm the fairy. The game is given away by my dad's hands holding me aloft, but I love it. My dad has always supported me, physically and metaphorically, and he still does, as does my mum and I love them to bits.

My dad and I have always loved Christmas and it is, without doubt, our favourite time of year. Every Christmas Eve, we sit down and watch *The Muppet Christmas Carol*, which is the best festive film ever. Our love of this flick hasn't faded with the passing of time, or by the fact that when we went to the pictures to see it, we and our fellow cinemagoers found ourselves playing a bizarre game of Chinese whispers.

Apparently, the management had a message for the Cherrymot family, whose presence was required outside. As this was clearly not us, we passed the message on, and happily continued to munch on our popcorn and chocolates, while enjoying the film.

When we emerged into the winter air an hour later, we were greeted with the warming festive vision of twelve firefighters merrily hacking the battery out of my dad's smouldering car, using a variety of shiny and well-loved axes.

It turned out that the rather important message, which was, 'your car is on fire,' *was* for us after all. But it had been repeated by so many people that by the time it got to us, it didn't sound remotely like our surname, so we ignored it.

It was harder to ignore the firefighters who were surrounding our car, though.

A fireman bounded over and happily handed Dad the remains of his car battery. 'Happy Christmas, mate,' he smiled, with not a hint of irony.

'I hope you've asked Santa for a new car,' Mum uttered, handing Dad the last chocolate from the bag in a bid to ease the pain. I don't think it touched the sides.

Anyway, despite that amusing anecdote, we still love the Muppets. Mum, not so much. She sits with us while it's on but does her crosswords. We've since introduced Paul to this tradition, who has duly purchased us a copy on DVD, because he is sweet like that. And our video player gave up the ghost, so it was kind of a necessity.

73. Always 'special'

One of my most prized possessions is a report card from when I was about five.

The health visitor stated that, 'I would only do as my mother told me' (quite right, if you ask me) and observed that I was, and I quote, 'consistently trying to push a square peg into a round hole.' The story of my life.

Things didn't get any better as I grew.

As I progressed (and I use the term very loosely), through junior school, a trainee teacher asked my parents if she could use me as a case study for her coursework portfolio, to which they agreed.

Afterwards, my mum got a letter from the trainee which said, 'thank you so much for letting me observe Holly in class. It's been an absolute pleasure and she's a very special child.' She said it.

That trainee probably passed her degree with flying colours based on that observation alone. She was also possibly left scratching her head as to why I hadn't been put back at least one academic year, if not several.

My defence has always been, that being born prematurely meant I was always going to be at least three months behind everyone else in terms of development.

Alas, this argument doesn't really cut any ice when you consider the fact, that Winston Churchill (military leader, two-time British Prime Minister and recipient of the Nobel Prize for Literature), Isaac Newton (who weighed just three pounds at birth and wasn't expected to survive, but who went on to describe the laws of motion and gravity) and eminent scientist Albert Einstein, were all premature.

I couldn't do maths and had trouble with spelling and grammar. But here's the thing: I absolutely loved reading and writing. My dad is a bookworm and thankfully, so am I. We devour books and adore the wonderful author Terry Pratchett, whose books should be prescribed by the NHS for anyone in need of cheering up.

My dad is also a wonderful storyteller. When he tucked me in bed at night, he never had to resort to storybooks, as he was quite capable of making up his own stories. Those magical tales and my dad's love of stories rubbed off on me and inspired me to want to be a writer.

So, while I can't spell for toffee (as my editor will attest), I've always loved telling stories, which would stand me in good stead when I became a journalist.

Many people will tell you that journalists just make stuff up (we don't) but telling stories has always been a passion of mine, and it was an honour to bring important issues to the fore, and interview people from all walks of life as a newspaper reporter. And it was my job as a reporter which led to me meeting my husband, who is the love of my life.

So I think that not being good at maths was a blessing, after all.

74. News In Brief

- Scraped together two A-Levels and a place on a journalism degree
- Obtained First Class BA (Hons) Degree
- Obtained a postgraduate certificate in news writing from the National Council for the Training of Journalists (NCTJ)
- Landed my first job as a journalist on a newspaper in Yorkshire (I applied because I loved the 1990s television programme *Heartbeat* and the books by James Herriot)

- Obtained a reputation as a tea and cakes reporter, by which I mean I loved writing about 'human interest' and good news stories. You know, charity fundraisers, cake sales, that sort of thing. Stories to warm the cockles of your heart, the kind that read, 'cat hit by burly, tattooed driver in massive truck is scraped off tarmac, revived, stitched back together and adopted by aforementioned burly, tattooed driver, who names the feline Piddles, that kind of caper. (I hated reporting on court cases and sad news, which didn't impress the editor.)

Note: The only feather in my metaphorical journalist's hat was acquired when I was covering a court case and the magistrate addressed us as 'the gentlemen of the press.'

On seeing me in the press box, the bailiff of the court, who had turned an interesting shade of green, perhaps envisaging, at best, negative press coverage and at worst, a writ, turned to whisper in his colleague's ear. A second later, the magistrate uttered: "I do apologise. I meant to of course, say, *ladies* and gentlemen of the press."' This was only in the 2000s, I kid you not.

I smiled and silently thanked the Suffragettes for all they had done for us, but at the same time, felt immensely sorry for churchyard maintenance staff the country over, who would no doubt have their work cut out putting all the soil back, from where these pioneering women would have presumably been spinning in their graves.

Here are some other important bits:

- I secured a job reporting for a B2B veterinary magazine and then,
- Became editor of its sister publication aimed at veterinary nurses

And it's here that I'll slow down the sightseeing bus, because this is where the romantic bit begins. Take notes, there will be a quiz at the end. Please don't think I'm joking...

When I left the newsroom with my fellow journalists to embark on a two-hour trip north, I was less than enthusiastic, not least because it was raining and grey, but because I knew that three long days of reporting lay ahead, which would mainly consist of sitting in lectures and hoping I understood enough to write a story.

I first set eyes on Paul at an awards ceremony, where he was presented with an accolade for his work. I smiled and clapped, like everyone around me, but was extremely taken by the handsome man who shyly made his way onto the stage. I was pleased to note he wasn't wearing a wedding ring, and decided I most definitely needed to interview him, purely for journalistic purposes, obviously.

The day took a definite turn for the better when I interviewed this gorgeous, soft-spoken and intelligent gentleman with a lovely, kind smile, bright eyes and lovely Northern Irish accent.

I dared not dream that he may have liked me in return, and tried to think nothing more of it, except that I'd enjoyed every moment in his company and how lucky I was to have met him.

That night, a group of colleagues gathered for the conference's annual quiz night. There was a spare seat next to me and who should come and fill it, but Paul! I was delighted and silently thanked whoever it was who had mixed up the seating plan, which meant he had to sit next to me. Happy days!

By the end of the night, we had lost the quiz, but I had won a bigger prize. I had Paul's phone number and a funny feeling it wasn't the last time I would see him.

I clutched the number close to me as he walked me to my room and bade me goodnight, before going back to his own abode. Suddenly, I was looking forward to the next three days! We arranged to meet the next day for a coffee and the rest, as they say, is history. Well, not quite, but you get the idea.

When my friend bounced over to me then next day to ask who I'd just had coffee with, I acted coy. 'Where's he from?' she asked, eyes as big as saucers.

'Northern Ireland.'

'Oh, that's a shame. It's so far away.'

I nodded, sadly.

'Still, there are trains and planes and automobiles.'

'Erm, no. Long-distance relationships are hard. And besides, the man has two-hundred sheep, so I don't think there's any question of him moving here, and I'm categorically *not* moving to Northern Ireland.'

Then I fell madly in love with him, got married and moved to Northern Ireland. As I said, I don't do things by halves.

75. Lambing

'It's nice,' Mummy-in-Law says over tea one day, 'that you've been able to help out with lambing.'

I nod slowly. My eyes are heavy with lack of sleep and my brain is fuzzy. Paul and I have been taking it in turns to get up in the night to check on the sheep, and we're both exhausted, but happy.

'Sure, it's been a nice quiet lambing, a good one to ease you in.'

I almost choke on my tea.

'Excuse me? What do you mean, "it's been quiet?"' I squawk. I can't remember the last time we slept through the night without one of us (though to be fair, mostly Paul), getting up every few hours to check on the lambs and the expectant ewes.

Mummy-in-Law chuckles softly. 'Oh yes. This has been relatively easy and quiet. You just wait until next time.'

I shuffle off to bed, with Mummy-in-Law's words ringing in my ears. What on earth will a busy lambing feel like? And more to the point, what state will I be in by the end of it?

Cold, unfinished cups of tea are scattered around our house, the yard and the lambing shed. I half expect John Humphrys to pop up from behind a bale and shout 'I've started so I'll finish.' Well good for you, Humph, because with lambs popping out all over the place, I won't be finishing a beverage any time soon.

76. Game on

In the mornings, we like to play the 'where has Holly left her farming clothing now?' game.

This is due the fact that when I get in from milking, I shrug off my coat and then forget where I've thrown it, absentmindedly remove my hat and dump it somewhere really strange, like in the fridge and scatter my socks about like they're confetti.

The first time I asked Paul if he'd seen my coat, his prompt reply was, 'You've probably left it at your behind.'

This made me laugh, as I hadn't heard it before, and he explained that it described the way in which I, and I quote, 'simply throw things behind me and saunter off'.

Now we've been married for a few months, the phrase has morphed into 'you've left it at your arse,' and it still makes me chuckle.

77. Cooking up a storm

'Have you banged your head?' my dad asks after I tell him I've made spaghetti Bolognese and homemade lemon drizzle cake.

'No, why?' I frown, as I tuck the telephone under my

chin so I can stir the sauce.

'Because when you lived with us, you classed making toast as cooking, and you even managed to burn that.'

'It wasn't burnt. It was… crispy.'

'Well, all I can say is, your mother and I look forward to a slap-up meal when we come to visit, or when you both come here, whichever is sooner.'

I smile. Yes, I suppose I *have* changed since getting married. As I dish up, I can't help but smile. I feel like Nigella Lawson. Only ever so slightly less glamorous, obviously.

78. Happiness is... calves with new straw

Today, after I'd thrown fresh straw into the calves' pen, I stood and watched, mesmerised as they sniffed at this new material which had magically appeared.

One inquisitive calf began swishing her tail excitedly as she prodded the straw with her nose. Seeing this, another calf swished her tail, and added a little jump for good measure. The others all replicated this happy little dance, each adding their own moves until they were all dashing about, leaping, kicking their heels together and mooing with happiness at this exciting event.

If only a new bed of straw was all it took for humans to be as happy. We could learn a thing or two from these beautiful beasts.

79. A big fan

Here's a tip; don't put your fingers in a rotating fan. It hurts.

How I didn't chop my fingers off, I don't know. Stupidly, I didn't look when I went to turn off one of the switches after milking. Instead, I reached over while gazing the other way and nearly mashed my fingers in the process.

I feared the worst and could hardly bring myself to look at my tingling digits, convinced that I was going to bleed all over the floor I'd just cleaned. Thankfully on this occasion, I got away with it. But still, beware.

80. Just like a local

I was happily listening to the radio today, when one of the interviewees said that sheep had 'fur.'

'They have wool, not fur,' I shouted, which, on

reflection, was stupid, as the interviewee couldn't hear me, and I was in the car on my own, so there wasn't even anyone around to appreciate the fact that I'd correctly identified the blooper. But I smiled anyway. Maybe I'm getting used to these farming ways, after all.

81. Calf out

Paul has bought a new container to keep the animal food in and the rodents out.

Oh, hang on, I'll have to park this story for a while, because as I type, Paul's brother has just shouted up that one of the calves has gotten out of its pen and is wandering around the calf house.

'They can't be,' I whisper, 'they're too big to fit through the bars of the gate, surely?'

'I think you'll find that if you go down there, you'll see that the calf has indeed managed to fit through the bars on the gate,' Paul says, a smile on his lips. 'Unless of course, she's learned how to undo latches, in which case, I'm entering her into some sort of talent show.'

'Very funny. I'll go and put her back in the pen,' I say assertively, sounding way more confident than I actually feel. They are big babies and if they don't want to do something, they generally won't.

As I head out, Paul says, 'try not let the calf dance on the milk bags,' and I have a sudden vision of her standing on her hind legs and doing an Irish jig.

'That would be an awesome sight,' I conclude, 'but is something I'll try to avoid.'

Wish me luck...

I nervously approach the calf house, worried about what I'd see; the calf chewing something she shouldn't be? Her head stuck through a gate? Or maybe she'd be sat in the tractor, all set to make a bid for freedom. I take a deep breath and slide the door open...

I'm relieved to see the calf standing in the middle of the house, staring straight at me, as if she's been caught red-handed (or should that be red-hooved?) Then I notice she's wobbling slightly. On further inspection, I see she has clambered onto a small pile of hay, as if to say to her friends, 'I'm the queen of the castle!'

Her pen friends, who have gathered at the front gate to get a good view of the show, turn to me and moo. I think they're saying, 'Look, she's so naughty. But we're good calves. Look at us, still in our pen. We ain't done nuffin.' (And yes, I know that's a double negative).

'How on earth did you get out?' I ask the calf, as if expecting an answer, because I really can't see how she did it.

'Commando rolls.'

I turn to see Paul entering the calf house. 'Thought it best I come and give you a hand,' he says, nodding at the calf.

'Thanks. But what do you mean, commando rolls?'

'She probably laid on the floor and rolled through the

gap,' he says, while walking slowly past her and getting a hand to the gate to open it.

We almost have her back in the pen when she jumps over the feeder that was put there to block her path, and pelts around the perimeter of the calf house as if she's competing in the Olympics.

Finally, we get her back to the open gate and I hold by breath as she stops, inspects the gap, looks at us and then, as if going home were all her idea in the first place, mooches back to join her friends.

'Wee shite,' Paul mutters.

'Yes,' I say, hugging him, 'but she's *our* wee shite.'

Now that's dealt with, back to the other story. Where was I? Oh yes…

Paul's very pleased with his new food container, which is big, shiny and sits in the corner of the sheep house.

Every time I finish working in there, I make sure I close and lock the door. This is because sheep are sneaky, cunning and clever, despite their reputation for being stupid. I have no doubt that they've been watching closely and have worked out how to open the door in theory. But, trying to turn a key without opposable thumbs would be tricky, if not downright impossible, so I'm not too worried. Or at least, I wasn't before today.

Having finished the breakfast feeding round, I closed and locked the door, as usual, and turned to see all the sheep standing at the front of their pens, staring at me. I could almost see the cogs turning as they worked out the best way of getting the door open, and I swallowed nervously. On reflection, I wouldn't put anything past them, and I quickly removed the key and put it in my pocket, just in case.

82. Careers

Our 'have you treated one of those' game is one of my favourites. Paul has done so many amazing things during his career thus far; from anaesthetising a Musk ox in Canada to picking a tooth out of a cat's trachea. (It wasn't the cat's tooth, it belonged to the other Tom it had picked a fight with. I'm not sure who you'd say had who won that fight. But, with one missing a tooth and one laid out on an operating table, I'd say they were both losers on that occasion.)

If I'd had the brains to be a vet nurse or vet, I would have specialised in farm work. For some reason, the idea of being outside in all weathers, getting muddy and soaked, always appealed to me. I suppose it's because it's the opposite of working in an office, where you're expected to be smart and squeaky clean while adhering to a schedule.

As editor of a publication for veterinary nurses, I was passionate about showcasing the plethora of career opportunities available. When asked where they predominately work, most vets and vet nurses will say in high street vet practices, which is true. But many work in other fields (literally), caring for animals on farms, in zoos and in stable yards.

I must admit, before I entered the veterinary sphere, I didn't understand the enormity of the tasks veterinary nurses can undertake. For some reason, they are often seen by some sections of the public, but not all, I hasten to add, as 'mini' or 'failed' vets, which is not the case at all.

Well, let me tell you that being a veterinary nurse is a career in its own right and you have to be very smart to qualify as a Registered Veterinary Nurse (RVN).

In fact, everyone in the animal care profession is very talented and clever, from farm assistants and zookeepers to technicians, veterinary assistants and auxiliary nurses.

Sadly, there's a lot of burn-out within the profession due to long hours, low pay and stress.

I came to love the nursing profession so much, that when I was editor, I created an award for veterinary nurses to recognise their hard work and dedication. I think that was one of my career highlights, because it was popular and made a lot of people smile and crucially, feel appreciated.

I've always been fascinated by animal doctors, or veterinarians as they're formally known. Human doctors are extremely gifted, and I admire them, but I'm even more in awe of vets, because their patients can't speak and so can't say what is wrong.

I mean, you don't see too many dalmatians strolling into practice saying, 'Alright mate? Give us some painkillers, will you, my leg's killing me since I ran into that tree trying to catch that bastard cat. I'll get it one day, I will.'

I understand that vets spend years training for these

scenarios (injured animals coming into their practice I mean, not talking dogs, although that would be pretty cool), but still, having to piece together a picture of what might be wrong based on an owner's feedback and an animal's behaviour, seems an extremely difficult, if not impossible, task. Yet, they do it. Amazing.

The veterinary profession has, like all frontline professions, been operating throughout the pandemic in a bid to ensure owner's animals are cared for, and I think this deserves more recognition.

Companion animals (dogs, cats, hamsters, gerbils, mice, rats etc.) provide companionship and purpose to many people, but they can also help boost mental and physical health, which is vital at any time, but especially during lockdowns. So I'm sure I speak for all pet owners when I say how much we appreciate all those who work with animals. Keep up the outstanding work, you are amazing!

Oh, sorry, that turned into a bit of a soapbox moment, didn't it? I would say sorry, but I'm not. I'm so proud of the veterinary profession. Thank you for all you do.

83. Awkward

I didn't recognise my own mother-in-law today. Awkward. To be fair, while I was physically in the local shop, I was miles away in my head, so when I turned

around and saw a lady waving, I was momentarily confused as to who it could be. I wasn't helped by the fact that,
nowadays, everyone wears masks, and the lady was wearing
a hat, which meant I could essentially only see her eyes.

'How are you?' I asked brightly, in a polite and formal
way, which not only shows manners but is also my 'go to'
response when I haven't recognised someone or can't
remember their name.

In that moment, I thought of my poor mother, who is
hard of hearing in one ear. When we're in social situations,
I always know when she hasn't heard someone properly
because she's either nodding manically in the hope the
action matches the scenario being described or saying in a
loud and dramatic voice, 'Oh, don't,' which is her cover-all
response.

I think is really rather clever, because it's not a question,
doesn't invite comment, but it shows she's been listening to
the best of her ability. Sorry to have blown your cover,
Mummy. Love you lots.

84. Follow the leader

I'm making my way to feed the sheep on the hill. It's so
windy my face is almost blown off me, as they say
around these parts.

I spot them on the other side of the field and call to

them, but they don't come straight over, which is unusual. Then I realise my voice is being whipped away on the wind and they can't hear me. I move closer, shake my bucket like I'm in the percussion section of an orchestra and shout my socks off. Finally, one hears me and looks up. She spreads the news and within seconds, they're hurtling towards me.

Keen to get out the wind, I pour the nuts on the floor in a line and retreat. As I get to the gate, I turn to watch the sheep eat, but they aren't there. Instead, they're all gathered at my feet, looking up at me expectantly and licking their lips.

'Aw, girls,' I smile, 'your food is over there, look.' I point, but they just keep staring at me. They must have locked eyes on the yellow bucket and not noticed I'd already put the nuts down.

It dawns on me that I'm going to have to walk them over to their lunch, which is easier said than done. I could only have walked a few paces, but can I see the food? No. So I trapse back and forth, with the sheep and lambs following me, as I zigzag across the area. It isn't even like the ground is muddy; it should be easy to spot brown food in green grass.

I hope I find the nuts before the girls lose interest, otherwise my weeks of training them to come when I call will have been wasted. Suddenly, and with a sense of relief, I spot the food and tap my bucket on the ground until the girls see it, walk over and start eating.

On my way back down the hill, I consider how hard it was to find the food in the grass. I thought I had been standing in one place but had actually gone a lot further into the field than I realised. This makes me shudder, thinking how easy it could be to get lost on a mountainside or hill walk. No wonder mountain rescue services are so vital and always in demand.

85. Milking it with the Mad Hatter

'Move down!' I shout, feeling like an (even madder), Mad Hatter than usual.

The cow I'm talking to ignores me the first time. The second time, she turns and blinks at me. The third time, she sticks her tongue out. Charming.

Finally, for the fourth time of asking and just when I think my voice is going to give out, she moves down the parlour very slowly, as if underlining the fact that she's moving because *she* wants to, and not because I asked her to.

She eyeballs me and then looks at her neighbour and sticks her nose in her ear, as if she's whispering, 'Look at her. Who does she think she is, strange English girl, talking all funny and ordering us about? Well, balls to that. We'll show her.' And they do.

86. An observation

Just in case you were wondering, yes it does hurt when a cow whips you in the face with her tail. That is all.

87. They grow up so fast

Our lambs are going to school today and I'm quite emotional.

Charlie, one of our farming friends, is taking them into her son's class as part of show and tell. Talk about setting the bar high. It will be the best show and tell ever!

I send her a text: *I hear the lambs are off to school. Should I make them each a packed lunch?*

If they're like typical small children, yes! comes Charlie's prompt reply.

I pack their lunch boxes, iron their ewe-niforms, teach them The Green Cross Code and reiterate the importance of washing their hooves when they've used the toilet. I think about telling them not to talk to strangers but there's no point, as they'll chat to anybody. That's why they'll be such a hit with the children, on account of being so friendly and inquisitive.

There's a tear in my eye as I watch them being loaded

into the trailer. Seeing my emotion, Charlie smiles. 'We'll be away an hour, max. Don't worry, I'll look after them.'

I nod and smile. 'I know you will.'

As they disappear up the road, I wonder what the morning will have in store for them. What will they make of all those children wanting to pat and cuddle them? I pray they are good and don't poo on the carpet. And I hope the lambs behave, too.

I clean the house, tidy the food cupboards and bed up the calf pens before glancing at the clock. Only twenty minutes have passed! I pace the floor, make a cup of tea, down it in one and make another, but it does nothing to calm my nerves. Now I know how Liz felt when she dropped her son off at nursery for the first time. How do people do it? I'm an emotional wreck. Gosh, being a parent is exhausting.

88. The naked truth

Having decided she's too old for a romper suit (or calf coats, as they're otherwise known), one of our foster calves has worked out how to undo the clasps and wriggle out of it. (No, I don't know how, either.)

Calf coats are, as the name suggests, coats for calves which we put on them when the temperature drops. The coats wrap around their middles and buckle under their tummies, leaving their cute heads and tails sticking out. The coats are blue, and make the calves look like giant sweeties in posh wrapping.

Having seen this display of defiance, one of the calves in the opposite pen decided to do the same. Thus, two naked calves greeted us when we went into their house today.

Paul looked about and decided that they'd all outgrown their coats anyway, so we went about removing them, or at least, trying to, as its easier said than done.

After ten minutes, we were both covered in straw and sweat and had managed to just about cajole one calf out of their attire.

Paul bravely attempted to remove the coat of the next calf on his own, but she took a dim view of this and showed her dissatisfaction by lifting her tail and liberally coating him in poo.

'My life sucks,' he said miserably, half-heartedly wiping the poo off his bodywarmer with a bit of straw.

'I don't think it's that bad,' I said cheerfully from the safety of the other side of the pen.

'You haven't just been shat on.'

A good point well made.

89. Mini moos on the move

Our mini (well, now not so mini) moos left us this afternoon and I miss them already. They were the first set of calves Paul and I raised as a married couple, and so will always be special.

Before they left, I gave them each a pat on the head and told them to be good cows and productive milkers, while reminding them that I loved them very much. I took photos of each of them in my mind, and on with my phone, obviously, as they will last longer.

They're going home to finish off their cow training (that is, they'll spend time out in the fields and hopefully, the sunshine, with other cows, days eating and resting, before becoming mums themselves.)

Pep-talk over, I helped load them onto the trailer and waved goodbye until they were out of sight.

I felt a knot in my stomach when I turned and saw the empty pens. 'I miss my moos,' I whispered, tears in my eyes.

After all, we had cared for them for months; right from when they were wobbly-legged calves, all bewildered and uncertain. We soothed and patted them, wrapped them in coats to keep out the chill, looked after them when they were poorly and taught them how to drink from the feeder. We watched as they got more confident and rushed madly about their pen when we gave them new straw, just like over-excited children on Christmas morning.

We watched as they became inquisitive and laughed when they had their noses literally in everything; buckets, feeders, drinkers, piles of straw, hay racks, you name it. We got a sense of satisfaction when they felt brave enough to call out for breakfast, and it was wonderful to see them happily sucking up their milk.

And now they're gone. Moos will no longer echo around the yard. There will be no more patting their soft noses, having cuddles or wiping the milk from their mouths.

I'm not crying, you are.

90. Laundry

Today I'm branching out and opening a calf laundry.
Well, no, that isn't strictly true. I'm not *washing* the calves, although that would be fun. (Can you imagine the size of the bath we'd need? Not to mention the loofah!) No, as much as I want to polish them until they shine, I don't think it would be allowed.

Instead, I've established a calf coat laundry but there's no business plan. We've set it up in ten seconds and our customers aren't paying, but we're getting lots of rewards, non-etheless

The wind is still biting, and rain is forecast. Despite the rotten weather, we hope to take delivery of a new set of foster calves in a few days, and so in anticipation of their arrival, I got the calf coats out and washed them by hand. However, they weren't as clean as I'd have liked, so I bundled them into our washing machine and they've turned out surprisingly well.

As such, every surface in our living room is now covered in damp calf coats, but the chaos is worth it, because the babies will be cosy and warm.

Talking of calf washing reminds me of a wonderful story about a Land Army recruit who was sent to a farm in Hertfordshire during World War Two.

Hailing from the city, she'd never been up close to cows or sheep before, so when the farmer asked her to clean the cows prior to milking, she took him at his word. When he returned an hour later, he found Daisy was gleaming from head to hooves, because the enthusiastic and tenacious volunteer had fetched a pail of water and some suds and cleaned the cow until she sparkled.

I've also heard stories of Land Army girls who ended up marrying the farmer they worked for, because, as one said, *'he couldn't manage without me.'* Although one hopes the union had something to do with true love, too!

We talk about feminism taking hold in the 1960s and girl power in the 1990s, but I believe it was the Land Army of World War One and Two who literally sowed the seeds of inspiration and change, so that future generations of ladies had opportunities to be brave, to try something new, to stand on their own two feet and enter a whole new world. And I for one, will be forever grateful.

91. Frazzle dazzles

I 'm delighted to report that Frazzle is doing well.

Against all the odds, he's pulled through thanks to his super mum, who clearly loves him to bits. He's still wobbly on his feet, which is understandable considering what he's been through, but he knows where to get his milk from and is suckling well.

He's also getting bigger by the day, and I can hardly believe how strong he is. You can see the determination etched on his little face as he stands unsteadily and sways from side to side, before crumpling down again, but once he's got his breath back, he tries again. I've never seen anything with such tenacity.

His wool is still stained but that will grow out, and if that's his only problem, we will be very happy and grateful foster parents indeed.

92. With a cherry on top

M y mobile rang this morning and I peered blearily at the screen. When I saw it was Paul, I answered straight away, and it took me a moment to realise that his phone was working, despite having been dropped in a jug of lamb milk the night before.

Later, Liz rang to bemoan the modern education system.

'School was much easier in our day,' she sighs, making me feel approximately one million years old.

'I've been trying to teach the children this new way of doing maths, but it's utter bollocks, if you'll excuse my French…'

'That's not Fren-'

'Fine, it's a load of *merde*. Better?'

'Yes.'

'No wonder you're a journalist, you're so fucking pedantic.'

'Thank you.'

'It wasn't a compliment.'

'Love, I've been told to f-off by politicians, felons and fellow reporters. You'll have to work harder than that to offend me.'

'I could if you like…'

'On with your point, my dear.'

'Oh yes, thanks. This bloody maths homework. Let me explain…'

I've no idea what she's talking about. Something to do with cherry systems which are apparently a good way of working out sums.

To be honest, she may as well have been speaking in French. I studied that at school, too, and after five years I still couldn't even say hello.

Undeterred, Liz sends me photos and videos of this new maths malarky, but my brain is having none of it.

'So, good luck with trying to teach that,' I say. 'Mind

you, that looks like degree-level stuff. How old is your son again?'

'Five.'

'Lord.'

'I know. I hope he gets to grips with this soon, so I don't have to help anymore. Let's talk about something else, this is giving me a headache.'

'OK,' I say innocently. 'What are you having for dessert tonight? Cherries?'

'Hilarious. After this, I never want to see cherries ever again.'

'Are you sure? Because I hear there's an offer on cherries in the supermarket...'

'You can take your cherries and shove them up your arse,' she laughs. 'And yes, you can quote me on that, Mrs journalist.'

Oh, goody.

93. New arrivals

We have new babies arriving tomorrow, but, unlike most expectant mums, I don't have any cravings and we haven't had to decorate a nursery or buy nappies!

Like some bovine conveyor belt, no sooner have our first cohort of calves grown up and moved out, than we get a new load to care for, and I'm beyond excited. The farmer is obviously pleased with the work we've done in raising his animals so far, which is why we're getting more.

I can't believe that feeding calves and wrapping them in cute coats is a job! You don't see that role on offer at many careers' fairs, do you?

Paul and I were going to go food shopping this afternoon, but we've scrapped that in order to get the calf house ready for our new babies. There are pens to be set up and straw beds to be made, oh, and I need to get a welcome banner and some cake.

'Getting ready for new calves is more fun than shopping anyway,' I smile.

'You're the girl for me,' Paul grins. 'I don't think any other person in the world would have reacted like that at not being able to go shopping.'

I take his hand and smile. 'It's like I said, square pegs can find their round holes, after all.'

94. Frazzle wants to be a big sheep

F razzle wants to eat solid food just like his contemporaries. The problem is, at four weeks old, he's only just now the size of a *newborn* lamb.

Also, let's not forget the fact that, thus far, he's spent his entire life in the pen in which he was born and has had his mum by his side throughout. His favourite spot, incidentally, is under the heat lamp. He is a very wise lamb.

Paul has decided that Frazzle is now strong enough to hang out with his fellow lambs in the main area of the sheep shed. Paul is excited about this. I am in bits.

'What if he gets trampled on?' I ask, biting my nails, although I know it's a silly question as Paul wouldn't put our animals in danger.

I hold my breath as we dismantle the pen, and the world opens up for little Fraz.

You can see the cogs turning as he realises there are no longer any barriers between him and his fellow lambs. He unsteadily gets to his feet and tentatively moves forward, putting one hoof in front of the other. Nose to the ground, he sniffs the straw beyond the pen and looks to his mum, as if saying to say, 'Look, Mummy, new stuff, new smells, exciting!

His mum nudges him forward in encouragement and then steps around him to make her way to the food trough. He follows and approaches the trough with gusto, just like his mates.

But while they guzzle mouthfuls, he carefully takes one nut at a time, which just about fits into his mouth and starts to crunch. His whole head bobs up and down with the effort, making his little ears flap from side to side as he does so. (To put this in context, this would be like me trying to stuff a whole melon into my mouth in one go. It would be difficult, messy, hard work and not pretty.)

But my little Fraz will *not* be beaten by a sheep nut. He

wants it and he will have it. He's tenacious; the fact he's even here at all is proof of that.

Ten minutes later, with saliva dripping from his mouth, Fraz swallows and I exhale with relief. 'Well done, my little boy,' I cry. 'You're amazing. You've certainly got razzle dazzle, my little Frazzle.'

95. A journalist's tale

As a journalist, you're always aware that you're very much on the outside of things. On the edge. A mere visitor in the lives of others. There to record a momentous occasion, such as a fiftieth wedding anniversary, or a promotion, for example.

Indeed, being a journalist can be a lonely job. Not to mention the fact that whenever you tell someone your occupation, they say, 'Uh oh, I bet you're recording me, aren't you? Best be careful what I say.' If only I had a pound for every time I'd heard that, I'd be a millionaire.

Members of the public seem to think that journalists can make up whatever they like, because they 'never let the facts get in the way of a good story,' and this winds me up no end.

For, if they ever took the time to look at the syllabus for a journalism degree or the criteria for the National Council for the Training of Journalists (NCTJ) news writing courses, they'd see that it's an extremely complex syllabus which covers law and politics in addition to a host of other key subjects. They'd also see that there are rules and measures in place to hold journalists and editors to account.

When I was a newspaper reporter, I was, as I've said, referred to as the tea and cakes queen, on account of the fact I loved covering good news stories and shied away from negative ones.

When I landed a job as a reporter for a veterinary magazine, I was over the moon. After all, it was the closest I was ever going to get to being part of the profession. But little did I know that one member of the veterinary profession would turn out to be the love of my life and would become my husband!

When I moved to Northern Ireland to be with him, I began a new and exciting life, which was a world away from my old one. I went from living half a life in a city to a full one in the countryside.

Here, you can breathe deeply without inhaling car fumes, run freely across fields and be at work in fifteen minutes as opposed to undertaking an hour and a half commute in choking traffic. Not a day goes by when I don't thank God for this new chapter and this chance. I know I'm very lucky and blessed, indeed.

This new life has also introduced me to the farming community, which is one of the most supportive groups I've ever come across. Everyone looks after one another and their animals.

If someone spots an escaped sheep, for example, they'll call to a friend who nips to a neighbour, who passes a message on and soon, the news is across the whole area, the owner located, and the sheep returned home.

As a vet, Paul is often called upon by his fellow farmer friends to assist when their sheep need help lambing, or if they are concerned about one of their pets. The pride I feel when I see Paul tending to animals and imparting his knowledge is enormous. Yet he's so modest. As my dad says, if something comes easy to you, you think anyone can do it, but they can't.

Here, everyone's keen to help when they can. Can't find a piece of equipment you need for a farm job? Just call a neighbour and they'll either drop the item off or leave it in their yard for you to pick up at your convenience. As I previously mentioned, even moving cattle is a community event.

96. Laps

Frazzle was doing laps of the pen with the other lambs today, which was beautiful.

The ewes get extremely excited when it's feeding time or when their silage (pickled grass) is topped up, or when they see us and think they're going to get fed. Basically, they get excited whenever there's the prospect of food, a bit like me.

As soon as they hear the key turn in the lock of the food store, the rustle of a bag or the rattle of a bucket, they're off, bleating for all they're worth. They all surge forward towards the end of the sheep house, like a crowd at a concert trying to get closer to the stage.

If you could hear the racket they make, you'd swear our sheep were starved and badly treated. They'd tell you, in two baas or less, that we're cruel hoomans who never feed them. But don't believe a word of it. They're the most loved and adored creatures in the word, so don't let them pull the wool over your eyes.

And just as human children watch and copy their parents in a bid to be all grown-up, so lambs mirror their mums.

Therefore, when the ewes rush forward and get all giddy at the prospect of food, their lambs do the same, even though they're not sure why. Then, like children in a playground, they start to run around the silage feeder, making themselves dizzy in the process. The scene puts me in mind of the Caucus race in *Alice in Wonderland*, where all the animals run around a rock to get dry, but don't get very far as the tide keeps coming in.

In addition to this show of athleticism, the lambs will also skip and jump, give the odd bleat and excitedly wag their tails, before collapsing into an exhausted heap on the nearest pile of straw.

As they get older, the lambs become more inquisitive, and will often push through the scrum of sheep at the troughs to see what all the fuss is about. But the pellets don't yet appeal, and they wander off in search of something more exciting to do.

While the lambs are off running in their groups, the ewes get to eat their silage in relative peace. It's a bit like when human mums get five minutes to themselves to have a coffee and a snack in the café, while their children burn off energy in the playground. What I wouldn't give to see the lambs on a seesaw or hurtling down a slide. So cute.

97. Ringing it

Paul has lost his wedding ring only months after I gave it to him.

I open the door to welcome him back from feeding the sheep. He approaches slowly, and at first, I think something's wrong with one of the animals. Then he holds up his hand and I begin to worry that *he's* hurt. I squint into the darkness.

'Sorry.'

'For what? Are you OK?'

And, because I have the observation skills of a brick, it isn't until he's really close that I notice.

'I've lost my wedding ring,' he says forlornly.

'Oh Paul,' I sigh, pulling him in for a hug.

'You sound angry,' he says. 'you said you wouldn't be angry if I lost it. You said, "these things happen."' Which is true. I did say that.

'I'm not angry,' I mutter, 'just disappointed,' as if he's a child whom I've just discovered has been truanting from school.

A wave of sadness hits me as I look at his bare wedding ring finger. Sad that the token I gave him, which we exchanged in church before God and in front of our family and friends, is lost, somewhere out there, glinting in the darkness.

'Let's retrace your steps,' I say suddenly in a bid to be constructive.

So, we grab torches and head out, buoyed on high hopes and optimism.

We take pigeon steps from our front door right down to the sheep shed, heads bent, pushing the darkness away with our beams of light as we scour the floor. I hold my breath with every sweep, hoping I'll spot it shining on the ground. I see myself in my mind's eye, lunging on it triumphantly and holding it aloft like it's the World Cup.

With every step I grow more disappointed and exhale loudly out of frustration and also, because if I don't breathe out, I'll faint.

The problem is the ring could have bounced and rolled in any direction. It could be nestling in the long grass or sinking into the mud. hiding at a jaunty angle under some straw or camouflaged by a pile of farm debris.

Many times, I've uttered the phrase, 'it's like looking for a needle in a haystack,' but never knew what it truly meant.

I do now. I know what it's like to search for a golden ring in a golden haystack. I also know what it's like to look for a golden ring in a shed full of hay. Knackering and nigh-on impossible, that's what it is. As we stagger home, it feels as if I've turned over every single piece of hay in the entire shed, which I probably have, and all to no avail.

The sheep stand and look at us, confused by our presence in their shed twice in one night. They let out a few baas in the hope that they might get fed again. 'Chancers,' Paul laughs.

One of the younger lambs comes and bumps my leg with her hoof. 'Have you seen a ring in here?' I ask her hopefully, but she just looks at me blankly and bleats. 'Oh OK, well, if you do, let us know, would you? Thanks.'

'Perhaps one of them ate it?' I suggest. 'So maybe we could install litter trays and train the sheep to poo in them, then we could go through each stool to check for the ring.' Then I stop, realising what I'm saying is crazy. I don't think they actually *make* litter trays for sheep. Hmm, maybe there's a gap in the market there.

'They're sheep, they're not stupid,' Paul says. 'Sure, they would've spat it out.'

I nod. 'Sheep don't like gold. Just like Tiggers don't like honey.'

'Let's leave it for tonight,' Paul says. 'We'll look again in the morning. And I'll borrow a metal detector from a friend. Well, you never know.'

I nod and rub my eyes which are sore from straining in the fading light. I scour the ground all the way back to the house, just in case.

To break the sad silence, I tell the only joke I know which seems fitting for the occasion. I shamelessly stole it from a guest panellist on the radio show *I'm Sorry I Haven't A Clue*. **Question:** What's rambling? **Answer:** Jewellery for sheep. (Geddit?)

98. Ringing the changes

I watch as Paul strides purposefully back and forth across the yard, metal detector in hand, head bent, face etched with concentration. My heart leaps every time I hear a beep which causes him to stop and paw the ground, but then he moves on, empty handed.

A host of Paul's friends have been quick to offer their services to help us locate the missing jewellery. Offers of metal detectors have flooded in, as have similar stories of wedding ring woe. It seems we're not alone in the missing ring field.

One of Paul's friends lost his wedding ring on honeymoon while swimming in the sea. A friend of mine lost their ring on a muck heap while shovelling manure from a wheelbarrow, just weeks after the wedding. Despite feeling the ring ping off his finger, knowing where he was standing, and even seeing it disappear, the ring was never discovered, not even with the aid of a metal detector. He now wears the replacement on a chain around his neck, which is very wise.

But the absolute winner (and I think this must be some kind of record), was the man who lost his wedding ring during his own reception. The mind boggles.

I turn from the window and relay the story of the missing ring to Mummy-in-Law.

'That's terrible,' she said, sadly. Then, after a second, adds, 'But do you know, his daddy did exactly the same thing?'

'What?'

'Lost his wedding ring not long after we got married. Somewhere out there.' She pointed out of the window to the fields beyond.

I sit down to hear the rest of the tale.

'As you know, we used to have cattle and my husband would feed them every morning before work. He always took the same route; out the door, through the garden and diagonally across the field, a bale of hay slung on his shoulder, head down against the wind.

'One morning, he came back looking distressed, his left hand aloft. It was devoid of a wedding ring. Well, you know yourself what a sinking feeling you get in your stomach when you realise it's missing. There was shock and horror all round.

'Well, we traipsed up and down those fields, following the route we knew he took every morning. We even borrowed a friend's metal detector, just like you have, but it was all for nought. At last, we had to admit defeat and we saved up for a new wedding band.

'During a mini ceremony in our yard, I placed the replacement on Ernest's finger and said: 'With this ring, I thee wed – again. And don't lose it!" She smiled at the memory. 'I wear the ring now, as Ernest was called Home in 2007.'

I blink back tears as Mummy-in-Law shows me her husband's ring which sits next to hers. We have a hug and I wish I'd been able to meet him. He sounds like a lovely man.

'And now, forty-seven years later, my son has gone and

done the same thing,' Mummy-in-Law says, her voice breaking with emotion. 'Talk about coincidences. You'll have to get him a new ring and have a little ceremony in the yard too, just as we did,' she smiles. I agree, it sounds like a great idea.

'And when you put the ring on his finger, you have to say, 'With this ring, I thee wed – again – and don't lose it!"

I keep an eye out for the ring as I'm feeding the sheep later.

One of the lambs shouts at me as I pass and I take a moment to pat her head and tell her how pretty she is. But as I walk away, she keeps bleating. I wonder what she's trying to say? Perhaps it's, 'Oi, hooman, my mam's just shat gold! It's amazing, come and see!' And then, as I walk away, I imagine her adding, 'Oh, charming that is, ignoring me. They don't listen to a word I say. How did hoomans ever become the dominant species?'

As I walk back to the house, my mind races with other possibilities as to what has become of the wedding band.

I imagine a magpie adding a shiny new ring to its nest, proudly placing it next to a more tarnished one, and thinking, 'My grandfather found treasure and so have I. What luck!'

I do like the idea of the two rings being side by side and it is rather a sweet notion, but still, I'd rather Paul's ring wasn't lost.

You just wait 'til I get my hands on the feathered critter. I'll be invoicing it for a replacement ring, if nothing else.

I look to the fields beyond and imagine Mummy-in-Law and her husband searching the network of fields, day in, day out, all those years ago.

While it's frustrating, I remind myself that metal can be replaced. People can't. And no matter what happens, nothing can take treasured memories away.

99. Game for a laugh

Today we're playing Sheep Tetris, not to be confused with Sheep Jenga.*

Sheep Tetris occurs during lambing, when we have to try and squeeze another pen into the sheep shed when room is running out. It's all about creative thinking and using every inch of free space, with pens at all angles.

Thankfully, lambs and their mums only stay in these pens for a few days. After that, they're 'released' into the fields as soon as the sun shines.

Sometimes, we keep the smallest and weakest lambs

*Sheep Jenga. A complicated game in which we pack away the sheep for the night by stacking them up, one on top of the other, a bit like Jenga, as the name suggests. Or the way in which you used to stack the stools in science class. Indeed, it's a great way to save space. (Only joking. We keep them in a very spacious sheep shed which boasts stunning countryside views. In fact, I'm seriously considering opening an estate agency especially for sheep looking for new abodes. What do you think? It could be called Baaagain Homes.)

inside with their mums a bit longer, just until they get better and bigger and can hold their own. We call this communal pen the pen-thouse (see what we did there?)

Paul, who thinks of everything, has even added a playpen with a lamb-sized door, so the youngsters can hang out with their contemporaries without their parents cramping their style.

He's even made a small feeding trough which is low enough for the lambs to reach into, so they can eat their pellets in peace without having to fight with the adults.

Frazzle's particularly taken with the playpen, which boasts lots of lovely straw and a heat lamp. He can often be found chilling out in there, often with a different lady every day. Such a flirt, that boy.

100. Siren sheep

Today I'm carrying the sheep nuts up the hill in my right hand. I know this is a very specific and boring detail to relate, but there's a reason for me sharing it with you.

I'm left-handed and predominantly carry and lift things with it. Unfortunately, I've managed to spill some household chemicals on my wrist and my skin doesn't like it one bit.

I say household chemicals because that's the only thing

I've come into contact with recently which could have caused such an adverse effect.

Paul kindly washed and dressed my wrist yesterday and I'm now sporting a lovely blue bandage which is an honour, as they're usually reserved for sheep emergencies only. Hence why I'm carrying the bucket in my right hand and giving my left a rest.

The wind is refreshing and makes me smile as I stride along. I'm hardly in the field before the sheep and lambs are around my feet. They must've heard the rattling of the bucket as I made my way up the incline. Gosh, they've got good hearing.

We'd just finished lunch when the doctor called to see about my wrist. I really struggled to hear what he was saying, not only because he was softly spoken, but because the phone signal was bad.

'I'm so sorry, but could you please speak to Paul?' I asked in the end, putting him on loudspeaker.

The doctor asks a variety of questions which Paul answered. I listen, fascinated as Paul uses medical terms to describe what we assume is a chemical burn. I hear the relief in the doctor's voice too, presumably because he can now understand the person he's conversing with, but also because his medical knowhow is helping him make a diagnosis.

He asks if we can send some photos of my hand so he can see what he's dealing with, which is fine, except to do that, we need to remove the bandage.

My pain threshold is somewhere around minus ten, so this is a very long and painful process, possibly more so for Paul, who has to listen to me whingeing.

'My sheep have to go through this too when I treat their feet,' he explains. 'I usually pull the bandages off quickly so it's over sooner, but I'm scared to do that with you in case that makes it worse.'

So, there you have it, the sheep are less troublesome than me and make for better patients. I'm not surprised.

While we wait for the doctor to let us know if we need an appointment or not, I consider the tough situations medical professionals have to deal with during normal circumstances, let alone during global pandemics. Talk about a rock and a hard place.

Not only are medical staff in practices and hospitals trying to deal with Covid-19 cases in a safe and effective way, they're also working around the clock to ensure they're available to treat other patients with non-covid problems. As such, doctors are conducting telephone triage consultations before they decide if a patient needs to be seen in person or not.

Now, I'm no medic, but I imagine it must be hard to try and triage someone over the phone, not to mention petrifying. The pressure to make the right call must be horrendous.

I sympathise with my doctor who is probably agonising over whether to bring me in or not based on a photo taken on my mobile. I don't envy him one little bit. And mine is a fairly minor injury. Goodness knows what they do when there's someone with something complex to deal with. God bless the NHS.

101. In a relationsheep

Frazzle's been fighting with the other lambs. I know this because Paul's just grassed him up.

Apparently, Frazzle was squaring up to some of the older ones this morning, spoiling for a fight. With head down and shoulders hunched, he galloped towards them but backed off at the last minute. I could almost hear him saying, 'Come an 'ave a go if ewe think you're hard enough.'

'He can't fight with them,' I cry over my porridge. 'He's too small. He'll get hurt.'

'I did try and explain that to him, but he wasn't having any of it. Instead, he took another charge at one of the big lambs and hit him, but Fraz is so small I don't think he made much of an impact.'

I put my hands over my eyes because I could just imagine it. 'And then what happened?'

'The other lamb charged at Frazzle, who wisely ran away before contact was made.'

I sigh with relief. 'Right, I'll go and speak to him.'

'No, don't. Having his mum go down to the playground to sort out the other kids will just make it worse. You'll embarrass him for starters, and then he'll get even more agro from the bigger lambs.'

Paul looks at me and sees the rage flickering in my eyes.

'You're going anyway, aren't you?

'Oh yeah.'

He shakes his head. 'If we ever have children, woe betide the school bully who picks on them.'

'Darn right,' I say, heading for the door.

102. Dance with me

Paul and I are dancing around in the kitchen to *Belle of Belfast City*.

We first danced together at a veterinary conference near Belfast, and while this song wasn't our first dance, it will always hold a special place in my heart.

To now be dancing together as husband and wife is magical and amazing, because, at one point, I didn't think we'd ever get here, but somehow, we managed it.

I'm out of breath, despite the daily farm workout. I used to consider myself quite fit, what with going to the gym a lot when I was a journalist, but that was before I tried ceilidh dancing with Hubby!

When we shyly and nervously took each other's hands for that first turn around the dance floor at the conference, I secretly felt quite smug, what with my daily gym sessions.

'This'll be a piece of cake,' I grinned.

I wasn't grinning for long. Instead, I was gasping for breath and looking for a glass of water.

'Wow, he can dance!' I thought as I chugged water and admired him from across the hall.

Just a few days earlier, I'd been feverishly packing my suitcase for the veterinary conference. I'd never visited Northern Ireland before, and I was excited. I'd even scribbled down two objectives in my notebook:

1. Get some great lead articles for the magazine
2. Don't flirt with the president (Paul) as I must remain professional

By the end of the conference, I'd achieved the first objective.

103. Not adding up

Question: If you have thirty-five sheep in a field and then you go on a work trip and leave your dyscalculic* wife in charge, how many sheep will she notice are missing from the field while you are away?

Answer: None!

That's right, number fans, I was merrily feeding the hill sheep for four days consecutively, not realising that fifteen, yes, that's fifteen sheep (half the flock), were missing.

*I was recently diagnosed with dyscalculia, the numerical equivalent of dyslexia. It comes from Greek and Latin and literally means 'counting badly.' Amen to that. Just ask the sheep.

Turns out the little scamps had pushed the gate open at the back of the field, snuck through and enjoyed a few days holiday.

Well, I say enjoy, but perhaps they realised the error of their ways early on but were prevented from going home because the wind caught the gate and closed it again. For all I know, they may have spent the next three days waving their hooves over the gate and shouting, 'Oi, hooman, we're over here,' while I was totally oblivious, just meters away.

And there I was thinking I was a shoo-in for The Sheep-sitter of the Year Award. After all, my charges were all still alive when Paul returned. (Though how, I don't know, because it turns out I was giving fifteen sheep enough food for twenty-five. I'm surprised they didn't burst.)

When I was asked for the millionth time how I hadn't noticed the sheep were missing (including by my auntie who lives in England – yes, news travels fast), I could come up with no reasonable explanation, except that I have the observational skills of a stone.

Paul gave me a 'thank you for looking after the sheep card' when he returned. I suspect it's now going to be rescinded.

104. Preconceptions

Research* has revealed that British people associate the following things with Northern Ireland: Leprechauns, green fields, The Giant's Causeway, Saint Patrick, shamrocks and The Troubles.

In the interests of parity, I also asked a Northern Irish friend what she thought of when she heard the word England. She said, 'Crowds, London, red busses, Buckingham Palace and motorways with more than one lane.'

In case you're interested, when I think of the island of Ireland, the following springs to mind: *Riverdance, The Lord of the Dance* and the 1990s band B*Witched (younger readers look it up. 'Cest La' Vie' was a tune!)

Thus, just days before I visited Northern Ireland for the first time, I was busy preparing. Activities included urgently looking for my passport while researching what currency and language they used. I'm only half joking.

I keep forgetting that Northern Ireland is part of the UK and as such, one doesn't need a passport to enter the county, just photo identification. They also use sterling and speak English, but with the benefit of that beautiful Northern Irish accent, which makes everything sound wonderful and interesting.

Until that point, I'd only ever seen Northern Ireland on

*Oh OK, by research I mean I messaged my friends asking 'What do you think of when you hear the words Northern Ireland and Ireland?'

television. It was, of course, in the news a lot when I was a little girl, due to The Troubles, but I only have a vague recollection of seeing grainy images on television. Of violence, yes, but mainly of people looking scared or angry, or both. It made me feel nervous watching it. The other time I saw it was when the Discover Ireland adverts were aired, which took my breath away with shots of stunning beaches and scenery.

I longed to visit Northern Ireland to take in The Giant's Causeway, walk the streets of Belfast and see where the Titanic started her life. Years later, I would also want to go and see The Dark Hedges, made famous by the television series *Game of Thrones,* and to scout out locations used in *Line of Duty.* But I didn't know that in the 1990s, because those shows didn't exist then.

I would also want to visit for reasons other than tourism. The main one being because my beloved and my betrothed lived there, and I longed to be with him. But I didn't know that then, either.

105. The Lamb Test

I was so excited when I stepped off the plane in Belfast and couldn't wait to see Paul. We'd been friends for years, and while I secretly longed for more, I was too shy to say anything. I remember spotting him as I came out of the airport and running over for a huge hug. It felt wonderful to be in his arms.

My job was to attend the conference and find news stories for the magazine I worked for. Paul was busy hosting all weekend, as the president of the veterinary association which was delivering the event.

Somehow, I managed to do my work while watching Paul. Admiring his professionalism, his kindness, his humour, his handsomeness, his cleverness. And I realised that I was falling in love with him from afar.

We first danced together at the conference's formal dinner. My heart was hammering in my ears and my hands were sticky. I hoped against hope that I wouldn't fall flat on my face and make a fool of myself.

The song was 'Shut Up and Dance', which was, looking back, very apt. Lyrics include *Don't you dare look back, just keep your eyes on me*. And I didn't want to take my eyes off him. I wanted to be in his arms forever. But we were just good friends. I didn't dare hope he would feel the same about me. And yet, I had to find out, one way or another and I'd taken a couple of days off work so Paul could show me his homeland. We'd chatted so much over the phone, that I had an idea as to what his farm might look like, but I couldn't wait to see it in real life.

Towns and cities disappeared into the distance as we made our way from the conference to Paul's farm. The rural beauty of Northern Ireland suddenly swam into focus, and it took my breath away. Sun-kissed fields of green and yellow, which stretched as far as the eye could see, were decorated with fluffy clouds (or sheep, to use

234

their proper name), while the hills and mountains beyond beckoned mysteriously and enticingly.

We passed quaint villages with lovely, lyrical-sounding names; Ballymoney, being a particular favourite. Rows of cottages with slate roofs, flower-covered front doors and neat gardens whistled by, as did seaside towns which were resplendent in the late afternoon sun.

As we got closer to Paul's home, main roads gave way to small, winding country lanes and houses became few and far between. Signs stated that if we were to follow them, we'd come across exciting tourist attractions such as castles and ruins. Alas, they'd have to be explored another day.

We careered past homemade signs which cheerfully informed us we were passing 'such and such' a farm. I turned in my seat to try and see the farmhouse, but the lane leading to it was long and winding, with trees obscuring everything, save for a chimney pot which glinted tantalisingly in the now fading light.

I pointed excitedly to signs featuring pictures of cattle and ducks (!) which warned drivers to be aware that animals could be crossing the road at any given point.

Then, we took a narrow road edged with hedges on either side, and slowly climbed a hill. Suddenly, the road dipped away, revealing a village which clung to the edge of a cliff. And while each cottage was painted a different colour, they all faced the sea.

As we passed the doors, picked out in pinks, blues and greens, I imagined the families that live behind today, and the generations who inhabited the buildings before them. The way they worked the land or served on the sea and the ways they contributed to the community. What hopes and dreams did they have for their lives? And what changes did they see in terms of political and scientific development? Whatever it was, the sea would have been there throughout; reassuring and unchanging. Indeed, that same sea roared up at us as we passed, like a guard dog warning us off. As we left, it seeped back, its secrets safe for another day.

Fog gathered in the distance, making the area look mysterious and mythical. I was stunned at how much the scenery and weather could change from one area to the next in a short space of time.

I was so taken with the scenery that Paul stopped at one of the beaches so I could explore. It was deserted and glorious and as I took my shoes off and trailed my feet in the sand, I felt like I'd stepped through the pages of a book and was suddenly the heroine of the piece, bravely exploring a strange but stunning land.

The waves rushed to the shore and soaked assorted rocks and stones. I could feel the salt on my lips and hear the roar of the sea. The wind picked up and played with my hair, making me feel like Demelza from *Poldark*. And my hero was there, walking beside me, though I dared not share my feelings.

Then we were off again, sweeping along a narrow track and then a bumpy lane. We then took a tiny ribbon of road which eventually narrowed to a lane. Then that I heard them, the legendary sheep and finally, after a few more minutes, I saw them! Field after field of gorgeous Dorsets, with their thick, creamy, woolly coats and friendly faces.

On seeing the car, they rushed forwards and bleated in greeting as if to say, 'Our favourite hooman is home! We've missed ewe!'

As I clambered out of the car, Paul disappeared into a field and returned a few minutes later carrying lamb, which, to my surprise, he plonked straight into my arms. I was a little taken aback, not only at being handed a sheep, which isn't an everyday occurrence, at least, not where I come from, but at just how heavy she was!

'Hello, lovely,' I whispered. Her wool smelt of fresh air and hay. She looked up at me with big brown eyes, let out a little bleat and my heart melted. I played with her ears and ran my fingers over her wool, surprised at how thick it was. 'You're gorgeous.'

I was also very nervous. Human babies always cry when I hold them (I think it's because they can smell fear), so I was expecting the lamb to react in the same way, but she seemed quite happy. She rubbed her pink soft nose against my face and, just like that, I was in love.

I learned later that this was The Lamb Test.

Apparently, Paul wanted to check that I liked sheep, and more to the point, to check that his sheep liked me. And bundling a new bubba into my arms before I'd even had a chance to take my coat off, was certainly a good way of testing my mummy-mettle. Apparently, I passed with flying colours.

The next day when I woke up in the spare room, the first thing I thought was, 'You don't meet amazing men like Paul, every day. He's the most wonderful man I've ever met. I want to be with him. I need to tell him how I feel.' I was going to tell him over breakfast, but I was too nervous.

It wasn't until later, when we were walking on a secluded beach, that I decided it was a case of 'now or never.' I turned to him, and, as the wind whipped around us, we shared our first kiss, and it was beautiful because we'd waited for it for so long. Years of looking at each other with longing, of holding each other's gaze and then turning shyly away. Years of hoping.

He wrapped his arms around me, and I snuggled into him. I wasn't dreaming, there *was* something between us. I couldn't believe my luck, that such a gorgeous man liked me too!

I remember thinking, 'So here you are. You're the man I've been looking for my whole life. You're the one.'

106. The proposal

After four months of long-distance dating, Paul and I found ourselves at the same conference where we'd first met all those years ago.

The veterinary conference calendar is very much a merry-go-round, and there always seems to be an event of some sort occurring somewhere in the country, whether it's for equine, cattle or small animal vets. From a journalistic perspective, this is wonderful, as it means there's always something to report on.

I was always on the lookout for good news stories and that conference was no different. But I had no idea that one of the biggest breaking news stories to occur at the event would involve me and change my life forever.

Living five hundred miles apart from one another meant Paul and I didn't get to see one another face-to-face very much, so I was grateful that our jobs meant we were often at the same events and could see each other during breaks and in the evenings.

On the last day of the conference, I was dressed in casual clothes: jeans, T-shirt and trainers, as I knew I'd have to help take down the magazine's exhibition stand. Paul was in a lovely suit, complete with a sheep-print tie, but that was nothing out of the ordinary as he always looks dapper at formal events.

I knew Paul was flying home that afternoon, which I was sad about, but at least we'd got to spend some time together. We'd arranged to meet in the foyer to say our goodbyes, but then he asked me to step into one of the conference rooms.

'Why are we in here?' I asked, checking my timetable. 'There isn't a lecture in this room for ages.'

'No, but this is the room where we first met,' he said, taking me by the hand.

'Yes,' I said, smiling at the memory.

I was still chattering away ten to the dozen, when Paul asked if he could get a word in edgeways and I obliged.

Then he said that the past year had been amazing, that he loved me very much and wondered if I would do him the honour of marrying him. He then got down on one knee and produced an engagement ring.

I didn't speak for a second (a first for me) because I couldn't believe what was happening. I had dreamt of such a moment for so long that I thought I was perhaps still asleep.

My eyes filled with tears as I threw my arms about his neck and whispered, 'Yes please,' (which has got to be a contender for the politest acceptance in history, surely?) I was so busy kissing and hugging him that I only looked at the ring properly as he put it on my finger. It was gorgeous, though to be honest, I would have accepted a Haribo ring at this point.

We dashed outside to call my parents, Paul's mum and my friends. In my haste and excitement, I also called Liz, who had only recently given birth to her fourth child and was asleep when I rang. 'Will you be my bridesmaid?' I asked breathlessly, without even saying hello. There was a second of silence then a hazy, 'Yup.'

'OK, thanks, speak later.'

Apparently, as Liz had gained more consciousness, her husband said, 'Did Holly just ask you to be her bridesmaid?'

Liz, whose brain was still fuzzy, simply said 'yes.'

'…So, she's engaged?'

Liz rubbed her eyes and looked at him. 'Wait. What? She's engaged?!'

'Well, she just asked you to be her bridesmaid, didn't she? So, unless she's finally lost it and has gone full Miss Havisham on us, I think we can safely assume she's just got engaged, yes.'

She rang me back, 'Sorry, just realised what's happened.

Congratulations to you both. Of course, I'll be your bridesmaid, you silly moo. You don't have to ask!'

Fiancé and I even managed to grab the official conference photographer who took our engagement picture, and it's gorgeous. Well, Paul looks gorgeous. I look like I've just been dragged out of a hedge. My makeup is smudged, my hair is mad. But my smile is huge and says, 'I'm the luckiest lady in the world.'

We began excitedly planning our wedding for May 2020. What could possibly go wrong?

107. March 2020

The world is shutting down.

Something called Covid-19 is spreading across the globe with alarming speed, and everything is closing with increasing rapidity.

I'm standing in Stansted Airport clutching my suitcase which I packed in approximately ten seconds. It contains three pairs of knickers and twenty books. (Always have a book in your bag, everything else can be sorted out later.)

Spain and Italy have just announced national lockdowns. Their hospitals are overrun with sick people and all events, including weddings, have been banned in a bid to stop the spread. It's becoming abundantly clear that England will be next.

My dad, who knows a shitstorm when he sees one coming, has decided the best course of action is to get me by Paul's side as soon as possible, so if our wedding is postponed, at least we will be together.

'We're right behind you,' my parents said as they pushed me out the door. (About five hundred miles behind, in fact.)

To be honest, I don't blame them. They've had to put up with my pain in the arseness (sic) for more than three decades and, having spotted a loophole which meant they could avoid having to put up with my meltdown, they quite rightly leapt through it.

So, to recap, it's taken me thirty-five years to find the man of my dreams who wants to marry me. We planned our wedding in three weeks and now, we are waiting to see if it will all be undone in a matter of seconds

108. 7.59pm

I'm huddled around the television with Paul and future Mummy-In-Law to watch Boris Johnson's latest Covid-19 briefing.

As I clutch Paul's hand nervously, I think that this must be how people felt just before war was declared in 1914 and 1939.

Citizens across the UK are leaning in and listening,

waiting to hear what's going to happen next, what's expected of them and how their lives will be impacted.

Of course, I'm not likening Covid-19, or the way in which the public have had to adhere to the government guidelines to a world war, but I should imagine that Mr Johnson, his cabinet and NHS staff feel like they're fighting a war now. It's an invisible enemy whose impact is sadly all too clear, with hospitals packed full of sick people, exhausted medical professionals and worried families.

In recent weeks, my friends and I have said that we don't know how people coped during the world wars or kept sane.

We're so lucky that, despite being in lockdown, we can call out family and friends, or see them on laptops. But during the war years, people were reliant on letters, which took weeks if not months to be delivered. The wait must have been excruciating. And how did the postal service even get letters to the trenches in the first place? Absolutely amazing.

I look at Paul and smile nervously. Maybe Boris will say that the lockdown is nearly over and everything can resume in May? Maybe he'll make a last-minute decision and say weddings are exempt and can go ahead? Maybe.

109. 8.12pm

B ollocks.

110. 9pm

T here have been a lot of tears in our household (mainly mine) but I should imagine the scene has been replicated in homes across the country. Future brides and grooms, who've been excitedly planning their weddings and waiting, now know their original plans will not be going ahead.

As we suspected, weddings are banned, meaning we'll have to postpone ours.

I can't say I'm surprised. By early 2020, our wedding preparation course had been cancelled, and our hen and stag parties swiftly followed. Then weddings were only allowed to go ahead with five people.

Now, I could just about cope with no reception, no guests and no photographer (My dad, who was already prepared to double up as Father of The Bride and Best Man, was also willing to wear a GoPro in order to capture the events on film, if required.) But I drew the line at having to choose between one of my parents or Mummy-In-Law.

I'm heartbroken.

I know there are so many people going through a hell of a lot worse right now, with relatives ill or dying in hospital, and them unable to see them, and I'm in no way comparing myself to them. We're so lucky to have our health and each other. I know that and thank God every day. I also know I'm blessed to be by Paul's side. Being apart would have been horrendous enough, but being apart while we unpicked our wedding plans would have been a bridge too far.

We have a big hug and a cry. There's absolutely nothing we can do apart from follow government guidelines and wait. It's hard, but it's also just tough.

We agree that we don't want to wait until next year to get married, which is what a lot of couples are doing. We just want to be married in church and say our vows before God and our family and friends. The reception and all the other twiddly bits can hopefully be done at a later stage. The wedding is the main thing.

And so, we wait. We speak to the amazing vicar at my church and to our wedding suppliers and formulate a Plan B, which is this: As soon as weddings can go ahead, no matter how small, we will get married. We send an email to our guests explaining our decision and everyone is so supportive and loving.

I'm so sad because I've wanted to get married ever since I was a little girl. Then, of course, you're just thinking about the frilly elements of the wedding; the pretty dress, your daddy walking you down the aisle, your mummy looking on, your friends and family standing in the pews, smiling and waving, your bridesmaids. You're thinking about seeing your groom, making your vows and having your first kiss, throwing the bouquet and enjoying your first dance.

Oh yes, the framework is all laid out, based on the fairy-tale weddings you read about in stories like Cinderella (how I longed for talking mice) or those you saw in old films.

But the main detail, the bit always missing from my day-dream, was who the groom would be. As a little girl, I wasn't worried about that. After all, adults were always saying, 'when you know you've found the one, you know,' so as far as I was concerned, finding a groom was the easy bit. The biggest problem, as far as I could see, was how I was going to train the unicorns to pull the glass coach to take me to the wedding.

Of course, life doesn't come with a manual and because I'm not the brightest light in the forest and have always been slow on the uptake (I refer you to the earlier report from the health worker about square pegs and round holes), I didn't think I'd met my future husband when I first encountered him at that conference all those years ago.

Yes, I thought he was gorgeous, I loved his accent and his smile, his twinkly eyes and the fact he was extremely clever, talented and most importantly, kind, but I never thought he would like me in return.

When Paul first saw me, he thought I was cute, was pleased I wasn't wearing an engagement ring and most importantly of all, noted my 'small hands' which would be, and I quote, "ideal for lambing!'"

It was Paul's kindness, generosity of spirit and chivalry that really shined through when I interviewed him. But I honestly didn't think I'd be able to sustain his interest.

By that stage I was in my early thirties, and had given up all hope of ever finding true love and getting married. However, Paul and I kept in touch and were friends for a long time before the penny eventually dropped, and I realised that the love of my life had been standing right in front of me all along.

That my future husband would be a farming-veterinarian from Northern Ireland, simply hadn't crossed my mind when I was that little girl planning her wedding. But I'm beyond delighted that he's all those things and so much more.

I have to keep reminding myself that I have found my true love and soulmate, and we will be getting married at some point, but we just didn't know when. But as I've said before, patience isn't my strong suit and I feel sorry for Paul already.

'I'd better call my parents and tell them about the wedding,' I say, dismally, 'though there's probably no need, they most likely heard my scream go up from here.'

As I dial their number, I remember that all our wedding stationary is stored in their house, including my wedding shoes, all the wedding gifts, sixty personalised chocolate bars bearing our new married name and a particularly peeved partridge in a pear tree.

'It's an ill wind that blows no one any good,' I say brightly when I speak to Dad. 'On the plus side, when the supermarkets run out of food, at least you and Mum can eat the chocolate bars and then use the wrappers to wipe your bum when the toilet roll runs out.'

111. Kind gift

We've just received a wonderful present from the ladies at the local church. It's a framed print of the 'Love Is Kind' verse from Corinthians. A note inside the box reads, *We're so sorry. Nobody should have to postpone their wedding day. Praying that you will be able to get married soon.* I cry with happy tears at their thoughtfulness.

112. Our non-wedding day

Today, I should've been up at the crack of dawn, excitedly chatting with my bridesmaids, trying to eat a bit of breakfast but struggling because of the butterflies in my stomach, nervously fiddling with my beautiful dress, having my hair and makeup done and hugging my parents while being full of excitement and anticipation, because today should have been the day I was getting married to Paul.

Instead, thanks to Covid-19, I woke up alone with no idea when we would be able to say, 'I do'. As reality sunk in, I pulled the duvet over my head and groaned. I was quite prepared to throw a full-blown pity-party and stay in bed all day.

But my lovely fiancé is made of sterner stuff and selflessly made every effort to make the best of it for me.

So, we went for a stroll in the garden (Covid-19 non-weddings don't stick to normal wedding day traditions, meaning we got to spend the morning together) where Paul presented me with a lovely bunch of wildflowers: my non-wedding bouquet.

While out on our daily stroll, we stopped outside the local church for the traditional church steps wedding kiss. Then, I got to walk down the aisle (OK, so it was in Sainsbury's, which wasn't quite what I had in mind, but beggars can't be choosers.)

Then we went milking, so at least we were useful.

We finished our shift at exactly 8pm, which was when we should have been having our first dance. Not to be dissuaded, we decided we would have our first dance after all, albeit in the milking parlour yard while wearing our farming clothes.

I couldn't stop smiling. After all, I had the most handsome 'almost groom' in the world and he looks gorgeous in anything.

Then it was homeward bound to get washed and changed. I put on my best dress and Paul wore a suit. Unbeknownst to me, he had lovingly prepared a buffet for us which contained all the food we were meant to have at our reception. And yes, I did cry, but in a good way,

After dinner, we took to the floor for a second first dance. It was the perfect end to what had been, under the circumstances and against all odds, a rather lovely day.

We made a video of our 'non-wedding' and shared it with friends, which not only proved popular, but also made them smile. We hope it will give joy and hope to those who find themselves in the same situation. Maybe it will inspire them to make the most of their own non-wedding day, too.

113. Unwrapping sheep

Our sheep are being unwrapped today and I'm so excited!

Covid-19 may have caused the world to come to a grinding halt, but farming life goes on. After all, cows still need to be milked and sheep need to be sheared!

A team of three professional sheep shearers and a couple of wool-handlers and their dad rock up with their equipment and set up in the blink of an eye.

The sheep have already been rounded up and are standing in a holding pen. From there, they'll go across a walkway (single file, no pushing at the back) and enter the crush (scarier than it sounds, just a smaller holding area), while the shearer gets ready. Then the sheep will be released one at a time onto a platform, where the shearer is waiting with his electric clippers.

Now, sheep aren't small or light and their woolly coats, which are tough enough to see them through harsh winters, are extremely thick, which means getting a grip on the relatively small sheep beneath can be difficult. But these guys make handling them look easy. Initially, the sheep struggle, their little legs pumping furiously, their heads wobbling from side to side, but they soon realise resistance is futile. You see, once sheep are sat on their bums with their legs in the air out in front of them (which is the position the shearer puts them in) they're helpless.

I watch, open-mouthed as the clippers are fired up. A high-pitched buzz fills the barn and the shearer proceeds to remove the wool (or to 'clip the sheep', to use the proper term) with ease.

Honestly, he makes it look as simple as peeling an orange, except this is a very wriggly orange and he's peeling it with one hand.

The fleece, which comes off in one piece, is handed to the assistants who roll and pack it into wool bags which we'll take to the Ulster Wool Board later. (Entire towns used to be built on the wool industry, but today, sadly, there's hardly any money in it. In fact, shearing the sheep often leaves the farmer out of pocket.)

The sheep look unrecognisable as they emerge from the shed, sporting sleek new looks. They are momentarily disorientated as they stumble into the light, but then they feel the sun on their skin and their mood visibly lifts.

I watch one newly unwrapped ewe as she realises she's

devoid of her heavy coat. She shakes herself vigorously, lifts one sleek leg experimentally and then the other, before twirling as if she's on a catwalk. For the finale, she takes a huge leap, lands beautifully and shimmies into the field. They must feel so much lighter for having all that wool removed.

The rams, on the other hand, are a different story completely; They strut into the shed all macho (their thick wool gives the illusion of extra bulk) as if they're spoiling for a fight and will take no prisoners.

Five minutes later, they emerge looking very sorry for themselves. They aren't so big or strapping without their coats and their swagger has gone. However, they look very respectable with their neatly clipped coats, like proper gentlemen, you might say. Although to my mind, they now look like freshly scrubbed potatoes.

'You look adorable,' I coo. One of them looks up at me, as if to say, 'Don't you say an effing word,' before slinking off into the field. At least they're cooler now. Well, in the true sense of the word, anyway.

But apparently, I'm not the only one who is confused by the animal's new look following their trip to the baaa-bers.

Braveheart and Canterbury, two of our stock rams, who've been hanging out in the same field quite happily for months and are best mates, are now merrily headbutting each other as if they've never met before and spoiling for a fight.

'They don't recognise each other without their wool,' Paul says.

'Are you winding me up?'

'Nope. They'll settle down soon once they realise who's who.'

Meanwhile, the lambs have got their own problems.

They're running around the field screaming their little heads off (they're too small to be shorn and so have missed out on this party) but their mums have returned without their trademark woolly overcoats, so the lambs don't recognise them. They shoot from one ewe to the other, have a frantic little sniff, decide she's not their mum and run off again.

One poor little mite is bleating so much I'm worried she's going to lose her voice. Her mum trots over and gives her lamb a big lick, but her offspring is unconvinced, and she does a few more laps of the field before she realises that she was next to her mum all along. Bless.

Mind you, I'm not surprised they're confused. I know of one lady who popped out to have her straight hair permed and when got home, her daughter, who was a toddler at the time, refused to look at her for the rest of the night, clearly, confused by the sudden change of appearance. I suppose that must be how the lambs feel, but on a bigger scale.

I mean, that's like going out with someone who starts the day in one outfit, then goes into a shop, gets changed into a totally new outfit, pops on a hat and a pair of sunglasses and then exists the shop. Chances are, they'd be able to stroll straight past you without you giving them a second glance, because you wouldn't be expecting them to look so different. Mind you, I'm oblivious all the time, so don't count on me.

114. The beach

If further proof were needed, and in case I haven't made it clear, I don't deal well with stress. Which is unfortunate, seeing as there's a global pandemic, the likes of which hasn't been seen for generations. The government, whose only line of defence seems to be to lock people indoors, is confounded by it, as is the medical world. There's no cure and to top it all, and on a selfish note, our wedding plans have been scrapped.

Don't panic! But, yes, I *am* panicking, rather a lot.

I have a brown paper bag in my handbag in case of panic attacks. I haven't had one since I was a teenager, but I always keep one on my person, just in case.

I've been doing some work around mindfulness and learning how being outside can boost one's mental health.

I appreciate that we're very lucky to be in the countryside and indeed, the middle of nowhere, during lockdown. My thoughts and prayers are with those who are in high-rise flats in cities and towns and especially those with children. That window for daily exercise must seem like a golden hour. No wonder parks and communal areas have become so popular.

I've taken to running (OK, jogging. Fine, moving a bit faster than walking pace) a route which takes me up a cliff path and down to the sea.

The clamber to the top is hard work, but well worth the effort. The first time I followed the route, I was initially disappointed as there wasn't much to see on the ascent, but then the grey ribbon of footpath gradually turned into a wider expanse of ground, dotted with an assortment of flowers in lollypop colours. The shrubs, which had been partially blocking the view, became less abundant and, after negotiating a particularly tight bend, I was rewarded with a view of the stunning seascape and an expanse of bold blue sky, which seemed to go on forever in all directions. A brave wind rushed up, as if in welcome, covering me in salt kisses, which I could taste long after my excursion had ended.

What a privilege it is to live somewhere as beautiful as this, and, moreover, 'what a view,' as Elizabeth Mapp of *Mapp and Lucia* fame, might say.

Since that first visit, I've returned to that spot many times. Not just because the exercise is good for me, but because standing up on that hillside makes me feel as if I'm on the cusp of something. As if the present is melting into the past and the rules of time no longer apply.

Do the people who've lived here all their lives still appreciate the view; I wonder? Would their feet still remember the way? Perhaps they come up here to see shadows of their former selves on the beach below, collecting shells and dreams and making wishes. Maybe they can even hear their own carefree laughter on the wind and recall the sound of long-forgotten voices.

Did people come here during the war years in a bid to clear their minds and bury fear?

I think of all the proposals proffered on the beach over the centuries and of all the people who discovered they were going to be parents or grandparents while walking the shoreline. In my mind's eye, I can see toddlers taking their first, tentative steps before tumbling onto the soft sand and giggling, and puppies bounding around, giddy and excited at being alive.

Sometimes, when I'm the only one on the beach, I imagine, just for a few moments, that I own it, which is a bit cheeky seeing as I've not lived here long, but still, a girl can dream.

Thus, I put my earphones in, play the music of Clannad and drift away on the waves of my imagination. In my head, I am no longer in modern attire, but in medieval costume, my locks flowing as I meet Paul, also clad in medieval gear.

The rugged coastline is stunning and the sea ever contrary. One minute, it's rushing towards the cliffs as if it is an enemy and clawing at the rocks with white gnarled fingers. The next, it's a suitor, kissing the stones and pulling them towards an embrace with gentle, sweeping movements.

If you listen carefully, you can almost hear the voices of ancestors whistling on the wind. This is, after all, an old land. Many have lived, loved and fought here.

Stories pass from generation to generation and new traditions are carved out with the creation of every new family, from attending church every week to a walk after lunch on Christmas day.

Memories collect on the beach as easily as shingle. And with one sweep of the tide, they're gone.

115. The time is now

I 've always wondered what it felt like, when the news came down the line. When the announcement crackled over the wireless. When readers feverishly turned the newspaper pages, hardly daring to believe their eyes.

Did strangers hug in the streets? Maybe neighbours ran into one another's houses without even knocking in order to share the news. To finally be able to utter the words they'd wanted to say for years, 'The war is over!'

British people celebrated the end of World War Two by having massive street parties where they sang, danced and hugged. Others gathered outside Buckingham Palace to see the king, while more determined revellers jumped in fountains and kissed strangers!

I know this because I've read about it in books and have watched countless documentaries. But despite this, I could never imagine what it must have felt like to hear life-changing, wonderful news over the radio and be able to share it with your nearest and dearest. I can now.

I'd switched on the wireless (which was what my nan always called it) to listen to one of my favourite radio programmes which aired after the news bulletin. Because I'd given up all hope of ever hearing any good news, I was only half listening to the headlines. Then I heard something which made me prick up my ears. Only, the newscaster's words didn't sink in at first. I suspected I was hearing things and turned the volume up to catch the discussion.

Then they repeated the statement and my heart leapt. I wasn't hearing things after all!

I jumped to my feet, threw my paperwork into the air, shot out the front door, ran back in again when I realised it was peeing down and I didn't have any shoes on, pulled on some footwear and ran across the yard to find Paul to tell him the news. But he was already running towards me, having heard the news on the radio in his shed. We stopped, inches from each other, breathless.

'Boris,' I began excitedly, 'on the radio, he just said,' then we both shouted in unison, 'weddings can go ahead!'

Paul burst out laughing. I burst into (happy) tears and threw my arms around his neck, my whole body shaking with adrenaline and relief.

Finally, we could get married! Yes, we'd have to cut the guest list in half and meet other criteria, but to me, being able to have twenty-five guests as opposed to five, was positively luxurious.

'I love you,' I whispered into Paul's ear.

'I love you too.'

We were back on track to becoming husband and wife! Hurrah!

Half an hour later, I'd gathered myself sufficiently to go back to work (after excited phone calls with my parents, family, friends and anyone else who would listen) and was sat at my desk when Paul appeared in the doorway. I looked up.

'What are you doing on Saturday the eighteenth of July?'

I shrugged.

'Fancy marrying me?'

I squealed and threw myself into his arms. 'Yes, please!'

The countdown was on. In less than a month, we'd be tying the knot. Hopefully.

116. Stand by your man...

I must really, really love Paul, because I'm standing on a windswept beach on a freezing day in the middle of June covered in oil, eggs and, by the smell of it, manure.

The question I'm desperate to ask is, 'What kind of place is this?' but I don't dare, because that would mean opening my mouth, which would be a very bad idea indeed.

Paul's friends and family have turned out (in a socially distanced way, I might add) to conduct a ritual which is common in rural parts of Northern Ireland and northeast Scotland.

The ritual, known as Blackening, stretches back generations and goes something like this: The engaged couple are kidnapped by family and friends, tied to a trailer, and taken to a beach where they are liberally covered in anything the partygoers can get their hands on. And, as this fun little activity originated in agricultural areas, the 'anything' usually includes, but is not limited to, animal faeces, food waste and any other muck which happens to be around the farmyard.

Apparently, the ritual is meant to ensure good luck for

the entirety of the couple's marriage. But, based on the amount of gunk we're covered in, I'd say our good luck will last for eternity, as will the smell.

Usually the betrothed couple are driven, firmly restrained, to the beach by their captors, but because of Covid-19 and social distancing etc. we've had to make our own way. So, we've effectively volunteered for this 'experience'. We must be mad.

When we arrived, everyone clapped and cheered. 'That's nice,' I said to Paul, smiling naively. It took me a moment to spot the buckets and bags people were clutching, but I was too afraid to ask what was in them.

As we got out of the car, some of Paul's female friends dashed over to me, their faces etched with worry, concentration and determination. They were on a mission.

'Put this on,' one said, throwing a boiler suit at me. 'And this,' another lady uttered, handing me a swimming cap. Someone else advised me to tie my hair up, remove my glasses and put on the goggles they'd kindly provided.

'Where's Paul's boilersuit?' I asked, clambering into mine.

'He refused to wear one,' explained the lady who had spoken first. She shook her head and tutted. 'The mad fool.'

'Well,' I said as I wrestled to get my hair under the cap, 'if he isn't wearing one, I don't think I should.' They stared at me, open-mouthed. 'What?' I thought they'd be impressed at the fact I was so stoically standing my man. 'It's romantic.'

'It's stupid' the first lady clarified, clearly not one for

beating around the bush.

'Aye, wise up,' swimming cap lady laughed. 'Noone will be expectin' you to go through this without some kindo' protection.'

'But..'

'Don't be an ejjit,' goggles lady said as she pushed a stray strand of hair back under my cap. 'Trust me, you'll thank us later.'

And with that, I was pushed towards the beach. Well, as much as you can be pushed while practicing social distancing. Paul was ahead of me and already being bundled into an open-backed tailor. Once I was up there with him, we were promptly tied to chairs.

'What madness is this?' I screeched, trying to make myself heard over the cackles and shouts of the crowd. 'It's like a witch hunt.' While I was not amused, Paul was having a whale of a time and laughing his head off.

The first egg to hit me in the chest took my breath away, but I quickly recovered. This isn't too bad, I can handle this, I thought, smugly.

But I wasn't smug for long, because then someone threw a bucket of freezing water over me and from then on, the onslaught was endless; More eggs, flour, slurry, hay and something I couldn't even put a name to.

After what seemed like hours, but could only have been a few minutes, Paul managed to break free from his chair and then released me. He then wrapped himself around me to protect me from the worst of the detritus. And that is where you find me now.

I can't see anything, because my head is buried, but I can

hear that Paul is having a great time and that pleases me. Apparently, this bizarre ritual shows that your friends love you and the community respects you, which is an odd way to show you care, if you ask me. Personally, I would have preferred a pizza and a trip to the cinema, but each to their own.

One of Paul's friends particularly enjoys liberally covering him in some sort of horrendous homemade concoction. I have no idea what it is, and I don't want to know. The one thing I am certain of is that it stinks to high heaven. I subsequently learned that the concoction was payback because Paul had covered his friend in something similar during his Blackening ceremony.

On some level, I *am* enjoying myself, if only because Paul has waited a long time to get married (as have I) and now we're one step closer to becoming Mr and Mrs. He's attended so many of these rituals in the past and now, finally, it's his turn. And I am his betrothed! I can't believe my luck! It feels like I've won the lottery of life.

Eventually, the group runs out of things to throw, and the pelting lessens. I breathe a sigh of relief as we are helped down and then wash ourselves in the bracing sea.

'They won't get to their second wedding at this rate,' one of Paul's oldest friends mutters to his wife, his arms folded resolutely, 'because they'll both be in hospital getting treated for pneumonia.' He has a point. Thankfully, and I don't know how, but we managed to get away with it.

To my utter joy, everyone stays behind to tidy the beach and take all the mess away, like very good and obedient *Wombles*. By the time we go home, there's no sign that anything untoward has occurred. I'm not surprised by this behaviour though, yes, the people of the community are fun-loving, but they're also caring, principled and care about the environment. Even if they do have weird traditions.

'Fair play to you,' one of Paul's friends says, bounding over. 'You are class for taking part,' she says nodding at me. I get the feeling that if she could've shaken my hand, she would have.

Safe to say, my English friends didn't understand the tradition and were confused when the photos appeared on social media.

What was all that in aid of? Liz asked via text.

I'll explain later, I replied, as I needed time to process it myself.

As soon as I got indoors, I headed straight for the shower. The warm water felt glorious compared to the cold sting of the sea and I smiled as I watched the muck disappear down the drain. Afterwards, I wrapped myself in a big, fluffy towel and latterly, fresh pyjamas.

But for days afterwards, even though I kept scrubbing my skin and washing my hair, I occasionally got a whiff of oil and rotten fish. Still, it could've been worse. I heard of one poor woman who, after a particularly messy Blackening ceremony, had to walk around with bits of pig bladder stuck in her hair for the best part of a week. Not a good look.

117. You gotta roll with it

O ne of my university lecturers once described me as tenacious, and I've worn it as a metaphorical badge of honour ever since.

You need to be tenacious if you're going to be a journalist. (It also helps if your hobbies include being told to f*** *** in a number of new and exciting ways by complete strangers, but that's another story.)

Tenacity does pay off, though. For example, when you're working on a story which requires you to keep making calls until you get that killer quote. Or, as happened to me on many occasions, a story falls through at the last minute and you need to find something else to replace it in two seconds flat, in order to fill what will otherwise be a gaping hole on the front page.

However, I'd assumed that my tenacious days were behind me when I moved to Northern Ireland to work with sheep. How wrong can one person be? **Answer:** Very.

Paul and I have convened in a field with Charlie, a friend of ours, who is kindly helping us sort the sheep. Some are staying in their current field (the one we're standing in) and some are being moved to pastures new. If they all stayed here, there wouldn't be enough food for everyone, so this is a pretty vital exercise.

The holding pens are all set up and I'm on gate duty. The idea being that when Paul or Charlie wrangles a sheep over to me, I open the gate and let them through.

I'm on the lookout for a really big stick which I can wield at the sheep who have to stay put, so I can say in a very Gandalfian way, '*you shall not pass.*'

My thoughts are interrupted by someone shouting my name and screaming, 'Don't let her in!'

I look up just in time to see a ewe careering towards me. She hits the brakes and I manage to grab her, much to my delight and surprise. 'That was easier than I thought.'

Alas, I've spoken too soon. The sheep obviously disapproves of my bragging and decides to make a bid for freedom by wriggling her legs – all four of them – frantically, as if she's peddling a particularly powerful bike.

'Don't let go!' Paul screeches. I'm not about to. I cling on with grim determination, despite the fact I know I'm losing my grip, because I can feel her wool slipping through my fingers.

Suddenly, and I have no idea how, I've gone from holding her shoulders to gripping her bottom. I'm not sure which of us is most upset about this. And then, looking for all the world as if we're participating in some weird human-sheep-conga line, we're off, sliding through mud, bushes and piles of sharp stones before finally falling into a huge pile of nettles!

I somehow manage to get some traction on the slippery ground and, like Bambi in reverse, push myself up and bring my feet together so I'm in a standing position. The sheep, who is also very tenacious, looks at me, decides I'm a wuss and makes another leap for freedom, chucking a right as she does so.

The sudden shift causes me to lose my balance and I find

myself gliding over the top of her and sucking in my stomach as if I'm participating in the pole (Dorset) vault. Unfortunately, I catch my foot on her side and we fall to the floor in a tangle of hooves and feet. We're both breathless, confused and ultimately, annoyed.

At first all I can hear is my own breath (which is good, as it means I'm still alive) but then I hear something which sounds like, although it can't be, *applause.*

The sheep, who now has her hooves on my chest and is using me as a cushion, looks at me and I look at her. We are both confused. Then we turn our heads as one to see Paul and Charlie clapping.

'At least you didn't let go,' Paul smiles, shooing the sheep off and helping me up.

'Thank you,' I sigh, bending down to rub the mud off my trousers.

'And you're not hurt, so that's the main thing.'

'No, I'm fine but thanks for ask-' I start to say, only to realise that Paul is actually talking to the sheep. She's snuggling into him and playing the victim card for all it's worth, but as soon as he looks away, she eyeballs me. If she'd flicked me the 'V' and stuck her tongue out, I wouldn't have been surprised. Unbelievable.

118. Excited sheep

One of the ewe's brakes failed today.

For some reason, the hill sheep were more excited than usual this morning when I appeared in the field with their breakfast. Normally, they surge forward as a big group and stop just before they run me into the ground.

Today, however, one particularly enthusiastic sheep started the charge early and was well ahead of the others by the time she got near to me. I didn't brace myself because I'm so used to them stopping just in time. As a journalist, you're taught never to assume, but I did, and immediately regretted it.

The ewe must have skidded on a patch of mud, because instead of slowing to a halt, she kept moving and barrelled straight into me.

Thankfully, she's quite small and I managed to steady myself so neither of us ended up on the floor. Despite being winded, I was fine and she showed no signs of distress. In fact, as soon as the food was in the trough, so was she. I smiled as she enthusiastically wolfed down (bad analogy?) a few mouthfuls before the others caught up.

Watching sheep run towards food troughs is like watching children excitedly run towards a playground; so cute.

119. Here we go

My hands are shaking and my breath is ragged. I'm holding the boarding pass which will get me onto a plane which will take me to England, so that in two weeks' time, Paul and I can get married! I turn and hug him with tears in my eyes as I hate saying goodbye, but we're counting down to our wedding day, so I'm not too sad. Fifteen days until we say 'I do'. Hopefully we'll make it this time.

120. Reflections

Once upon a time, there was a woman who had given up on love and on finding a man just as lovely and kind as her daddy. She just couldn't believe that there was a man out there who would love her just as she was. And she was, it seemed, always the bridesmaid and never the bride.

Then she met a man at a conference, who showed her that gentlemen did still exist, that chivalry was real and that she *could* be loved for who she was; she didn't have to change or be a performing seal, be cleverer or more accomplished or prettier or thinner. That it was OK to have OCD and depression and be nervous, while still being a whole person capable of loving and being loved. Because he loved her just as she was. In his eyes, she was beautiful, inside and out.

And to her, he was gorgeous, inside and out, too. Not to mention gentle, caring, honest and handsome, clever, accomplished, supportive and loving. They made each other laugh, both loved animals and were equally bewildered at having found love in the most unexpected of places and later in life. They were there for, cared about and loved one another. They were both square pegs in the round hole of life, but together, they were the perfect match.

And so, on Saturday the eighteenth of July 2020, reader, I married him*.

121. The small big day

I worry non-stop about anything and everything. I even worry that I haven't got enough to worry about. And so it's rather ironic that I wasn't the slightest bit worried on my wedding day. Not nervous or anxious or agitated; just blissfully happy and excited.

*Thanks to Charlotte Bronte for penning *Jane Eyre* just so I could nick that line. So thoughtful of her to pre-empt our wedding by more than a century and write a bestselling book, just so I could quote it in mine. Yes, it's all about me!

When I awoke, I felt as I did as a child on Christmas Day, when I would slowly blink myself awake and see light peeping through the curtains, proof that the long night was over. Sighing with relief, I would wriggle my toes to feel the stocking at the end of my bed, and my stomach would flip with excitement at the rustling of paper which told me Santa had been! I resisted the urge to bolt downstairs to see if Rudolph had eaten the carrot I'd left for him.

As I lay there, I wondered if I was still dreaming. Then, just like I had done all those years ago, I wriggled my toes. But I wasn't listening for the rustle of paper in a stocking now, but the sound of my duvet gently brushing against the bag which contained my wedding dress. I got goosebumps when I realised that I hadn't imagined it, I really was engaged to Paul and we were getting married in a matter of hours!

I thought of him, waking up in his hotel down the road, eating breakfast and getting ready. I suspected he wasn't nervous. After all, this is a man who takes animals apart, fixes them and puts them back together again, so I couldn't imagine that standing up in church and saying vows would really phase him.

One day, he was busy picking bits of plastic out of a dog's intestine during one particularly tricky surgery, while his friends, who are also professional builders, were building his new house. I was probably faffing about with press releases in an office five hundred miles away at that point. Well, we all have our talents.

Back in my room, I listened for any movement. Nothing. I rolled over and looked at the clock which told me it was ten minutes past six.

I've always loved Christmas Day. As a little girl, I would shoot out of bed at five o'clock, run into my parents' room and shout, 'He's been, he's been,' while bouncing on their bed. Once they'd scraped themselves off the ceiling, they'd hug me before muttering, 'Great. Why not go back to sleep for a bit?' Then I'd snuggle between them and fall fast asleep for at least two hours. (Again, ironic as for the rest of the year, my poor parents couldn't get me out of bed with a crowbar.)

The thought had crossed my mind that it might be fun, on the morning of my wedding, to bound into my parents' bedroom and bounce on their bed, just as I had done as a child. But I resisted, on the basis that I was thirty-five years old. Instead, I crept downstairs and made tea as quietly as I could, aware that my friends were sleeping in various parts of the house.

When Daddy came downstairs, we hugged and I presented him with tea and a present; cufflinks engraved with the words 'Father of the Bride'.

He smiled and thanked me, and we hugged some more. At last, it was his turn to walk me down the aisle and give me away, as he had seen so many of my friends' fathers do over the years.

The rest of the house slowly came to life, and I greeted Mummy and my friends with hugs and kisses. I felt like I was floating on air, but at the same time, it was all rather surreal. Every time someone asked where the bride-to-be was, I found myself looking around the room for them, before I realised that it was me!

Looking back, I think I wasn't letting myself get too excited, just in case the government did a last-minute U-turn and said we couldn't get married after all. I think that's why I was quite sedate; I didn't want to get myself all excited for no reason. I think I was also exhausted from the emotion of our first wedding being postponed and then months of watching and waiting.

Most mothers of the bride have to force their daughters to sit down and eat something on the morning of their wedding, but my mum had no such problem. I happily wolfed down cereal and toast and had to be told to back away from the fridge when I tried to help myself to more food.

I watched excitedly as my friends had their hair and makeup done. I was going last so as to be as fresh as possible for the ceremony, and so hung around in my penguin PJs for a while. My dear friend Ben, who didn't need his makeup or hair doing, got himself ready while he waited and looked utterly dashing in his suit and tie.

Then it was my turn to be made up and have my hair curled. I felt like a princess and the ladies, including my dear friend Flora, did wonders.

Then, it was time to put on the dress. I was shaking as Mum helped me step into it. When I turned and saw myself in the mirror, I couldn't believe it. Was this really happening? Was it really me? I couldn't stop smiling. When my dad came to see me, he smiled and said, 'Well, you aren't going to get better than that, are you?' My parents smiled at me and I beamed back at them; their little girl had at last found her prince.

Liz, who had done her own hair and makeup at home (and she looked cracking) had arrived by that point and I walked downstairs to greet her. She looked wonderful in her Grecian pink dress, as did all the bridesmaids. She looked at me, tears already welling up in her eyes. 'You look fabulous,' she smiled. 'Don't cos you'll set me off,' I whispered.

We first met in senior school when we were twelve years old. We studied together in the library, had countless slee-povers, giggled until we were giddy and made plans for the future, including the places we'd visit, the people we'd meet and the posh jobs we'd invariably have. We chatted into the small hours about the difference we'd make to the world while we were in it. The weddings we'd have, the handsome grooms we'd bag ourselves and, in Liz's case, the much longed for and loved children she'd have.

Liz, I am delighted to report, is now a happily married lady, for she found herself a very kind and handsome man and they have four lovely children together. In addition to being a brilliant mum, she's also an entrepreneur. She's the most tenacious, feisty and funny person I've ever met, who also has a heart of gold.

She stood by me over the years, even when I went spec-tacularly off the rails, got my priorities wrong, moved away and was only in contact intermittently. Despite that, she never left my side or stopped being my friend. Not once in all that time. She forgave my many misdemeanours, wiped my tears, encouraged and cared for me and I love her to bits.

All of these thoughts came to me as we stood in the

kitchen on my wedding day. I was humbled and delighted that she'd agreed to be my bridesmaid and I couldn't have been prouder or more thankful for my dear friend.

Of course, the bridal party consisted of all my dear friends whom I love to bits, whom I met in school, at college or at work, and they've all stuck by me. They're amazing and I'm blessed to have them in my life. Thus, to have them with me on my wedding day was the icing on the cake.

Talking of which, Paul even made and iced our wedding cake! He's so multitalented! But what made it even more special was the fact it was baked and decorated with love. It was beautiful and the attention to detail, which summed us up as a couple, was stunning.

A collection of sheep stood on the bottom tier in a field of green food dye. On the next, our initials were picked out in blue icing, my favourite colour, while the top tier had space for the cake topper I'd ordered as a surprise (well, I had to contribute something.) The cake topper depicted Paul and I in our wedding attire, and even had his kilt picked out in the correct Crawford tartan! The picturesque scene was completed with some extra sheep standing at our feet! We couldn't have asked for more.

The wedding car was a 1960s Beetle (I love the television series *Heartbeat,* which is set in that era, did I mention?) and the bridesmaids travelled in a VW campervan. (Paul's family used to holiday in a similar van, and so the vehicle was a nod to them.) Both had blue ribbons tied to the front and they looked resplendent on the driveway.

My bridal party and I had photos in the garden, before

returning to the house so I could put my sheep earrings in and my crucifix necklace on. The bridal party then joined Mum on the driveway, while Dad and I took a few minutes to gather ourselves. Then we hugged, took a few deep breaths and stepped outside.

Our immediate neighbours, those who lived down the street and even our friends in the next village had gathered to wave us off, which was wonderfully touching and I felt like a princess as I waved back. But then they started to clap, and that set me off crying again. For, while I understand they were clapping in a congratulatory way, I think they were also saying well done for getting married despite everything, for understanding the true meaning of marriage, for scrapping all the bells and whistles so we could say our vows in church.

And of course, the fact they'd made the effort to come out and see us off in a socially distanced fashion meant the world to me.

Afterwards, our neighbours said it had been a tonic for them too; from seeing the cars to watching me emerge in dress and looking so happy with my parents and the bridal party. In fact, many said it had been the highlight of lockdown, which meant so much to Paul and me.

After climbing into the car, Dad and I posed for photos and then it was time to go. Except, the car wouldn't start. My grin stayed in place. Just a glitch, I thought. The driver turned the key once more, but again, no joy. I tried not to panic.

Meanwhile, Liz, who was driving herself to the ceremony, was already in her car and throwing her kids' car seats and toys in the boot, utterly convinced the Beetle had conked out and she was going to end up driving us.

Happily, the car eventually kicked into life on the third attempt, and we were off.

Elsewhere, two of our guests were having fun and games of their own. They had planned to meet at our house so we could drive in convoy. The reason being that the high street leading to the church was closed for pedestrian social distancing, meaning guests would have to take an alternative route through narrow, congested streets, and we thought it best to tackle that particular navigational challenge as a group.

But on a whim, the duo had decided to take the country lanes instead of the main roads in a bid to dodge the traffic, which was a great idea in theory. Unfortunately, they got stuck behind not one, but two combine harvesters. Then, just to put the tin lid on it, the combine harvester drivers stopped in the middle of the narrow road, got out and started chatting. The air, I think it's safe to say, turned blue as they pipped their horns and tried, but ultimately failed to squeeze past.

By the time they got to our house, we'd already set off for the church and they finally caught up with us on main road. Thankfully, we weren't difficult to spot on account of the fact Dad and I were in a 1960s Beetle complete with blue ribbons, and our bridal party was following in a VW campervan. They tried to overtake us, in what was increasingly becoming a posh episode of *Wacky Races*. On the sixth attempt, they succeeded.

Back in the bridal car, I was also getting increasingly

bemused and confused. Somehow, we had ended up leading the procession, when I was convinced that as the bride, I was meant to arrive last. But seeing as I was the only one with alternative route logged into my phone, we were at the front, like some really expensive taxi navigation service.

It was a surreal journey. I squeezed my dad's hand, hardly believing the day had actually come, and peered out the windows, beaming at everyone.

I'd passed so many bridal cars in the past, and always beeped my horn to show support. On that day, drivers did the same for me, and I couldn't have been happier or prouder.

As we neared the church, our driver pulled in so the bridesmaids and my mum, who was driving herself, could get ahead and park up.

On our approach, I saw people waving and clapping, and fought back tears, again, as I realised my old school-teacher and her husband were there to see us, as were my dear friends from church and some of my friend's parents. None of them, sadly were allowed into the church as we were restricted on numbers, but the fact they'd made the effort to come and see us on our big day meant the world to us.

The roof of the car was down at by this point, and my dad and I waved to them all as we went by – talk about feeling famous! The memory of them standing in the sunshine and waving to us will stay with me forever.

As we pulled into the church, bang on time, I might add, I was taken aback to see Paul still getting changed. I ducked down, squealing, 'He can't see me before the service.' The little outburst was my one and only Bridezilla moment, which I think was pretty good going, considering.

Thankfully, Paul had heard the cars approaching and quickly made his way into church so he didn't see me before the ceremony!

I discovered later that the poor man had basically organised the wedding single-handedly. He was in Asda buying flowers to decorate the church just hours before the service. By that point he was wearing his kilt but had teamed it with an old T-shirt and battered brown leather boots, as he didn't want to get fully dressed until a few minutes before the ceremony. Which meant he sort of stood out among the Saturday morning shoppers.

The staff, who were intrigued, asked what he was doing. 'Getting married in an hour and a half,' he smiled. One of the women got on her walkie-talkie and updated her colleagues, 'Everyone, he's the groom, I repeat, he's the groom.'

From there, he went back to the church to unload the milk churns and Wellington boots he'd brought over from Northern Ireland, in what was a lovely nod to his working life.

Once in position on the church steps, he filled them with fresh flowers we'd bought from the market the day before; we specifically wanted ones with roots attached so they would live after the service. In fact, they're still blooming in my dad's garden to this day.

Multicoloured bows were meant to have adorned the

chairs at the reception, but of course, there was no reception, so, unbeknownst to me, Paul had hired the bows anyway and tied them around the pillars of the church. They looked stunning and everyone commented on what a wonderful touch it was. It was such a beautiful gesture on Paul's part, because he knew how disappointed I was at not having a reception, and so had tried to tie in as many elements from it into the service as possible. Thank you, Paul. You are so kind, amazing and very much loved.

A friend of mine took a wonderful photograph of Paul standing outside the church, car keys and paperwork hanging from his mouth as he organised the rings. (The poor guy had no best man, meaning he had to look after the rings himself. To complicate matters further, our rings had to go into isolation seventy-two hours before the service and only we could touch them.)

Liz dashed into the church to check the groom was safely inside, and then I got out of the car and made my way to the side entrance. I was shaking with excitement, disbelief and adrenaline. Liz held my hand throughout and said reassuring things like, 'Enjoy every moment. This is your special day,' and, 'You've finally met the man of your dreams, which is all you ever wanted.' Finally, she said, 'I'm so proud of you,' before handing me the handkerchief I inevitably needed.

Then the Vicar came out and said a prayer with us before we moved into the foyer, where Paul had tied a blue bow around the font and left me a single red rose. He is amazing.

As I held my dad's hand and got my breath back, trying

to drink everything in and sear it into my memory, I heard one of our chosen songs being played inside the church. It was *The Wedding (Ave Maria)* by Julie Rodgers which includes such lyrics as: *I see the church, I see the people, your folks and mine, happy and smiling…Oh my love… can this really be? That one day you'll walk down the aisle with me… I see us now, your hand in my hand, this is the hour, this is the moment,'*

And it was our moment. I smiled at my gorgeous daddy (who looked so smart and was even wearing a tie, even though he hates ties), my beautiful bridesmaids and my lovely man of honour, Ben.

Liz did a cracking job of sorting my dress and fluffing my skirt, then the music started, Dad looped his arm around mine and we were off!

Dad looked so proud and I couldn't stop smiling, especially when I saw my dear friends and family. My thoughts, however, seemed to be stuck in a loop: I'm a bride, I'm actually the bride! Where's my lovely groom? Remember every second. Don't fall over!

Then we were at the top of the aisle and I saw Paul waiting for me, arms behind his back. He looked resplendent in his Crawford tartan kilt, complete with long white socks, shiny shoes and smart black Bonnie Prince Charlie jacket, from his days living and working in Scotland. I almost burst with pride. I looked about and back at him, by which point, he'd turned and was smiling at me. Then my thought loop changed to, 'There's the man I'm going to marry. He looks gorgeous. He will soon be my husband. Don't fall over!' I didn't take my eyes off him from that second on, and as we got nearer, I saw he had tears in his eyes, as did I.

After all these years, my dear friend had become my best friend and was about to become my husband. He was willing to stand up in front of family and friends and most importantly, before God and take me as his wife. I couldn't wait for him to become my husband and to spend my life by his side. I felt like the luckiest woman ever. Indeed, I *am* the luckiest woman ever.

'You look beautiful,' he whispered, as I stood by his side. 'You look amazing,' I replied (equal rights and all that).

The guests were crying, then my dad started to cry, so I hugged him, which made my mum cry. Liz meanwhile, was having issues of her own. Not only was she trying to hand me a tissue, but she was being told by the vicar to 'please sit down,' except she couldn't, not until she'd taken my bouquet (which was made out of an old copy of *Jane Eyre*.) Finally, she managed to wrestle it out of my hand and took her seat, shaking her head incredulously. Bless. Then we turned and got on with the business of becoming husband and wife.

Before the ceremony, we placed a sign in the entrance to the church which our guests read as they made their way in. I think it summed everything up beautifully. It read: *Dreams really do come true for on this day we said I do.*

122. The Mystery of The Self-Turning Tap

One of the taps in the milking parlour keeps turning itself on. Today, I heard the water gushing out and rushed down the walkway to turn it off.

The taps are on levers which you pull down to turn on and push up to turn off. They're linked to long hosepipes which are used to wash down the areas where the cows stand to be milked.

During milking, the cows face the troughs with their bottoms towards us, so we can more easily reach their udders.

Two seconds after I'd turned the tap off, it was on again. Cursing, I dashed back and put it firmly in the 'off' position. Very mysterious indeed.

123. The Mystery of The Self-Turning Tap – Solved

Today, we worked out that the cows are turning the taps on with their tails.

We know this because one of the girls was more than happy to give a demonstration. While she was being milked, she started swishing her tail from left to right and then up and down, and sure enough, after a few minutes of this, her tail knocked the lever and turned the tap on. Mystery solved. I know, it's like reading a *Sherlock Holmes* mystery, isn't it?

124. A tale to tell

As I was making notes in the field today, notebook resting on my knees, I felt a hoof tap my leg.

I turned to see One Ear standing next to me. She looked at the notebook and then back at me, as if to say, 'What doing?'

'Yes, Mrs, what can I do for you?' I asked, although I already knew.

She's annoyed that I've got this far in the book without

telling you her story. But I've been putting it off because hers is a very *special* story and I need to take my time telling it. You see, One Ear wasn't always called One Ear. Well, I've started the story now, so I had better carry on.

Now, it's quite rare for ewes to give birth to quads, so I think Paul was rather surprised when one of his sheep did just that. But what was even more unusual, was that they were all ewe lambs. One Ear (although that wasn't her name then) was one of the four, and they all had the correct number of ears.

But when she was about twelve months old, dogs somehow got into the field she and her sisters were grazing in and attacked them.

One of the dogs ripped off her ear and chewed her tail, breaking it in the process. There was blood everywhere and sadly, one of her siblings didn't survive. But One Ear, as she came to be known, clung to life, as did her other sisters.

By the time Paul got there, it was all over, and the dogs had been rounded up. He was devastated but tended to the casualties as best he could. Yet little One Ear didn't make a noise, not when she was picked up, put in the trailer, or even when she was placed in a safe, warm pen with her sisters. Not one solitary bleat.

Paul lovingly nursed her and her remaining siblings back to health. He cleaned their wounds, gave painkillers and antibiotics and liberally dispensed hugs. It took months and was a slow and painful process, but he got there in the end, and so did they.

'Did you find her ear?' I asked, when Paul recounted the sorry tale one day.

'Yes, it was in the field, but there was no point trying to sew it back on because it would've just come off again.'

'And her poor tail?' I asked, watching as she swung the top half back and forth, the lower section limp and lifeless.

'Broken. It will never heal.'

'Poor bubs.'

'Yes, but she manages.'

I watched as she flicked flies away from her face with her remaining ear.

Whenever I check on the hill sheep, I always try to spot One Ear first, but if she's facing the wrong way, she looks like all the others (i.e., with two ears) and it's only when she turns to face me that I declare happily, 'Hey, one ear!' Incidentally, she can hear perfectly well, especially when I shake a meal bucket.

She has the most beautiful, fluffy, white, symmetric face with huge dark brown eyes which shine with intelligence, and a pretty pink nose. The symmetry is a little out of kilter now due to the missing ear, but it only adds to her charm.

Her left ear is a beautiful shade of grey and thins to a perfect point. Then you follow the ridge of her head and the sweep of her skull to the right-hand side, where the lack of an ear just shows even more prominently, her lovely eye and the most exquisite cheekbones which models would kill for.

Whatever she physically lost on the day of the attack, she's since made up for in personality and sass. She's a survivor, she's strong and she's a fighter. I wish she could speak, because she'd be so eloquent and passionate.

If she were human, she'd be a journalist or a politician,

because she's that tenacious. Or, if she were a human born in a different era, she'd be a Suffragette, fiercely fighting for women's rights. She certainly fights for her right to be fed, that's for sure, and asserts her place in the flock by pushing to the front of the queue when its feeding time.

One morning, I was out feeding the sheep when I stopped to chat to a visitor who was making a delivery. As such, I was holding a big paper bag of meal, which I was going to pour into the trough just as soon as the conversation ended.

But One Ear, who was clearly bored of waiting, decided to take matters into her own hooves by ripping the corner off the meal bag, spitting it out and sticking her mouth underneath the flow of food. I got the message and fed them there and then, before she went pop with overeating.

Nowadays, she positively struts around the fields. I'd stop short of calling her *diva*, but she's full of confidence and knows her own mind. She currently lives with the younger lambs who are the toddlers of the group, and they definitely look up to her and follow her lead.

'Has she had any lambs yet?'

'Oh, lots,' Paul says.

'And did they each only have one ear too?' The question is out of my mouth before I can stop it and I cringe, but Paul doesn't judge.

'No, it's not genetic. They all had two ears.'

How cute.

One day, we wanted to move One Ear's gang from their field to the holding pen down the lane, so we could tend to their feet. Unusually, One Ear remained at the back of the group as we walked them down the hill, as if she were making sure nobody got left behind. As she trotted along, she swung her head from left to right, as if scanning the group and making sure they were all accounted for.

The young sheep filed out of the gate and turned right (we'd blocked the left-hand side of the lane with gates) and made their way up the lane, which is just wide enough for two sheep to trot happily side-by-side.

No sooner was the last youngster out the gate than One Ear was off, weaving her way through the group as easily as a bike through stationary traffic, and was at the front in no time. She clearly didn't want to miss out on anything and was keen to reassert herself as the leader. She strutted with such confidence that she looked for all the world, as if she'd been up at the front the entire time. As I said, she's calm, collected, sure of herself and very cheeky! Our gorgeous One Ear, who makes our sheep collection complete.

125. One Ear disappears

Paul had to go out tonight to pick up a dead sheep from one of our rented fields. It's always sad when we lose one of our little woolly friends, but she was an old girl, and it looks like she died in her sleep while surrounded by her companions, so in the circumstances I suppose it's the best we could have hoped for.

With Paul out, I was in charge of giving the twin lambs their bottle (although we just say, 'we're going to feed the baby,' seeing as they're practically the same lamb, just in two bodies). Afterwards, I take a walk to check on the hill sheep.

It's been a scorcher of a day. In fact, it was so hot I wore my gym kit to go milking as it was the lightest thing I could find, and I was still melting. My legs felt like lead throughout, and I was sweating buckets. Goodness only knows how the sheep felt, what with being outside. That said, they do have lots of trees and bushes to shelter under, as well as access to plenty of water. Thank goodness we sheared them when we did.

Most of the girls are tucked up under their favourite tree, which is nice, but they always emerge looking like they've been Tangoed (younger readers look it up) as the orange dust around the base of the trunk temporarily dyes their wool. Some are standing in the middle of the field, happily munching grass and the rest are under hedges, chilling out.

After one lap of the field, I still haven't seen One Ear, which is a worry. Knowing she's alright is like knowing the captain of the ship is on the bridge. She's a good girl, our One Ear, and she looks after the youngsters.

'Where is she?' I ask the other sheep. 'Have you seen her?' They don't reply. I walk around again and check under every bush and tree. I even go into the other field to make sure she hasn't wandered in there and the gate has closed behind her. With every step, my heart rate quickens and panic rises into my throat. I peer at every ewe, hoping that when they turn their heads, I'll see one of them only has one ear, but they're all intact.

By the time I do my third lap, my mind's racing. What if she's fallen in a ditch? Or is in the long grass, feeling unwell and I can't see her? By now the other sheep are getting twitchy, and some are staring at me, no doubt wondering what I'm up to.

From up on the hill, I can see Paul making his way back in the car. I slope back down the field, clamber over the fence and walk to greet him and to admit I can't find One Ear. It's not the news I want to give him when he's just returned from dealing with the sad case of the dead sheep, but I'm going to have to.

I give him a hug and then just say it really quickly, 'I can't find One Ear please help me look for her sorry please.'

There's a pause as Paul deciphers what I've said. Then he states, 'She's not there.'

'I know. I just told you that.'

'No, I mean, she's not there. We took her to one of the other fields yesterday to put her to the ram, don't you remember? I saw her today, she's fine.'

I almost cry with relief. Thank goodness for that. As we walk back, I tell him how I've just spent the best part of half an hour looking for a sheep that wasn't there, which was why I couldn't find her.

The ewes who were looking at me oddly were probably saying, 'Er, hooman, One Ear isn't here! You moved her yesterday, remember?' And as I continued frantically searching, they perhaps looked at each other, shook their heads in disbelief and added, 'Hoomans, they don't listen to a word we say!'

And the less said about my failing short-term memory, the better.

126. Squeakums

O h dear. Now I've told you One Ear's story, Squeak has come over and wants me to tell hers too. OK, here we go...

Well, first things first; Squeak is as wide as she is long and not very tall, but she walks confidently (she's a bit like One Ear in that respect). She has the most beautiful mottled grey and white face and lovely white coat. As such, I'd assumed her body would be white, too. But when she was shorn, I realised that the mottle grey and white pattern covered her entire body and went right down to her tail. The result being that she looks as if someone has seasoned her with salt and pepper. So gorgeous!

Squeak was an orphan and would shout for milk so often and so loudly, despite being bottle fed regularly, that she went hoarse. So instead of being able to make traditional bleating sounds, she could only emit a high-pitched squeaking noise, hence her name.

By the time I met her, she was an adult, and I longed for her to have a lamb so we could call it Bubble (geddit?) I was delighted when we discovered she was in lamb, and she soon ballooned. In fact, she was huge, bless her! She'd wobble around the field with her belly protruding from both sides and her heavy udder swinging. She looked very hot and uncomfortable and I hoped the lamb would arrive soon, for everyone's health and happiness.

I got my wish one morning when I was doing my rounds and noticed, to my horror and delight, that her waters had broken! Not that she was phased by it. She just looked at me as if nothing was out of the ordinary and carried on eating.

My first reaction, of course, was to panic. I felt like a servant whose queen had gone into labour. Well, Squeak is certainly the queen of her flock! I took to my heels and ran to the house, shouting, 'Quick, call the vet.' Then I stopped as I remembered we didn't need to call a vet, because I was married to one, which was double handy – and a very handsome vet he is too!

Paul was calm as a cucumber, as usual, and we were soon by Squeak's side. She'd laid down by this point and I was sat by her head, chatting away, ready to offer soothing words or ear rubs when she began to bleat in pain, but she didn't. Just like her favourite hooman, she was calm. In fact, you would've hardly known she was lambing.

'And the good thing about the name Bubble,' I rambled, as much to keep me calm as anything else, 'is it can be applied to boys or girls.'

Then I saw something out of the corner of my eye. It was Paul, leaning over and placing a gorgeous, soggy but as far as I could tell, healthy, long-limbed lamb next to Squeak. 'Bubble!' I whispered. 'Hello, gorgeous. Welcome to the world.'

I was instantly in love, as was Squeak. The lamb had her mum's white and grey markings around her nose, and a few splodges about her eyes and cheeks.

I was so busy admiring the new arrival, that it took me a minute to notice that Paul was in the process of placing another lamb next to Squeak. Then I was the one doing all the squeaking. 'Twins. You've got twins, you clever girl!'

The second little bundle was just as gorgeous. She had a few specks of grey on her face, but nowhere near as many as her mum or sister, which, on reflection, was a good thing because it meant I had more chance of telling them apart!

'Well done, Squeakums,' I whispered. Twins. No wonder she was so huge!

I looked at Paul. 'Now what are we going to call them? I'd only had one name picked out and now there are two.'

As it turned out, the twins' cheeky characteristics meant that naming them was no problem at all. Ladies and gentlemen, meet 'Bubble and Trubble!'

As you can imagine, having twins is physically and mentally draining for the poor ewe, who must keep an eye on two youngers who are frequently demanding milk. To help out, we supplement the milk the lambs get from mum with powdered milk, which we give to them in bottles. (We use old glass juice bottles which have been sterilised, and replace the traditional screw lid with a teat. It looks like a human baby bottle but twice the size!)

At first, the lambs are dubious and don't want anything that hasn't come from Mum, but they soon learn that the bottle means extra portions, and so come running over at feeding time!

Feeding lambs is an honour and a delight, and I can see why volunteering on farms can help people with depression and other mental health issues, because it is such an uplifting activity. As soon as the lambs see you, they bleat and come running over as fast as their four little legs will carry them. They then come to a grinding halt and look up with big, pleading, beautiful eyes.

They suck on the teat so enthusiastically, that their heads bob up and down with the effort and their little bodies ripple. They also wag their tails, just like dogs do when they're happy.

One day, I was tasked with feeding the twins on my own, a challenge I accepted, despite being nervous.

Bubble was the first to notice me. She dashed across the field, sniffed the bottle and started sucking enthusiastically. But of course, Trubble was hot on her heels and soon appeared by her sister's side. Clearly afraid she was missing out on something, Trubble reared up, as if she were a horse in a western film, and used her front hooves to boof her sister out of the way so she could get to the bottle!

Bubble, momentarily stunned at having been displaced, shook her head, looked at her sibling and mirrored her action, boofing her out of the way so she could carry on drinking. This pantomime went on for some time, until I decided the only way to deal with the problem was to hold one of them between my legs while they had their half of the bottle, and then swap over. This worked quite well, although I was continually swatting the non-drinker away, as they would sneak around the back and try to butt their sibling from behind!

As they got bigger, they moved onto solids and didn't need, or indeed want, much milk from their mum or the bottle. Despite this, they continue to make a fuss and compete for the bottle, even though they don't want it.

Trubble, for example, would sprint over, take a few half-hearted sips and then wander off. But on seeing Bubble going for the teat, she'd return with gusto, boof her out the way and clamp her mouth around the teat again. The funny thing was, she wasn't even sucking, she just didn't want her sibling to have something she didn't! Just like human children with their toys, I suppose.

And just like children, they're prone to the odd strop now and again. Take this morning, for example. There was Trubble, happily enjoying her breakfast bottle, when the lid came off – I subsequently discovered it was cracked and had to be replaced. Thus, the poor little lamb got covered in a shower of warm milk, as did Bubble, who was standing close by. Somehow, I managed to right the bottle quickly and save most of the contents.

The duo momentarily froze in shock and then shook themselves vigorously, which made their ears flap. I wiped their faces with a tissue and apologised. 'But there's still plenty left,' I said, offering them the teat. But they were having none of it. They just looked at me in disgust, as if I'd done it on purpose, turned around, flicked their tails in my face and walked off. Well, that's gratitude for you.

127. Happiness is... (part two)

A cow coming over to say 'hello,' which she does by putting her head so close to yours that all you can see is her pink nose. The feel of her warm breath on your face is comforting, like a hairdryer thawing you out on a cold day. Bliss.

128. What's in a name?

We call our sheep and lambs various names, ranging from munchkins, Wombles and flumps when they're being good, to weasels, giant balls of wool, over-sized cotton buds or occasionally wee ****** when they're being sneaky, trying to dodge us, refusing to get into the trailer or generally misbehaving.

I was tidying the kitchen after lunch when Paul called up the stairs. I thought I heard him say, 'The sheep have escaped and are down the road trespassing in the gardens of the big houses.' But surely not.

'What was that you said?' I asked, tea towel in hand.

'The sheep have escaped and are down the road trespassing in the gardens of the big houses.'

'Ah.' Nothing wrong with my hearing, then.

'Well, thanks for letting me know,' I said, quickly retreating.

'Could you give me a hand please?'

I winced. 'They haven't eaten anything they shouldn't have, have they?' I asked with trepidation. 'Or damaged anything?' I could just imagine a line of petite little hoof marks going diagonally across a neat lawn. Or a heap of sheep happily munching on some poor sod's prize-winning petunias, as if they'd been planted solely for their culinary delight.

'I don't know, but we can find out together.'

'But they're your sheep.'

'Oh, so they're *my* sheep when they're being naughty, but *our* sheep when they're being good?'

'That's right,' I said, glad to see he had a good understanding of the situation. He looked at me over the top of his glasses. 'I'll get my coat,' I sighed.

So here we are, traipsing up the road towards the big houses which are down a long, narrow lane overlooking the sea. As you can imagine, I've already used some of the alternative words to describe them. Safe to say, I wasn't referring to them as flumps or Wombles.

The field from which they've escaped is one of the rented plots and, despite having acres of grass on which to feast upon, they've obviously decided that the grass is greener elsewhere and scarpered. Thus, as we speak, they're probably busy ruining some poor person's garden. Or perhaps several gardens.

I hear them before I see them, as contented bleats emanate from various bushes. I pop my head over a hedge and spot them. One of the escapees stops munching and looks up at me with big eyes, as if butter wouldn't melt.

'Number Six,' I growl, 'I might've known you were leading the charge.' He eyeballed me and then continued eating.

Paul has been getting the lowdown from the people who own the houses. Thankfully, they're very good natured and aren't the least bit cross.

The sheep haven't caused any damage, and no harm's been done, well apart from giving one of the residents a start when they opened their front door to discover their front garden covered in huge cotton buds. Oh, and they've had a few mouthfuls of stolen grass, but the humans have forgiven them, which is nice.

We ascertain that Number Six has been flirting with the ewes non-stop. He has also been leading them astray, literally, by finding a gap in the hedge and taking them on a merry dance down the road.

'Get away with you,' I say, waving my arms in circles in a bid to move them on, but they dig their hooves in. Thankfully, Paul, who knows his sheep of old, is on the case, and has bought a bucket of food to tempt them back to the field. 'You go on ahead,' he says, handing me the bucket, 'and I'll make sure there aren't any stragglers.'

Number Six, fickle beast that he is, then decides that he *will* follow me after all, because the food in my bucket is much better than the front garden buffet.

He's in big trouble. We've just found out that he's been picking fights with the other rams in his field, in a bid to be the new leader, even though he shouldn't be having such notions at his age, which means we're going to have to separate them.

'What goes on in that head of yours, Number Six?' I ask, picking up the pace in a bid to make it up the hill. 'Did you think, "I know, Mummy hasn't had enough exercise today, despite being up at 5.30am to milk cows. Nor is she tired enough, so what I think I'll do, is pick a fight with a ram twice my size, almost kill myself in the process, then hightail it down the road, pee in someone's prize flower bed and make her tramp through three fields and back again to get me home."' I turn to look at him. 'Am I along the right lines?'

He stops and looks up at me with his big, sad eyes until I feel my heart melt. I can't stay angry at him for long. I crouch down to pat him and as soon as I do, his head is straight in the bucket.

'Children,' I utter. 'Who'd have 'em?'

129. What a team

p aul has potentially found a new field for the ewes. The possibility of renting a new piece of land is very exciting, because the more land we can rent, the more sheep we can keep for breeding.

As amazing as the whole sheep-breeding process is (cute and cuddly lambs etc.) you just can't keep them all. Not unless you're a millionaire with acres of land. So, until I win the lottery, some of them have to be sold for breeding or as pets.

Being a farmer, or even owning a few sheep, is a complex business which requires military-style organisational skills and a sharp brain. All fields are monitored for their sheep friendliness and sustainability long before any hoofs get anywhere near them.

Indeed, ensuring sheep have enough grass to keep them nourished and happy throughout the year, is an eye-wateringly big responsibility and thus, I avoid it.

Thankfully, Paul is made of sterner stuff and always has a plan. Hence, why we're surveying a new piece of land long before we need it. I think Paul should take up chess, as he's great at forward thinking and planning.

Farmers can share fields for the purposes of keeping animals at different times of year, but there should always be a window between one group leaving and another arriving, so that the risk of passing on any nasties, such as scab, is minimised.

It's a bit like a holiday let. I mean, you wouldn't rock up at the accommodation at the exact moment the other group was leaving the property, would you? There needs to be at least a few hours or, even better, a few days break in between, so the cleaner can go in, put the bins out and make it feel fresh and welcoming. Otherwise, you may enter and discover dust, dirt and some questionable cereal choices.

Let me tell you that sheep have equally high standards and expectations when it comes to where they stay. Well, why wouldn't they? If, for example, you put them in a field which they consider to be below par, they'll soon be back at the gate making it clear in no uncertain terms, that they want the problem addressed *pronto*. As in, they want to be moved to a better class of hotel, thank you very much. Thus, I feel the weight of responsibility when we go to view the potential new field.

As we arrive, the kindly farmer, who looks as old as the hills, comes to chat.

He has sky blue eyes that seem faded with age, a craggy face and a wonky smile. A woolly hat is rammed on his head and he wears a threadbare jumper over a crisp white shirt, while waterproof trousers and boots complete the countryside look.

'Windy day, so it is,' he says, by way of greeting.

'Aye,' Paul responds.

'Rattling the windows down here, it was. Did you hear it?'

'Not so much where we are, no.'

The old man whistles through his teeth and shakes his head. 'Wild here, it is. Sure, look at the way it's rattling those gates.'

We turn as one. Indeed. I shrink into my bodywarmer at the mere sight of the shivering gates, pleased to be wearing a thermal vest and several jumpers.

'I like eels,' the man says, *apropos* to nothing. 'Rivers full of 'em.'

I'm briefly knocked off balance by this sudden swerve in conversation and change in topic. But a quick scan reveals that the two fields are divided by a little stretch of water. I wouldn't say it was a river, more a tributary, but it's his land, and if he wants to call it a river, then a river it is.

'Glad you're thinking of taking the field,' he smiles. 'Be good to get it into shape again. Always things to do. So many things to do... and everything is harder nowadays. Dodgy knees,' he says, sadly.

He looks across the yard to his farmhouse with haunted eyes, watching ghosts only he can see, performing scenes from long ago which are painted bright by the technicolour of nostalgia.

Sensing we should leave him with his memories, Paul and I go to look for a walk.

When I found out that Paul was going for a preliminary visit, I jumped at the chance to attend. I feel like that parent who visits a potential senior school on behalf of their child, with a list of questions with which to bombard the teacher: 'Will they have enough grass? Access to shelter? Do you provide fresh water? Can we access the field easily and around the clock? What extracurricular activities do you offer? How many of your students go on to university?' (OK, maybe not the last two...)

The fields boast plenty of lush grass for the ewes to munch on, and there are lots of hedges for them to shelter under when the rain comes. The little tributary also means they can go down for a drink whenever they want. The sheep are going to love it, and I can't wait for them to see it.

The current sheepy residents are off yonder, as people say around here. They aren't Dorsets, like ours, but crossbreeds. Mules mixed with something else, I think, and the effect is stunning. They have beautiful black deer-like faces, mottled with specks of white, which has a marbling effect. They're well fed and fluffy, making them look like big marshmallows and their long black ears flap as they run, which affords them the maximum one million cuteness points.

As we approach, they form a circle with their heads pointing inwards, as if they're having a conflab.

Then, from the middle of the huddle, a sheep springs up, shoots us a look and disappears. A second later, another sheep appears in the air, flips her ears and vanishes. The girls continue this caper for a few minutes, all the while swapping places with ease, as if they're on a trampoline.

Then, the circle breaks and the sheep form a line, trotting towards us as if they're in the army.

It's so beautifully choreographed that I'd swear they've been rehearsing. They look like a rhythm gymnastics team, and it wouldn't have surprised me in the least if they had 'rounded off' the routine by standing on their back legs and extending their hooves in the air.

'I booked the entertainment,' Paul says, proudly.

That is a fib. But I almost believe him.

When we return to the farmer, he's feeding his chickens.

'We'll take it,' Paul beams.

The man's face breaks into a smile.

'Cracking news,' he says. 'I'll get you the key.'

I smile. Everyone is happy. A good day all round.

Subsequent investigations reveal that his name is Morris. We can't wait to work with him.

130. Lamb tails

I wasn't sure what it was at first. A piece of rope, maybe, or a ribbon? But why would a ribbon be in the sheep shed and how did it get there? I went over to inspect, gingerly picked it up between finger and thumb, and then felt a bit sick as it dawned on me what it was.

'A lamb's tail!' Paul beamed when I showed him, as if I'd just presented him with a prize bunch of flowers.

'What?' I said, panic rising in my throat, as I madly looked around for a lamb missing her tail. 'That's not good, it is?'

'Well, it wouldn't be good if the lamb lost its entire tail, no, he chuckled, 'but the end is meant to fall off. We put elastic bands around them for that very reason when the lambs were young, remember? It keeps their tails short but leaves just enough to cover their bottom, which protects them from flies and prevents flystrike.'

Ah yes, flystrike. I'm on firmer ground, here. A horrible condition where flies lay their eggs on the sheep, meaning the poor creatures are eventually crawling with maggots. Keeping tails short and dosing helps prevent this terrible thing from happening, but if the flies do get hold, and if intervention treatment isn't given quickly (i.e., clipping around the infested area to get rid of the maggots), it can often prove fatal.

I remember seeing Paul treating a poor sheep who had flystrike once. It gave me the creeps and I'm not afraid to say it. Her lovely wool was full of maggots, which you were hard-pressed to see at first, but on closer inspection, it was clear she was crawling with them. I shuddered and began to itch as Paul shaved around the infected area. (This is usually around their bottoms, as the flies are attracted to the faeces. Once the infested section of fleece is off, and the maggots are away from the sheep's body, they die quickly.)

The poorly sheep was treated with cream and medicine and thankfully, made a full recovery. But I've since developed an aversion to flies and am forever swatting them, knowing what pain and suffering they can cause our poor sheep and other animals.

Anyway, once I get over the initial shock of holding a tail in my hand, I can see that the remains are actually quite pretty; all white and fluffy, like a duster. I decide to do a 'show and tell' with Liz.

'Look,' I say, holding the tail to the camera phone, so Liz can see.

'What the actual fuck is that?'

'A lamb tail,' I say proudly, as if I've just discovered a treasure trove.

'It fell off?' she squeaked. 'Can you sew it back on or something?'

I told her what Paul told me, about shorter tails being better for the sheep etc. which seems to placate her.

'It looks like a piece of rope, doesn't it?' I observe.

'Or a tampon.'

I tilt my head. 'Or that.'

131. New balls, please

Today, I learned how tennis players must feel when participating in a big match.

It also became painfully obvious why I never took up the sport and sadly, why I'll never be a Wimbledon champion.

Ok, for this section I need you to imagine the sound that tennis players make when playing at Wimbledon or similar. You know, when they hit the ball with all their might and make a 'meheaaaaah' sound? Got it? Good.

Next, imagine how they look when they're waiting for their opponent to serve: feet planted squarely on the floor, forearms resting on bent legs as they rock from side to side, trying to anticipate which way to run. Then they're off, sprinting to the ball, smashing it across the net and running off again. Imagine also, how they stop abruptly when the opponent hits the ball into their own side of the net.

If you have all of these images in your head, you will have some idea of what Paul and I looked like in the field today. It felt like we were having a game of tennis, but we were trying to return thirty fluffy balls, which were very much alive, hot, bothered and in no mood to play.

All we wanted to do was get them into a pen. We'd done well to get them to the edge of the field and to the gate, but they just wouldn't cross the threshold. It was like there was an invisible barrier stopping them. One line of sheep blocked the entrance while the others piled up behind them like dominos. Meanwhile, the ones at the back kept trying to break away from the group and scarper across the field.

Hence, why Paul and I were adopting the tennis stance; knees bent, forearms on legs as we tried to anticipate their next move. I was eyeballing them. The sheep were eyeballing me. Every so often, one would make a run for it, and Paul and I would sprint after them, head them off at the pass and return them to the group. The first time it happened, it was fun, and I felt a sense of achievement. After the twentieth time, I was beginning to lose enthusiasm and patience.

Whenever one of the sheep started eying up a gap in the group and jolted forward, I ran towards them, which stopped them in their tracks, and also made it look as if we were playing a complicated game of musical statues.

Finally, one of the sheep decided to explore inside the pen and the rest followed, well, they are sheep. By this point, I was dripping in sweat and out of breath, but happy, because it meant we could start vaccinating them.

But boy, did I ache the next day! Alas, I think I'll put my dream of winning Wimbledon on hold. I might get some tennis whites though; I've always fancied a set of those.

132. Colourful creations

On another note, and just for your information, when the ewe is 'put to the ram,' as they say in agricultural fields, the ram has a harness placed over his shoulders which wraps around his tummy. The harness holds a crayon (colours vary, but are often yellow, red or green), which sits at chest height. The idea being that when the ram serves the ewe, the crayon leaves a mark on her fleece so we know which ones could be pregnant. Each ram has a different colour crayon so we can tell who has mated with who.

The first time I was sent to buy a crayon for the ram, I asked if he got a colouring book to go with it. I was disappointed to discover it wasn't that sort of crayon. Very disappointed.

133. It's a small world after all

It's not the first time this has happened and I'm sure it won't be the last.

Today, a local tradesman came to measure up for a job. We want to have cameras installed in the sheep shed so that we can keep an eye on the expectant ewes from the comfort of our living room. Apparently, we'll be able to turn our television to a preselected channel and see them on screen. I can't wait to get SheepCam up and running!

Anyway, this tradesman started chatting away, but I interrupted because I was so excited. 'You're English,' I said, clapping my hands.

'Yes,' he said slowly, obviously worried I was about to make some accusation.

'Me too!'

He gave an unsure smile.

'I mean, it's not as if I actually needed to clarify that,' I rattled on, 'I should think it's quite obvious that I'm not local. It's just nice to hear someone speak like me. A voice from my homeland,' and with that, I got all misty-eyed.

I know some people will say, 'Well if you don't like the Northern Irish accent, go home then.' But I do like it. In fact, I love it. I adore the Northern Irish accent and Northern Ireland itself. But I also love my homeland and get homesick sometimes. But for all that, I'm pleased to have been accepted here.

'Ah yes,' he said, visibly relaxing. 'I see what you mean. Whereabouts you from?'

'Hertfordshire.'

'Me too.'

Unbelievable. I move five hundred miles from home and end up chatting to a man who used to live less than thirty miles from my parents.

'What brought you here?' I asked, clearly unable to stop being a journalist.

'I used to love holidaying here with my family when I

was little,' he explained. 'We had family out this way, you see and I always thought of Northern Ireland with fondness. When I got married, my wife and I came out here on holiday and she fell in love with it too.'

In fact, they loved it so much that they relocated, and haven't looked back since.

'It's a better pace of life here,' he continued. 'We could afford a house by the sea and our son is in a great school with small classes, so he'll get a better education. On the way home, he looks out of the car window and sees the tractors in the fields and the boats on the sea. We go for walks by the seaside on weekends and our neighbours have sheep and cows. It's idyllic.'

And he's not the only one. There are lots of Northern Irish-English pairings in these parts.

Indeed, it's not hard to see why someone, having already fallen in love with a Northern Irish native, would pack up and relocate so that they could be with them in their homeland. Clearly, the Northern Irish charm is still very much alive and well.

Of course, that goes the other way, too. I know of many Northern Irish people who've left their homeland to start a new life in England or even further afield. Whatever makes you happy, that's what I say.

134. Box babies

Looking at the four ewe lambs happily munching away in their field, it's hard to believe that just a few months ago they could all fit inside one cardboard box — at the same time.

Now, before anyone sends us strongly worded letters and accuses us of being cruel, please let me clarify: We don't pack our lambs into boxes for ease of storage. No, no. Rest assured that they have plenty of room inside the spacious sheep shed to run around and do lamb things, such as skipping, jumping, clambering over each other, eating, drinking, nibbling hay, jumping in piles of straw and snoozing in sunny spots etc.

I previously thought that farmers would have been pleased whenever ewes gave birth to triplets. More lamb from your ram! More bang for your buck! (If you'll excuse the mixed metaphors.) I mean, who wouldn't want three identical bubbas running about the place? Well, lots of farmers, apparently. Not because they're mean or don't like lambs, but because it's often extremely problematic for humans and animals alike.

Sheep are better suited to caring for single or twin lambs because they only have two teats.

Now, you don't need to be a veterinarian, farmer or mathematician to work out that the equilibrium would be quickly knocked out with the addition of a third hungry mouth to feed.

In the case of twins, there's always one smaller than the other. And triplets are even smaller again. The first lamb's often a good enough size, the middle acceptable, but the third is often the smallest and weakest. And of course, if you have to compete with your siblings every time you want a nutritious drink from your mum, the odds of survival are stacked against you.

For this reason, farmers will often remove the biggest lamb in order to give the other two a fighting chance. But just because one of the lambs is bigger, doesn't make removing them from their mother any less upsetting.

The first time I gently removed the biggest of a set of triplets from the sheep shed, the ewe was shrieking her head off and the lamb was bleating like his heart was breaking. Meanwhile, the only thought going around in my head was, 'I'm definitely going directly to hell for this. Do not pass go, do not collect two hundred pounds.'

I tried my best to calm and comfort him: I patted his little head, fluffed his ears, rubbed his back, kissed his little nose, whispered softly, but it did no good whatsoever. He cried until he was hoarse (not *a* horse, it didn't transform into a different animal, although I would've liked to have seen that).

I carried him into the calf shed where we'd created a lamb playpen. Moving the lamb to a different building is an important part of the process, as it means they can't see or hear their families, which helps a little.

Slowly, I lowered the little mite into the pen which had been freshly fluffed with straw and contained a big box which was also filled with straw. No sooner had his little hooves touched the floor than he was straight inside. He was still shouting, but at least he was comfy. And he wasn't on his own for long, a few minutes tops, because Paul was directly behind me with Box Baby Number Two.

'You have a step-sister,' he said as he gently lowered the bawling lamb into the pen, where she stood for a minute or so, shouting for all she was worth. Not to be outdone, Box Baby Number One cranked up the volume until I couldn't hear myself think.

Box Baby Number Two stopped and looked around, as if she'd only just noticed she'd been relocated. Then she spotted Box Baby Number One, who was still bawling. She skipped over, put her little nose against his and immediately, he stopped shouting. Then she clambered into the box and they snuggled up together.

'What just happened?' I said, eyes as wide as saucers as the silence settled like dust.

'They're a comfort to each other,' Paul said. 'Sure, it doesn't matter that they're not blood relations. They don't know that, anyway, they just thrive on each other's company.'

'Instant siblings?'

'Something like that.'

I smiled. 'That's beautiful.'

135. The drinks are on me

The first time I was given the task of feeding the Box Babies, I was a nervous wreck. The weight of responsibility was heavy on my shoulders. These little babies were effectively motherless, confused and hungry. I could give hugs (I wore my fluffiest jumper to emulate a sheep) and I could provide milk to alleviate the hunger, but I have a knack of causing chaos and confusion in any given situation, so I knew I probably couldn't help on that score.

I entered the pen nervously, clutching my bottle as I made my way to the pen. On seeing me, the lambs shot into their box, turned and poked their little noses out as if to say, 'Go away!'

'I've got a bottle,' I said, shaking it to show them. Then I scooped one of the smaller lambs up and tucked her between my legs. Initially, she wriggled furiously, but I managed to steady her head long enough to tilt the bottle and get the teat into her mouth. She resisted for a while and glared at me as best she could, but then I squeezed the teat to show her what to do and her eyes light up as the milk hit her tongue.

I squeezed the teat a few more times until she worked out how to suck, and then there was no stopping her! I smiled as she drank enthusiastically, her little head bobbing with every pull. Occasionally, she'd stop to get her breath and I'd wipe the milk from her mouth, but then she was straight back on it again.

Meanwhile, the other box babies, who had been watching all this from the safety of their house, had crept out and were forming an orderly queue to get their drink. But such politeness didn't last long once they worked out that human visits meant food and from then on, it was pandemonium!

I only had to open the door a slither and the lambs were up on their feet, bleating and running in circles. They gathered at my feet as I clambered into the pen and climbed all over me as I sat down. I felt very popular, but of course, with all the jostling, it was almost impossible to feed them, so I employed the tried and tested method of scooping one up at a time, forming a human barrier to keep them in my arms and the others out!

The other problem was that I struggled to remember who I'd fed. Some of them had milky mouths, which was a giveaway, but the neat and tidy ones weren't so easy to tell apart. And this was before they had ear tags, so I couldn't even clock their numbers.

'Well, that's charming, that is,' Paul said when I told him my plight. 'You can't tell your own children apart!'

We got around it in the end by spraying them with different coloured dots using temporary spray, which meant the little munchkins' days of running around the back and re-joining the queue for a second drink were well and truly over!

The lambs would always be known collectively as the box babies, but it wasn't long before they couldn't fit into their box at all. But we let them keep it, as they enjoyed using it as a climbing frame. So cute.

136. What's that you say (part two)

Another spectacular misunderstanding occurred at milking today.

But before I divulge, let me give you some context. Once the cows have been milked, they walk through a footbath which leads to their living area, where they chill out for the rest of the day until milking time comes around again.

Milking was over and I was busy cleaning the living area, when a cow shot out of the footbath, closely followed by one of the other milking assistants.

'Don't let her bite you,' he squealed.

My first thought was, 'What one earth have you done to make her want to bite me?' But I wasn't scared, as I'd never seen a cow bite anyone before and anyway, she'd calmed down by that point and was just mooching about. However, I stepped out of her way and let her amble past me, just in case.

It was as I was stepping back that my brain caught up, and it dawned on me that the assistant hadn't said, 'don't let her bite you,' but 'don't let her *by* you.' Which I had.

He shot off around the other side of the living area and managed to walk her back to where she was meant to be, which was in the queue with some of the other girls who were waiting to have their hooves treated.

On reflection, perhaps I'm not getting used to the lingo after all.

137. It's very different in the countryside

Today, Paul and I drove past a field, and the conversation went something like this:

Paul: 'Look, a scarecrow.'

Me, craning my neck to see, 'Oh good, I like scarecrows.'

But despite turning my head this way and that, I couldn't see anything which resembled Worzel Gummidge or Dorothy's companion in Oz. Or, come to think of it, anything that looked remotely like a traditional scarecrow.

I was looking for a stick standing proudly in a cornfield which had been lovingly dressed in big, old, floppy hat, a shabby workman's coat and raggedy trousers. But try as I might, I couldn't see anything of the sort.

'Where?' I said, getting increasingly frustrated because patience isn't my strong suit.

'There.'

'Ah.'

The reason I didn't see it, children, is because it wasn't a nice old-fashioned type of scarecrow at all. It was, in fact, an *actual* crow nailed to a wall. (Dead, I hasten to add. Long dead.) But, just to clarify and in case you missed it, it was *literally* a crow, put there, I assume, to scare other crows away. A stark warning which said, 'Don't come here and eat our crops or this could be you.'

Its jet-black wings were splayed out on either side of its body, making it look like some sort of ornamental fan. Its head flopped to the side and its beak pointed to the floor. The pale brickwork behind made the scene even more stark and depressing, and I felt a bit sick and very sad.

In short, it was the most horrific thing I had ever seen. But, as I am always being told, it's different in the countryside. You're telling me.

Yet, I suppose, as a farmer, your options are limited.

It must feel as if they're constantly taking part in some sort of never-ending and very bizarre game show, where a cheesy and irritating 1980s-style quizmaster bombards them with surreal questions every five minutes.

'So, Farming Contestant Number One...' the quiz master hollers in the depths of my imagination, kitted out in a snazzy, sequined jacket while brandishing brightly coloured, oversized cards and grinning at the camera – 'here are your options:

1. Keep the birds off your crops so you actually have something to sell, which means scaring off or having to kill said birds, or,
2. *Don't* keep the birds off your crops, which means you and your family will slowly die of starvation but at least the birds will be happy.

'So, what's it going to be? And either way, you don't win the speedboat.'

138. And that's the end of that

Another day, another lambing, and I am delighted to report that mother and lamb are doing well. It also gives me great pleasure to announce that that is the end of lambing. Thank goodness!

I collapse onto the sofa, put my feet up and close my eyes, but all I can see emblazoned on my eyelids, are sheep. Lots of them. I open my eyes and check under the sofa to make sure one hasn't snuck in. Just in case.

'Well done on all your hard work, Paul,' I say as he joins me. 'I really enjoyed lambing. Another new but exciting experience.'

'I know it can be a bit of an anti-climax when the last lamb arrives.'

'Well, I wouldn't say that,' I counter, 'more of a relief, really.'

'But don't worry,' he continues, 'not long to go.'

'Not long to go until what?' I ask, with a sense of mounting dread.

'Until winter lambing.'

'What?'

'Winter lambing. Well, the ewes who got pregnant in July have to have their babies some time. In fact, they should arrive right in time for Christmas.' He smiles and I try to smile back, because he seems so excited.

'Yay,' I beam, while crying inside.

139. It's the way you tell 'em

'**I** love my chickens.'

Morris leans on the gate and looks out across the field to where his little brood are pecking the ground and strutting, clearly enjoying the early morning sun on their feathers.

'That's nice,' I smile, taking in the beauty of the countryside and the serene scene.

'Except that cockerel, he's a little bastard,' Morris adds. 'Attacked me the other day. Mad he is, I tell ye. Pecked right up the back of me legs.' He paused while he took a sip of tea. 'So, I chased him over the field and kicked him right up the arse.'

I know, it's like listening to *Jackanory*, isn't it?

140. Spiders

Today I walked past a spider which was bigger than my head (who says I exaggerate?!) It was just hanging out on the wall in the entrance hall, chilling.

On seeing it, I backed up the stairs and refused to move until Paul came to get rid of it. After all, he is a vet and I'm pretty sure 'spider removal' is in the job description.

'The spiders over here are huge,' I gasp as he confidently scoops it up and puts it back on the floor.

'What are you doing?'

'You don't want me to put it outside, do you? It's freezing.'

'What?'

'Well, it's used to being in here.'

'Well, it can just get used to *not* being in here,' I retort. Then I look at the spider, who has stopped stock-still in the middle of the floor, as if waiting for permission to stay. I can feel all eight of its eyes looking up at me, which are possibly brimming with tears.

If it has been in here for a while, it might have a family, and who am I to cause all sorts of arachnoid anguish? If it goes outside, it will spend the rest of its life searching for its family in a state of eight-legged peril.

'Fine,' I say, 'but if I wake up and it's in bed with us, you're in big trouble.'

141. Freeloader

I go to the greenhouse in search of some flowerpots so we can plant vegetables for later in the year. I don't know this person who, all of a sudden, or at least, since moving to Northern Ireland, has started to enjoy cooking and housework, baking, gardening and vegetable growing, but I like her.

Before I return to our house, I stop off in the store to wash the pots before I add the compost.

As I run the first one under the tap, a spider approximately the size of my head, drops out and lands in the sink. I immediately turn the tap off and, instead of hitching up my (metaphorical) skirts and making a run for it, guide it back into the pot and out of harm's way. I'm just about to take it to the garden when it occurs to me that if I do that, it'll be disorientated. No, it needs to go back where it came from.

With a sigh, I take him to the greenhouse and put him back where I found him, or at least, where I found the pot, just in case he has a family nearby. I know, I'm getting soft in my old age.

142. Hamsters and spammers

I 've just discovered that the small rodents who like to whizz around in wheels and are popular companion animals, are called hamsters, as in ham and not hampsters, as in picnic. So, it's true, you *do* learn something new every day.

Incidentally, I have no idea why I thought they were called hampsters. Perhaps it's because they, like me, love food, and try to stuff as much of it into their mouths as possible. I know, it's fun inside my head.

My first encounter with a hamster was when I was about five years old, and sitting on the carpet in my cousin's front room playing a board game. Meanwhile, my cousin had put her hamster in his exercise ball for a bit of cardio. As the hamster merrily trundled by, minding its own business, I spotted it and, thinking it was an ordinary ball, picked it up and hurled it across the room to my daddy.

How I didn't kill the poor thing, I don't know. I think my dad managed to catch the ball before it smashed into the wall.

Apart from being completely disorientated and possibly having a sore head, the hamster lived to tell the tale. Unless, of course, the adults lied to me, and as soon as the pet was back inside its cage, it keeled over and died. I hope not. I'm going to have to look into that now. And, despite showing promising bowling skills, I never did make it onto the school cricket team. Shame.

143. Bankety Bank

I've just had a text from BigGlobalBanketyBank (not it's real name, but you get the idea) informing me that my account's been compromised and as such, I must email them forthwith with my existing bank details and an admin fee of three hundred pounds to rectify the situation. Which is interesting, because I'm not a member of BigGlobalBanketyBank. And I'm not a complete idiot either. There are parts missing.

144. Who's Who?

Roger Daltrey is being interviewed on the radio as we drive out to do our sheep checks.

'What's the name of the band he was in?' I ask as we stop to negotiate a junction.

'The Who,' Paul says.

'The band. The name of the band that man was in.'

'The Who.'

'The man talking on the radio, wossname, Roger Daltrey?'

'I know. I just answered you.'

'So which band was it?'

'The Who!'

I tap my hands on the wheel, 'No, I know who he *is*, I'm asking what band he was in.'

Paul doesn't know whether to laugh or cry. 'Are you serious? I'm answering your question. But let me say it again, this time very slowly: Roger Daltrey was in the band The Who.'

The penny drops. 'Oh,' I say, dissolving into giggles. 'I see!'

'I thought you were winding me up, as that's exactly the sort of wordplay joke you like.'

'I wish I was joking,' I laugh. 'But no.'

145. Winter's a wonder in this land

Winter nights are different in rural Northern Ireland. I haven't been here long enough to pin down what it is, but it's special, that's for sure.

Darkness folds slowly into the bay and even the waves grow quiet, as if exhausted by the movement of the day. We pass cosy cottages emitting rectangles of light which fight against the gloom, while the smell of woodsmoke pierces the air, tempering the frosts.

Darkness descends and settles wild animals into the safety of the shadows. Fields slip into darkness as tractors are trundled back into yards and parked up for the night. A hush descends.

A soft breeze pats down the leaves as we walk down the lane towards the house, which welcomes us with twinkling lights; decorations from Christmas which we're keeping up as a symbol, in the hope of an even brighter year ahead.

From the living-room window, we can see the outline of the hills and the jagged headland, silhouetted against the raven black sky and highlighted by a full moon that looks as if it's about to dip into the sea.

Cocoa is poured into our new, stripy blue and white mugs, themselves reminiscent of the sea. We sit on the sofa, arms around each other and doze, wrapped in the warmth of our love and happy memories of a day well spent.

146. Ramalmadingdong

'We're looking for the ram,' I tell dad over the phone, as Paul and I drive around the huge perimeter of one of the rented fields.

'Why, where's he gone or meant to be?' Dad asks.

'Well, he's been out mating with the ewes, but now he's finished and we're going to pick him up. Hopefully we'll have lots of new arrivals come lambing time.'

'And how many ewes was he in with?'

'Thirty.'

'Blimey, he's probably dead in a ditch somewhere, having conked out with exhaustion,' Dad snorts. 'Or he's had it away on his toes and is heading to the Bahamas to get away from all those women. Poor sod.'

The first time I went to a sheep sale, I was mesmerised and, like a child at a fairground, didn't know which way to run first. There were ewes, rams, ram-lambs and ewe-lambs. Of course, I wanted to take all the lambs home, but there just wasn't room in the car.

Paul was looking to buy a new ram, and I was being helpful as usual, by giving my expert opinion.

'Get that one because it's cute.'

'Catch yourself on,' he laughed, 'sure, I'm not buying something based on how cute it is.'

'How about that one, then? I feel sorry for it because no one is paying it much attention.'

'It's probably had lots of attention; we've just come at

a quiet time.'

What fascinated me most, however, was the farmers. Having read the catalogue and had a browse, they would identify the ram they were interested in buying and enter its pen to inspect it: from looking inside its mouth to check its teeth to feeling along his legs and back for muscle tone, before finally, and rather surprisingly, having a good old feel of his chutneys.

'That's charming, that is,' I observed. 'They haven't even been formally introduced. The farmer could've at least bought him a drink first. Chancer.'

My silly observations aside, buying a new ram is, of course, a big decision and a huge commitment, both financially and emotionally. Farmers must also check that whoever they buy isn't somehow related to their flock, because nobody wants incest. And, as I've said, sheep, and especially rams don't come cheap.

The latter are more expensive because one ram could serve dozens of ewes, and subsequently produce around one hundred lambs per year, which is good going!

The sale catalogue is posted to potential buyers before the event and one day, I picked up Paul's copy in the hope of seeing some nice photographs of sheep. Well, I was horrified to discover there were no photographs. Not one! And, to quote Alice before she popped down the rabbit hole to Wonderland, 'What is the use of a book without pictures?'

Instead of looking at photos, farmers merely rely on a chart which lists the ram's lineage and name. Ah, names, I'm on firmer ground here.

'This one's called Digger,' I say to Paul, 'we should get that one.'

'Why?' Paul says hesitantly, but he already knows the answer, and we say it together, 'Because it's cute.'

This year, all the names, well in the Northern Ireland Dorset Club, anyway, have to begin with the letter D. This means there are some charming entries including Deliveroo, Delboy, Dancer, Dozer and the rather scary sounding Dictator.

This meant that last year, as you've probably already worked out, all the names started with C. As such, the ram Paul purchased already had a name when he came to us, and I was delighted to discover it was Canterbury.

Frazzle was born a year later, but I'd already started calling him Fraz by the time I learned of the official naming protocol. In order to get around this, please let me introduce you to DazzleFrazzle!

Now, it might not surprise you to know that I had never been in an auction ring before, so when Paul said he was considering buying a new ram, I was raring to go and see everything for myself.

We got there early to give us time to look around the pens and see the sheep before the auction. The sound of bleating filled the air, which was already sweet with the smell of straw and hay.

Some pens contained only one sheep or ram, while others held up to six, but the pens were spacious, meaning the animals could spread out. Each pen was decorated with bunting which listed the breeder's flock name and contact details. Some were adorned with rows of colourful rosettes which the animals had been awarded earlier in the after-noon. Places ranged from first to seventh, and the person who had scooped seventh place – and received a rosette for it, had proudly, and quite rightly, put that on display too. Good on them.

'I like this one,' I said, pointing to a rather old-looking boy vigorously chewing some hay, his mouth working in circles as he chomped happily, revealing some interesting-coloured teeth. He looked over at me with big dopey eyes, nonplussed, his ears twitching.

'He's old,' Paul said, 'Too old for us, really.'

'How about that one?' I said, looking at a chilled-out ram next door. 'Another old one,' Paul said, consulting the catalogue.

'What can I say? I just like all the old, scruffy-looking ones.'

'Charming.'

'Not you, silly,' I said, 'The sheep.'

Laughing, we carried on looking around.

Now, you may know this, but I certainly didn't before I came to live here, but Polled Dorset sheep have no horns (the poll bit) whereas Horned Dorset sheep do.

'That ram is gorgeous,' I said, pointing to one with par-ticularly huge, cream-coloured horns that curled again and again into smaller loops before coming to two sharp and magnificent points. The ram was particularly handsome, with a big, smooth skull and a striking, blemish free, white face.

'Aye, he's a fine-looking beast,' Paul agreed, 'but I wouldn't want him running down a hill at me, especially when he's got those sharp bits and all I've got is a bucket of meal in my hand.'

Amen to that. I've been butted by one of the rams *without* horns and that hurt enough. It was completely my fault, of course. You're meant to carry buckets of food at arm's length when walking with rams so that they can see it, and don't try to run through you to get to the food. As I said, it was totally my fault, and I received a little butt to the backside for my troubles, which shocked and knocked me off balance, but did no more harm than that. The ram wasn't being vicious, he was just trying to get to the food, and I had confused him.

But if he'd wanted to, he could've charged properly, and trust me when I say that's the last thing you want to happen. Rams have huge, strong heads and hulking muscles and could cause some considerable damage if they hit you at speed. It makes me cringe when the rams head-butt each other when fighting, let alone anything else. In fact, such fights can be deadly, which is hardly surprising when you see how they attack one another.

After sizing each other up, the rams step backwards in order to get a good run up, rear and then charge, their hooves ripping up the grass beneath them as they run, before putting their heads down at the last minute, just as knights would have lowered their lances at the last, before smashing their heads together with an almighty crack.

Rams can reach speeds of up to fifty-miles-per-hour and the fights can last hours, so it's easy to see how the impact can often cost one, if not both rams their lives.

It's such a shame and such a waste. But wildlife is red in

tooth and claw.

Back at the showground, the auction is about to begin and I'm excited. The auction room is circular, like an amphitheatre, with bidders facing inwards and looking down onto the ring where the sheep will be shown, while the auctioneer sits above the ring and faces the bidders.

We take a seat at the end of one of the rows and watch as the first two sheep, Lots one and two, are brought in. The sheep are quite skittish and run around in circles for a while, but soon calm down enough for the bidding to start. And when it does, all I can hear is something which sounds like 'hmanana-banananaan.' I look over and realise it's the auctioneer, who is leaning into a microphone and stating bid amounts, which are increasing with frightening rapidity, and the only reason I know *that*, is because I've seen auctions on TV. But other than that, I don't have a clue, but everyone else does.

I watch, mesmerised, as people making bids by waving their hands at, or nodding to the auctioneer. I keep stock-still throughout, petrified that if I make any movement at all, even to simply push a loose strand of hair from my face, I'll inadvertently end up buying fifteen prize rams which we can't afford, which would be awkward.

Before the sale, Paul asked me to download the bidding app onto my phone, just in case we couldn't stay until the end. Having the app meant he could potentially bid remotely if he saw anything he wanted to buy. It was a request he quickly came to regret, however, when I realised that the store lamb sale (lambs being sold for fattening in readiness for the meat market) was the next day.

'I'm going to come home to two hundred store lambs sitting on our sofa, aren't I?' he said.

'Yes, you are.'

If only. I want to rehome them all, but alas, we can't. Otherwise, we'd be overrun with sheep and broke.

Back at the sale, I hold my breath as the auction continues apace. I'm proud of Paul, firstly, for being able to understand what the auctioneer is saying, secondly, for knowing what makes a good ram based on, from what I can make out, the barest of facts and thirdly, that he's saved up for one.

Lots one and two have been sold and are off to a new home and a lovely life which will consist, mainly, of eating and attempting to get many ewes pregnant. ('I'm coming back in the next life as a ram,' Dad said when I explained the role of the ram.)

Suddenly the swing-doors open and in trots the lovely ram we saw earlier. Before the auction, he was getting spruced up, so as to look his best in the ring. His owners had cleaned his nose and polished him with a big white cloth. They sprayed his back with water to ensure he glistened and brushed him all over. And I must say, he looked very dapper. He's strong and proud-looking, but with a kind and friendly face.

Picking the right ram is important. This is because we want to breed lambs with a particular look and certain characteristics, half of which will come from the ram.

Paul is currently pleased with his sheep but says they're on the verge of getting just a bit too big. Therefore, he doesn't want to buy the biggest and heaviest ram, but nor does he want to sacrifice good shape and appearance. I suppose it's a bit like Goldilocks who didn't want her porridge too hot or too cold, but just right.

Having found a ram somewhere in the middle in terms of size, but still with a very handsome face and a good body shape, Paul checked him over and felt his testicles to make sure they were nice and firm. After all, we want him to give our lovely ewes lots of beautiful lambs!

I suppose it's a bit like looking for a new car; you don't want to buy one which looks all snazzy when it's on display in the showroom, only to get it home to discover a catalogue of problems.

All of this, of course, went straight over my head. I just like looking at them.

Paul always smiles when we're at the sales, and it's a special smile. One which says he's content because he's among his animal friends who make him happy. He speaks their language and they speak his. You don't have to be rich, or a showman for animals to love you, just be kind, gentle and, if possible, have a bucket of meal with you.

It's a smile which says he's excited about the prospect of adding to our flock and this makes me happy.

Having assessed the ram, Paul says he'd like to put in a bid, but thinks he might be out of our budget, so I am not to get too attached.

Back inside the ring, Paul makes a signal which the auctioneer sees and accepts. For now.

I twitch uncomfortably and find myself getting nervous and protective, glaring at everyone in the ring in an effort to dissuade them from bidding. I want Paul to get the ram he wants. *And I* want the ram too, because we can give him a good and loving home with lots of lovely ewes.

Time seems to stand still until, suddenly, the auctioneer locks eyes with Paul and brings down his gavel. Sold! I breathe out, shaking with relief. As we get outside, I squeal with delight, clap and kiss Paul.

'Well done. You did it! We're ram parents again. I'm so proud.'

When we get our new boy home, we take photos and plaster them all over social media, in the same way as parents share photos of their newborn baby when they bring them home from hospital, or on their child's first day at school. We're proud and want everyone to know about our beautiful boy.

Paul puts a new harness, complete with orange crayon, onto the ram and releases him into the field.

In the ring, the ram looked all big and brave but now, he looks small and lost. He peers around, confused by his new surroundings and lack of companions. But then the ewes appear from behind a row of trees, whereupon he bleats happily and races after them, all worries suddenly forgotten. He's up the hill like a shot and is big and confident again, surrounded by his new girlfriends.

When we go to check on him the next day, it's not hard to see which ewe is his favourite. She looks like she's been tangoed and there's not a patch of white wool to be seen. There are crayon marks on her head, her side, her neck... the mind boggles. Best not to ask.

But what I *can* tell you, is his name. We used to have a wonderful ram called Wordsworth and we also have a lovely boy called Canterbury. As such, I wanted to keep the literary theme (as tenuous as it may be), going. And, as you know, this year the sheep have to have names beginning with D. So, let me introduce you to...Dickens!

147. We will not be moo-ved

Technology is a wonderful thing that no doubt expedites the milking process. Except when it breaks, of course, at which point it ceases to be helpful very quickly indeed, as one of our neighbouring farmers recently found out when the meal auger broke down.

Please don't ask me to describe what it is, but from what I can gather, it meant that the hoppers (or food chutes as I call them) had stopped dropping meal for the cows to eat during milking time.

Of course, the first time this happened, the cows were already inside the parlour and couldn't do anything about it. They were milked regardless but didn't get any dinner at that point, although they did get fed later to make up for it. However, once the grumpy cows (because by that point, they were *very* grumpy cows indeed) got outside, word quickly spread to their companions.

'The cows are refusing to go into the milking parlour because they know they won't get fed,' the very bemused and tired-looking farmer told us the next day.

Yes, the cows were protesting, and nothing could induce them to go inside. Oh, they'd lined up outside the parlour as usual, and poked their heads around the door inquisitively, but when they didn't smell any food, they quickly retreated.

It was only when the farmer yielded and filled each hopper by hand, that the cows allowed themselves to be milked. But this caper meant that milking took hours, because the farmer was basically providing table service for two hundred cows. Still, at least his girls were happy.

And people say animals are stupid.

148. Lambs, lambs everywhere... but not in our yard

I have lamb envy. It's not pretty and I'm not proud, but that's just the way it is.

Perhaps this is what women feel like when they long to be mothers but are yet to have a child. Everywhere they look, they see babies in cute outfits being carried by exhausted but ecstatic-looking women. They see dads, mums or indeed, grandparents proudly pushing prams with sleeping tots inside, while toddlers skip along high streets, hand-in-hand with their parents.

In my case, it seems that every field I pass is full of lovely lambs, while friends who are in the middle of lambing or calving plaster their social media pages with photos of newborns, while I scroll through them, envy building like a rage, until I stomp off, unable to take any more.

I walk into the sheep shed and the silence is deafening. I stare at the empty troughs, hay racks and water buckets. The hurdles and pallets which we use to make pens are stacked against the wall, no longer needed. We aren't lambing at the moment, which is why everything is so quiet.

The calf house has an equally sad atmosphere, as our latest batch of babies went back to their farm recently. Again, I imagine this is how parents feel when their children leave the nest. Empty and sad.

I go outside for some fresh air and lean on the fence to admire the ewes in their field. 'Hey, Skinny.'

She's called skinny because when she was born, she was, yes, you've guessed it, skinny. But she's since bloomed into a very confident and contented ewe.

Somehow, she picks up on my low mood and walks over for an ear rub. Well, I say walk, but it is more of a waddle, as she's pregnant, so it takes her a while to get to me, but when she does, I rub her ears while absentmindedly telling her all about my lamb envy. I thought it was so nice of her to listen, but it turns out she was doing much more than that. She was planning to take matters into her own hooves and do something about it.

A week or so later, Paul and I were on our way back from the airport after a little break and decided to stop to see the sheep in one of our rented fields. Skinny was there too, as we'd relocated her before we left.

336

Skinny was sitting by the gate, as if waiting in welcome. Then she stood up, turned and promptly delivered a lamb right in front of us! She had literally waited for us to get back before giving birth!

Skinny wasn't meant to get in the family way, but one of the rams had obviously taken a shine to her when he snuck into the ewes' field unexpectedly one day and thus, she was soon with lamb.

Obviously, we were delighted, but because we hadn't been expecting her to lamb so soon, and we were on our way from the airport, we had no trailer or anything of use with us.

Paul handed me the lamb and picked up Skinny with ease, carefully placed her into a one tonne bag he found in the car (left over from a building job) and placed her in the boot. She looked so cute with her head sticking out the top and her lamb snuggled in beside her. Then we all went home.

I was delighted with the new arrival and took lots of photos for social media and our family album. And I also managed to squeeze in lots of cuddles!

The new addition also meant I was able to join in with lamb conversations again, which ensured my lamb envy disappeared. Thanks for coming to my rescue, Skinny, you are amazing.

149. Brontë hunters

I'm excited on two counts. The first being that we're going on a day trip, which will be our first family outing since we got married.

The second is because we are visiting The *Brontë* Trail in County Down. The route, which consists of various stop-offs at cottages, schools and churches, charts the early life of Patrick *Brontë,* who was born in these parts and would go on to Father Anne, Charlotte, Emily and Bramwell, arguably the most famous siblings in English literature.

I was so excited when I discovered the *Brontë* link in Northern Ireland that I had to investigate. I contacted the Tourist Information Centre and spoke to tourist information officer Jason Diamond, who was indeed a diamond, for not only did he give me loads of information about the trail, but he invited me to take the tour!

Mummy-In-Law is an avid reader too, and Paul likes a day out, so we all piled into the car and set off. It's pouring down, but the rain does little to diminish my mood or dampen my enthusiasm. In fact, it enhances it, because it all seems very *Wuthering Heights*-esque.

As we pull up at the schoolhouse, I look across the rolling hills and catch my breath. It is a beautiful view, and one which would have changed little since Patrick explored the area as a boy.

The schoolhouse is as basic as can be, with two fireplaces at each end (one is original) some benches and a blackboard. There would have been about thirty children crammed into this classroom during Patrick's day, all trying to learn and keep warm at the same time. It's cold enough now during winter, let alone when they would have been taking lessons.

It must be said that the various stories which run through the *Brontë* family tree, some romantic, some brutal, others tragic, wouldn't be out of place in one of the sisters' own books.

Patrick was born to poor but loving parents and spent his early life in a tiny cottage. It looked like he was destined to be a manual worker, but his thirst for knowledge impressed the local priest so much, that he not only encouraged Patrick with his education, but helped him train as a teacher and apply to Cambridge to read theology. Patrick was successful on both fronts and went on to become a member of the clergy himself.

He visited his homeland briefly after graduating, but after that, he never stepped foot onto Northern Irish soil again. We don't know why this was, but there are theories. One is that he was ashamed of his humble origins. Another, that he wasn't close to his family. Jason, however, is more forgiving. He said: 'History depicted Patrick as a distant and cold father, when he was actually generous. He gave his mother an annual allowance paid out of his wages and on her death, transferred it to his youngest sister, Alice.'

By the end of the tour, I felt like I'd gotten a little closer to discovering the true nature of this man, who, for so long, has been shrouded in mystery, mistreated by history and is something of a side note in the bigger, more famous story of his daughters' lives.

By the time we head home, I'm sopping wet but happy, my brain buzzing with all sorts of stories. In fact, I feel a feature coming on.

It feels good to have stretched my journalistic muscles. I feel useful and excited to share what I've learned with others. I'm full of endorphins, having forgotten just what a buzz I get from interviewing and writing. Not to mention the joy of discovering a story and the excitement of piecing it all together, like a giant jigsaw.

I love playing with words, weaving and shaping them into sentences that are powerful and effective. Into paragraphs that make readers think and feel and hunger for knowledge. Words can be our companions during the darkest times, transport us to new worlds and make us laugh, cry and smile. They are powerful pieces of magic.

And I feel, for the first time in a long time, like I'm back in the game.

150. Lambkin the great

All lambs are special, and I love each one, but some stories are more traumatic than others.

He looked like a teddy bear or a real-life cuddly toy. His coat was dark brown with a little curl to it, all thick and

340

soft. He had long legs and big feet and the most gorgeous face! Deep-set, big brown eyes which crackled with brightness and life, a strong jaw and big ears.

'What a lovely-looking lamb,' I said to Paul, thinking nothing of it, as he placed the new arrival next to his mum.

I'm still overwhelmed at how something so big – especially in this lamb's case, could fit inside a modestly sized sheep. But here he is.

Even his mum looks a bit surprised at her huge baby, but is soon licking away at him as he snuggles into her. As births go, it was straightforward enough and there was no indication that anything was wrong. But when I checked on him later, I was surprised that he wasn't on his feet. Normally they're up and about quite quickly, but as far as I could see, he was still in the same position we'd left him in. I fetched Paul, who examined him but found nothing amiss.

'He might just be exhausted,' Paul concludes, 'he's a big lamb and it was quite a long delivery. We'll feed him and see how he gets on.'

The next day, the lamb still isn't on his feet and my heart plummets. I stop what I'm doing and sit with him. 'What's the matter, mate?' I ask, stroking his big ears. He turns to look at me, and it's almost as if he's smiling. He has the happiest little face I think I've ever seen on a lamb.

After a while, he starts to rock forwards and backwards, which is the standard starting point for any lamb finding their hooves. Eventually, he gets enough sway that he's able to put one hoof on the floor and then the other. 'Come on,' I say, clasping my hands.

He struggles and strains, but eventually and with much effort, gets the third leg straight. 'There's a good boy, you can do it,' I whisper, feeling like a mother encouraging her toddler to stand.

Indeed, I'm that moved by this big life event that I whip out my phone and film it. I'm a proud foster parent and I want to show everyone what this lamb can do.

He's up on his hooves for a few seconds, his whole body quivering with the effort but then, as if he's a beanbag whose beans have fallen to the bottom, he flops down, exhausted. I wipe away a tear.

On one hand, I'm proud of him. On the other, I'm aware that he should be up and about by now. I'm extremely concerned and so is Paul. 'I'm beginning to wonder if he didn't develop properly in the womb,' he says.

'Surely not. He's huge and looks well developed to me.'

'I don't mean just physically,' Paul says as gently as he can, and the penny drops.

'You mean his brain might not have developed as it should?'

'Possibly. It looks like his brain is having trouble sending messages to the rest of the body.'

'But that's OK, we could keep him as a pet, couldn't we?'

'Sure, if he's able to stand, but he needs to do that first.'

Not being able to stand meant the poor thing couldn't even suckle from his mum, which was devastating. There's nothing more rewarding than seeing a lamb suckle for the first time, not just because it's incredibly sweet, but it means they receive that first vital dose of colostrum, which provides newborn with antibodies to fend off a host of respiratory and intestinal diseases. In fact, newborn lambs should receive at least ten percent of their body weight in colostrum by the time they are eighteen hours old, which this bubba just wasn't getting.

In the first instance, Paul milks the mum for her colostrum and gives it to Lambkin (now his official name) via a feeding tube inserted into his mouth. Usually, we only feed lambs in this way until they are big enough to suckle from their mums.

However, when a lamb is orphaned, their mum isn't producing enough milk, or as in this case, when a lamb is very sick, we continue to feed them as they grow, usually via a bottle filled with powdered milk.

I tried to be optimistic about Lambkin, convinced that he was just having a few beginners' issues and would soon get the hang of being a lamb.

Every time I popped into the lambing shed to do a job (and sometimes even when I didn't) I would pop over to see how he was getting on. Sometimes, he'd be in a slightly different place, having wobbled a few steps, but he never went far.

But after a few more days of this, when the lambs born after him were merrily skipping around the pen and Lambkin was still in his corner, I began to lose hope. He would watch the others dashing around as if thinking, 'What are they doing, then? Why they rushing about?' It broke my heart.

I would often hold his hooves or stroke his ears while explaining how important it was that he stood. But he would just look at me with his smiley face, oblivious to what I was saying, to the severity of the situation or to the tears pouring down my face.

His mum would nuzzle him from time to time, and even sit with him. 'That's it, Mum,' I said softly, my voice breaking with emotion, 'You show your baby how much you love him.'

By the end of the week, his mum had all but given up on him, choosing to spend her time caring for her stronger lamb. It seems that ewes know when one of their lambs is sick or dying, and when this is the case, they won't waste their energy caring for it. I still find this hard to grasp, but that's nature's way.

To top it all off, Paul had bought out the dreaded heat lamp. I say dreaded, because it seems to me, to signal the loss of all hope. It says, 'the only thing we can do now is keep him warm and hope for the best, because even the professionals have run out of options.'

Admittedly, Lambkin had gone downhill very fast, and so the appearance of the lamp didn't come as a great surprise. He was laying more than sitting and not eating or drinking much. And to add insult to injury, the beautiful spark had disappeared from his lovely eyes.

We took him into the house and set him up in a big box under the heat lamp. I wanted to wrap him in a blanket, but Paul said we didn't want to overheat him. Sometimes, I forget that these creatures spend their lives outside in all weathers, so being in a hot house would be alien and scary to them.

I laid with Lambkin as much as I could. I pulled out my biggest, woolliest jumper and stroked him with it, hoping he'd think his mummy was next to him. 'We love you, Lambkin,' I said, my head against his, while Paul's hand rested in mine. 'Just you remember that, OK? You are so very loved. Come on, you can pull through.'

I didn't even know, by then, if he could hear me. His breathing was shallow, and his eyes closed.

'Come on, pet,' Paul said, kissing my cheek. 'It's time for us to get some sleep too.'

I nodded and wiped my eyes which were red raw from crying. I turned and kissed his lovely head. 'Sweet dreams, lovely Lambkin.'

The next morning, our big, beautiful boy was gone. We don't know if his organs were ever fully formed, or if there had been another problem. But at least he was at peace.

His once pink lips were now blue and his body stiff and lifeless. His lovely, long limbs splayed out, as if he'd had one last attempt at trying to stand. I wasn't afraid to touch him, he was still the same sweet Lambkin.

'He didn't even get to suckle properly,' I sobbed as Paul scooped me into a hug. 'Let alone go outside, run in fields or play with his friends.' I cried for him and the life he'd never know.

'But he got so much love,' Paul whispered. 'Sometimes that's all you can give.'

The tears just wouldn't stop coming. But I wasn't just crying for Lambkin, as sad as I was, no, the whole experience had unblocked something within me. I was crying for parents who had lost children, either through miscarriage or after they had been born.

I was crying for them and praying that they were able to

get the help they needed in order to mourn and maybe one day, have another baby or adopt. They'd never forget their first, of course, but they'd be able to pour all their love onto the next child, and tell them all about their sibling, who was equally loved.

Later, when I was out in the fields watching the other lambs skit about, I said a prayer for Lambkin and his mum. I hope she wasn't too sad, and I prayed that Lambkin was in heaven. I imagined him running about, bleating and having lots of fun with his friends. I hope he knows he was loved. Because he was, very much.

151. Snow scene

This morning, I opened the curtains to find a flock of sheep staring at me through the window. The field opposite doesn't belong to us, but a neighbour, who obviously moved them in either late last night or very early this morning. I wave and smile. I love living in the countryside.

152. Cows

I t's a freezing cold morning and I'm on milking duty. I had to drive extra slow on the way in because of all the ice. I'm wrapped up in layers of clothing with a thick hat rammed over my head and I'm still cold. In fact, the warmest thing in the whole parlour is the cows' udders. 'Oh lovely,' I whisper as I clean their teats, 'nice and warm.'

I'm still stunned by the fact that the milk comes out of the cows warm! I don't know why this should surprise me as they're warm-blooded creatures, but there you go. If only we were still allowed to drink the milk straight from the cow, I could bring my own powder and make hot chocolate!

As we finish up, shards of sunlight start to filter through the gateways and light up the darkest corners.

Ten minutes later, shafts of sunlight are running down the walls like happy paint, highlighting the cows' intricate black and white patterns.

Bars of buttery yellow light peep through the windows, as if saying, 'a new day awaits, come and play.'

Yes, getting out of bed so early is a struggle, and I'm tired for about the first hour, but then it lifts like fog, my brain kicks into gear and I get excited about the fact that when the shift is over, I practically have the whole day to myself!

It's also wonderful knowing that the cows are milked and back in their beds, just chilling, or enjoying a well-earned breakfast or dinner, depending which shift I'm on.

Sometimes, I just walk through the barn and chat to them while they sit and look at me with their beautiful big, brown eyes. Sometimes they'll swish their tails in greeting, but for the most part, they just watch me walk on by. They look happy, as if they haven't a care in the world, which is as it should be.

Driving home, I see people emerging from their houses clad in office attire, clutching bags, mobiles and laptops. Bleary-eyed, they clamber in cars to embark on their daily commute into the city. And I feel thankful that I'm not joining them.

153. Teacher training

SheepCam is up and running, meaning Paul and I can have the TV on in our living room and flip between watching our favourite soaps and the sheep in the shed. To be fair, the latter is often more dramatic than anything the TV schedules can offer.

The cameras have been installed at various points so we can see what everyone is up to; be it snoozing, eating or, most importantly when lambing begins in a few weeks, going into labour. For now, we have a test group in there. This is so we can make sure everything is working and/or iron out any glitches.

When I finish milking, I pop my head into the shed to

say hello to the girls. 'We'll be keeping an eye on ewe,' I grin. 'Geddit?' Some look up at me briefly, then go back to the hayrack, others just blank me completely. 'Tough crowd.'

That night, Paul and I retire to the sofa. 'Shall we test out SheepCam?' Paul says excitedly.

'Good idea.'

I grab the remote, switch channels and squint at the screen. Funny. I can't see any sheep, only straw. 'They must be having a party down the other end,' I say, slowly.

'They'd better be, otherwise they've escaped.'

I laugh a little too loud and too long, as the camera flips to reveal an empty pen.

We shoot off the sofa, put on our boots, fight with our waterproofs for a few seconds before abandoning them, open the door and run into the rain to look for the missing weebles.

'How has this happened?'

'They're sheep. They follow each other.'

'Right.'

'If one discovers an open gate or a gap in a fence, they'll go through it and the others will follow.'

Makes sense. I try to shake off the horrible feeling that I was the one who left the gate unlocked. Again.

Paul shines his torch down the lane, but the wee weasels aren't there. And if not there, where?

We walk on for a while, then Paul stops suddenly, his head tilted to one side, listening. 'They're over there,' he growls, pointing to the next field along, as he shines the torch into the thick darkness.

At first, all I can make out is the outline of trees, but as my eyes slowly adjust, I see twenty twinkling stars. Then I realise I'm actually looking at ten pairs of sheep eyes which are staring back at us out of the darkness.

'Get back in the house, now,' Paul shouts in his best teacher voice. It's so authoritative that I turn around and start walking. 'Not you,' he says, 'the sheep.'

The escapees slowly but surely oblige, giving us sidelong glances as they trot by, as if they're school children who've been told to go back inside after playtime, and are doing so reluctantly. They file in, nonplussed, as if it isn't freezing cold and midnight. As if they hadn't been naughty and given us a fright.

'You should all be in your pyjamas by now,' I yawn when we eventually get them inside. We tuck them in and read them a bedtime story, because we are big softies and they are very much loved.

154. All hands on Deck

My friends and I have just finished one of our online quizzes and are having a chat, when Paul rushes into the living room holding a cardboard box with a blood-covered lamb inside.

'What happened?'

'I'll explain later,' he says, placing the box in front of the oven so the lamb can benefit from the heat, before disappearing back outside.

Mummy-in-Law, who has fostered many lambs over the years, swings into action and goes to the 'lamb linen section' of the hot press (airing cupboard) where the freshly laundered towels live, while I explain the situation to the quizzers.

'Well don't just sit there, woman,' Liz says. 'Go and look after your baby.'

With that, my friends wish the lamb well and say good night. I have a sneaking suspicion it's going to be a long one, but I don't mind if a lamb needs me!

I kneel next to the box and stroke the lamb's head. He is blood splattered, wet and bleating his little head off as he calls for his mum. He looks frantically from left to right as if trying to find her, and it is heart-breaking to watch. 'Hello, lovely lad, what's happened to you, then?'

Mummy-in-Law gets to work drying him off with a towel, moving her hands in brisk, circular motions to replicate the nuzzling his mother would do if she were here.

He's a good size and is clearly strong as he's standing already. When Paul returns, he has a bottle in hand. 'There you go, mate.' The lamb is also a fast learner and sucks quickly and contentedly.

I'm afraid to ask, but I have to. 'What happened to his mum?'

Paul looks at me with sad, tired eyes. 'She was having problems with the birth and I needed to perform a caesarean to save the lamb. It was too late for her.'

I reach out, hold his hand and squeeze it. 'I'm so sorry.

You tried your best and it's a miracle you were able to save him. It's thanks to you that he's alive.' I hope my words are of some comfort, but I doubt it. Vets, like doctors and all medical professionals, I suspect, have a huge responsibility. They literally have animal or human lives in their hands and it must weigh heavy.

'I should have done something sooner, I should have...'

'Don't do that,' I say softly, 'you *always* do your best. If it wasn't for you, lamb wouldn't be here either. You have such knowledge and expertise. You're amazing and I'm so proud of you.'

I certainly couldn't do his job. I can't even decide what to have for breakfast in the morning, let alone make life or death decisions based on ever-changing circumstances.

'What shall we call him?'

'It has to be another name beginning with the letter d.'

I nod. 'How about Deck, as in December and *Deck the halls with boughs of Holly*? After all, it is nearly Christmas.'

Paul nods sadly. 'Yes, pet, if you like.'

'That's decided then.' I reach out and stroke Deck's ears. He has finally settled down and is nodding off, lulled by the heat of the fire and the milk in his tummy.

'Can he come home with us?'

'No, pet, it's best he goes back to the sheep shed so he can see and hear the others.'

Well, it was worth a try.

Later, we take him down to the shed and settle him into a pen. Soon, we will see about getting him a new adoptive mother, but until then, we wish him sweet lamb dreams and turn out the light.

155. Cuddle quota

While we're working out what to do about Deck's situation, I make the most of the scenario by getting in as many lamb hugs as possible. I give him his bottle three times a day, make sure he's warm enough and have a chat whenever I'm passing. When I climb into his pen, he'll come bounding over, put his hooves on my knees and push his head towards mine. And we'll sit in silence, our heads touching, eyes closed contentedly. I feel his warm breath on my nose and smile. I hope he feels loved, even if it is only by a hooman.

156. Sheep substitute

Deck's getting a new mummy today and I'm so nervous. The ewe we've selected for him sadly lost her own lamb, and so we're pairing them up. As is the way of things on most farms, the coat of the dead lamb has been removed and placed over the would-be adoptee. This is so the mum gets the scent of her own lamb, which increases the chances of her accepting the new one.

On a side note, seeing the coat removed from the poor dead lamb was the closest I've come to being sick on my own shoes. It wasn't so much the gore that got to me, as the sadness. It also made me cry to think that, even in death, the lamb could serve a purpose by uniting an orphan lamb with a grieving mum.

The dead lamb was much bigger than Deck, so now it looks like he's wearing a Superman cape. I don't think his new mum is convinced either, but she desperately wants a lamb to look after, so is willing to overlook this discrepancy.

At first, Deck just bleats and bleats, confused as to why he is in a new pen and presumably, wondering where I've gone. All the while, the ewe stands at a distance. Every fibre of my being is screeching out to go and scoop him up, cuddle him, tell him it's alright and that I'll look after him. But I don't, because I know this is for the best. But, unable to take any more, I slip out of the shed and leave them to get acquainted.

When I pop back later, the ewe has moved a little closer to Deck, who has at least stopped shouting. I watch as she gives him a few cautionary sniffs and then begins to lick him. I breathe a sigh of relief.

Now, I *know* Deck's mum can look after him better than me because she is, after all, a sheep; she can snuggle up to him with her big woolly coat, give him proper milk on tap and talk to him in his language. But I still miss him.

I pop my head around the door one night to check on them and grin as I see them sitting with their heads pressed together, while Deck slowly drifts off to sleep. It is a beautiful vision and just as it should be. But the pain of separation is still raw for me.

'How do people foster children?' I wail into Paul's shoulder. 'It's so hard. You get attached to them so quickly and then they're gone.'

'Dear, you only looked after him for one night,' Paul says, stroking my head.

'Details,' I say, blowing my nose loudly into a handkerchief. 'I miss my baby.'

Despite my selfish reasons for wanting to rear Deck myself, I cannot deny that the mum and baby both seem content in each other's company, and my heart swells with joy for them.

There was poor little Deck, literally crying out for a mum, and there was the ewe, her heart breaking and her milk flowing for a lamb that died, and now the orphan has a new mummy and they're healing and loving one another, which is beautiful.

Deck is rapidly learning how to 'sheep' thanks to his new mum. I still miss being on mummy duty, but you have to let your children spread their wings, don't you?

Having resigned myself to the fact Deck doesn't need me anymore, I go into the shed the next day to give one of the other lambs their bottle. As I pass his pen, Deck runs over to me. Thinking he must be hungry, I offer him the bottle, but he only takes a few sips and stops.

Concerned, I step into the pen and kneel down. To my utter delight, he runs over, places his hooves on my knees and puts his nose to my nose. We sit there for a while, head-to-head, eyes half-closed in contentment, and I smile. So, he does remember me and enjoys our cuddles as much as I do. Amazing.

157. SheepCam

I 've said it before and I'll say it again, watching Sheep-
Cam is better than anything on television.

The new cameras mean Paul only has to venture as far as
the living room to check on the girls in the shed and, if
nothing's happening, can go back to bed.

I have offered to take my turn on the night shift but
seeing as I don't actually know what I'm doing, and would
just have to get Paul out of bed anyway if something was
amiss, it's probably best all round if I just stay put.

I can't remember when a new television programme was
last aired, mainly because no new content is being made
due to lockdown. At the moment, it's all repeats of repeats.
So instead, we sit for hours just watching the goings on in
the sheep shed, and it really can be more dramatic and
interesting than anything the soap scriptwriters could
come up with. In fact, they could probably get inspired by
watching our sheep for a day or two. Now there's an idea,
offering residencies to writers...

There are the box babies, who pile inside their box when
small, sit half in and half out as they grow and eventually,
when they can no longer squeeze inside, they abandon the
box altogether and pile on top of each other in a corner.

Then there is Frazzle and his mum, although he is so
small you can hardly see him. This is made even more
problematic as he blends in with the straw. But we know
he likes to sit in the top corner under his heat lamp, and

his mum snuggles next to him, so we have a fair idea of where to look.

Then there is One Ear, her and her twins, who get bonus points for being the laziest lambs I have ever seen. They don't even stand to suckle! Instead, they simply stay seated and call to their mum who trots over and stands over them while they drink. Talk about spoiling them rotten!

And of course, there's Deck and his mum, who have moved to the pen-thouse in the corner, which they share with other lambs and their mums.

Lockdown has been tough for everyone and as I write this, we are now in our third. The whole process has been emotionally draining and, I, like everyone else, miss my family and friends terribly. So much so, that I set up a lamb fan club to keep everyone involved and updated. I share photos and videos on my social media pages and I like to think they lift people's spirits.

Animals give us so much in terms of love and joy. We're lucky to have them and I'm honoured to work with them and try, in my small way, to repay them for the kindness and happiness they provide, even though they probably have no idea just what a special job they do.

158. Riddle me this

I 've been banned from hosting quizzes because:

   a. My questions are too hard and
   b. I'm useless at technology

The first quiz I hosted was fine, because I was asking the questions and Paul was in charge of the technology, meaning the entire thing went smoothly.

However, the second time around, Paul was busy and couldn't assist. Safe to say, it was pandemonium.

'Can you see anything?' I asked as I tried to get the images on screen.

'We can't even see you,' Liz sighed. 'You've turned your video off.'

'Oh.'

I pressed a few buttons, but to no avail.

Ben, one of my oldest and dearest friends, managed to have a small nap, a three-course meal and a shave before I got sorted.

'OK,' I said, with joy in my voice. 'Onto question two.'

'We've been here an hour and we're only on question two?' he wailed.

'What was Rudolph the red nosed reindeer originally going to be called?' I continued, ignoring him.

'Not a fucking clue,' Ben said.

'No' I said, 'try again.'

'Hang on,' Ben said, suspiciously, 'are all the questions about Christmas?'

'Yes. It's called The Christmas Quiz. The clues is in the name.'

'Oh, for fucksake.'

Well, that's not very festive, is it?

I am pleased to say that I am a very organised and dedicated quiz planner. I have spreadsheets for different rounds and lots of questions stored on my laptop, just in case I am ever called upon to host at the last minute, although strangely, that is yet to happen. I send email invitations with login details very early on, so nobody can wriggle out of it at last minute. I even send prizes out afterwards. You're jealous, aren't you? I knew it.

Mind you, I'm not sure which my friends find more irritating, me hosting a quiz or being a participant. This is because whenever I know, or think I know the answer to a question, I put my hand up.

'You aren't in school,' Ben says, 'just write the answer down.'

I also sometimes forget that my microphone is on when I say the answer out loud. Of course, everyone hears me and writes it down. So, it serves them right when I'm wrong, which I invariably am.

159. Big choices

Deck's beginning to eat solid food now, but he can still have milk from the bottle if he likes. Today, I offered him a drink just seconds after he'd stuffed his little mouth with food. He was so excited but couldn't decide whether to spit the nuts out in favour of the bottle, or swallow what he had and then go for the milk. In the end, he opted for the latter. It's a bit like me when I'm offered a biscuit just as I've taken a sip of tea. Indeed, difficult choices are all around us.

160. Christmas TV

I'm looking forward to watching the festive episode of the *All Creatures Great and Small* reboot. I have the popcorn out and my favourite pyjamas on.

SheepCam is on television when I get in from feeding the sheep, so I make a cup of tea and head to the sofa. But my bottom doesn't even get within touching distance of the cushions before I spot something of concern on the screen. I squint. Is...is that sheep lambing? *Now?* How? I *literally* just came in from visiting them and nothing was happening then. I leap up, almost pouring tea over myself in the process, slam the mug down and run to the door. Happily, I don't need to put my jacket on, because I never got the chance to take it off in the first place.

I enter the shed at such speed, that I crash spectacularly into the gate and ricochet into a pile of buckets behind me. The peaceful environment is shattered and the sheep start shouting. Well, all except one.

'There you are, my lovely.' I clamber over the fence and slowly move towards the ewe, who is clearly in some discomfort, because she doesn't even try to stand, which is good. I think.

I gently stroke her nose in what I hope is a reassuring way. I pull the lambing gloves from my pocket and put them on, before taking a look at the business end.

Suddenly, I'm overcome by imposter syndrome. (Well, perhaps it's not that. Imposter syndrome implies you have the expertise but not the confidence, whereas I have neither the confidence or the expertise.) Despite this, I remember to breathe and keep calm. I'll be no good to her if I'm in a tizz. Paul has gone out to check the sheep in the rented fields, so it's just us.

My fear is slightly tempered by the fact that the lamb's hooves are already poking out. I gently take them in my hands and pull. To my relief, the lamb slides along nicely and in no time at all, its lovely little nose is out. I pull enthusiastically and the lamb's long, glistening body slips out. 'Hello, little one,' I whisper. I wipe the lamb's mouth to make sure it can breathe and quickly lay her (I just checked) next to her mum, who nuzzles her enthusiastically.

I sit back on my heels and giggle, marvelling at how brave and calm ewes are. I'm sure they are in pain during labour, but apart from a few bleats here and there, they are often just focused on getting the job done.

I decide to get them into a pen so that they can have some bonding time away from the others. The lamb is already trying to stand and will be up and about in no time.

I dash off to get some straw and busy myself making the pen nice and cosy. When I turn around, the other ewes have gotten brave and are excitedly inspecting the new arrival. I hope they are congratulating the new mum in their own special way, with all their bleats and snuffles. Maybe they'll club together and buy some bunting, or perhaps a banner stating: *Well done ewe, it's a girl!*

I'm so impressed with how ewes just crack on with motherhood. They quickly get to grips with feeding their lambs and are extremely protective from the start.

As predicted, by the time the pen is ready, the lamb is on her feet. As such, it takes me just a few minutes to guide her and her mum inside.

'How are you getting on?' Paul asks as he enters the shed.

'Ok, I think,' I smile. 'I was just about to get her some food and water.'

'You'll need to change your gloves,' he says while looking at the sheep in the pen. 'The next one will be putting in an appearance at some point.'

I do a double take and realise that the ewe is indeed marked with a red spot, meaning she's expecting twins. How comes I hadn't noticed that before? But there isn't time to ponder and so I dash to change my gloves.

Minutes later, I'm back in the pen but very confused after examining her. 'She's so tight. There's no way I can get my hand in to help her lamb.'

'That's OK. They don't always come out straight away. Let's give her some time.'

As I clamber out, I spot another sheep in the first throws of labour.

'I'll have a look,' Paul says as he heads over to examine her.

'The envelope's empty,' he says a few minutes later, confusion etched on his face.

'What do you mean?'

'There's no lamb in there.'

'A phantom pregnancy? It can't be,' I say confidently, like I know what I'm talking about.

'No,' Paul says, with the look of a man who is beginning to realise what's happened in his absence. Realisation is dawning on him and it's about to dawn on me, only I wish it wasn't.

He has a little chat with the ewe he has just examined, then turns her around to look at the blue spot on her wool. The *blue* spot. The symbol that says a ewe is having a *single* lamb, not twins.

You know when you're flicking through the television channels and come across a horror film (and you hate horror) so know you should turn over, but for some reason, you just can't stop watching? Well, this is a bit like that.

Paul comes back, examines the ewe in the pen and then confirms what I suspect.

'That isn't her lamb.'

'Of course not,' I say, nodding wholeheartedly. 'Sorry, what?'

It took a while, but we eventually worked out what happened. Would you like to know? I thought so. Take a seat, this may take a while...

When my back was turned, the newborn found her feet, but was unable to get a drink from her mum because she was still sitting down. Therefore, the cunning youngster wandered off to try and get a drink from one of the other ewes and when her mum did eventually stand, she was immediately surrounded by inquisitive sheep. The upshot of all this was that when I turned around, I didn't notice the mix-up and merrily led the new lamb and the usurper into the pen.

The usurper was quite happy with this arrangement: Pregnant sheep have a habit of stealing other ewe's lambs while waiting for their own to arrive. The lambs are also fine with this, as it means they get milk from two ewes. Double helpings!

I feel a bit sick and very sorry for the usurper. Not least because I'd just stuck my hand in a very intimate place when she wasn't anywhere near ready to lamb. I also feel bad because she seems quite happy with the little lamb and is contentedly nuzzling it. But now we're going to have to split them up, and all because I didn't look properly at the spots on their wool.

It doesn't take long for us to resolve the situation, and soon, everyone is back where they should be. Happily, usurper went into labour overnight and is now the proud mother of twins. I'm so pleased she didn't have to wait long for her babies to arrive.

'No real harm done,' Paul says, giving me a hug.

'This time,' I say, miserably. I still have so much to learn.

161. A present for the present

A parcel arrives from my parents and as I remove the lid, I can smell the scent of home; my mum's perfume, my dad's aftershave, the air freshener they use around the house.

To my delight, the box contains a bundle of my old toy sheep. One of them has a handwritten sign hanging around its neck. It reads: '*We want to live with you, please. We're cheap sheep! We don't need feeding, just loving.*' I smile and hug them. The smell of home, of childhood and of love is embedded in their wool. I miss my parents and wish they lived here. Then my life would be complete.

162. More presents

Another box of my belongings arrived today, delivered first class, no less. And it has just dawned on me that my parents are dismantling my old room, one box of belongings at a time, and sending them over under the auspices of wanting me to 'feel at home,' when, they're making the most of my absence and seizing the opportunity to make some space, Fair play.

My parents were bitterly disappointed when they realised that I'd be living in Northern Ireland, mainly because they couldn't just load up a van with my stuff and ceremoniously dump it in Paul's front garden before driving and shouting, 'She's your problem now. No refunds, no returns!'

'I was really looking forward to that, as well,' Dad said, forlornly.

163. Christmas shopping

In the best display of panic-buying I think I've ever seen, a man pitched up in our yard this afternoon, just two days before Christmas, looking to buy some sheep as 'a present for his wife.' Full marks for effort and originality.

'She'll love them,' he said, in the slightly manic tone of

a man who has clearly clean forgotten to buy a gift for his beloved, and is now hammering down the door of last chance saloon.

To give him credit, he must have swung into action pretty quickly when he realised his error. After all, we'd only put the advert online that morning and he was standing in our yard an hour later. He'd only seen one photo of the sheep, but apparently that was enough to convince him that his wife would be smitten.

He could have barely had time to focus on the ewes before he said, 'Yes, I'll take them. All of them. Right now.'

Turns out he'd bought his trailer with him, but left it at the top of the lane so as, and I quote, 'not to seem too keen.' Although, to be frank, the only way he could've been any keener was if he'd rolled in mustard before he arrived.

'Well, it's certainly an unusual gift,' I mused. 'Would you like them gift wrapped? I've got ribbons in assorted colours.'

I'm still not sure if he thought I was being serious or not, but nonetheless, he declined my offer. Shame. They would've looked really pretty with accessories.

As we watched him drive away with the best gifts ever, I started to worry.

'Sheep are for life, you know, not just for Christmas,' I tutted.

'It's OK,' Paul soothed, 'I know the family and his wife has been farming for years. It's not like he's taking them to a second floor flat and is going bung them under the tree.

'Apparently, he's going to put them in the outhouse and send his wife in there to get something on Christmas morning, whereupon she'll discover a heap of sheep to give her seasons bleatings. I don't know how he's going to keep them a secret for the next two days, but sure, that's not our problem.'

I'd love to know the thought process that led him to conclude that the obvious gift choice for his wife was not a box of chocolates, a bunch of flowers or her favourite perfume, but a selection of sheep. Surely the former items would've been, if nothing else, easier to wrap? But I also love the fact that his wife is clearly not materialistic.

'What a lovely gift,' I say as Paul puts his arm around me. 'Oh, which reminds me, have you got enough paper to gift wrap my goats?'

I ask for goats every time my birthday or Christmas rolls around but sadly, they're yet to materialise. But a girl can dream!

On a side note, did you know that when goats give birth, it's called kidding? I kid you not!

164. Christmas 2020

'Oh my gosh, it hasn't got a head,' I shout, although I don't know why, as I'm the only human in the sheep shed. 'I don't remember putting that on my Christmas list to Santa: A clementine, some chocolate coins, a new book, a headless lamb.'

I was just making my second attempt to acquaint my bottom with the sofa and watch *All Creatures Great and Small,* when one of the ewes decided it was a great time to push out a lamb. Down went the tea mug (again) I stood up (again) and went to the door, still in my jacket (again).

My confidence is growing with every lamb I deliver. But what's that saying? Pride goes before a fall...

'Oh, my Lord, it hasn't got a head,' I say again, just to remind myself of the severity of the situation.

I close my eyes and try to envisage what I can feel: Leg. Gap where head should be. Leg.

For a second, I almost forget how to breathe as I wonder what we're going to do with the distraught mum. Deciding I'm well and truly out of my depth, I dash to find my wonderful veterinarian husband who will help.

Minutes later I'm standing next to the ewe and fiddling nervously with the buttons on my jacket while Paul inspects her. I try to read his face, but he's giving nothing away. Slowly, he removes his hand.

'Carry on,' he says calmly, as if he has asked me to do something simple, like open a can of cola, instead of continuing to try and extract a headless lamb from a labouring ewe.

'I'm sorry, what?'

'As you were. The lamb isn't headless,' he says, a smile playing on his lips. 'It's just positioned backwards.'

Apparently, this is quite a common occurrence and means that instead of coming out in the traditional 'diving position' of front hooves followed by head, this lamb will come out back legs first.

'I can't deliver it,' I insist, 'I've not delivered a backwards lamb before.'

'Well, now's your chance.'

In the event, it was easier than I thought. That said, it wasn't exactly a picnic for the ewe, who had to deliver the largest part of her lamb last. Ouch! It's enough to make your eyes water. But mother and lamb are doing well, so that's the main thing.

If I had to, I think I could cope with a backwards birth again. But I'm going to send a memo to all ewes asking for them to resist the temptation, if at all possible.

165. Wrap star

It's gone midnight by the time Paul gets in from a problematic, but ultimately happy lambing. The ewe was marked for twins, which was fine, except the lambs had got their hooves and legs in a tangle inside the womb. This is, I am told, quite common, but means that whoever is on midwife duty has to untangle them while they are still inside and then deliver them safely. Thankfully, Paul's a dab hand at complicated deliveries and all went well.

All the excitement means that, while Paul has bought some lovely unicorn paper for my presents, he hasn't had time to wrap them.

This means that on Christmas morning, I find a

selection of items wrapped in old farming newspapers and binder twine, which is used to keep hay bales together. I smile and hold them close. I'm so happy because I know they've been chosen and wrapped with love, by a man who is so tired he can hardly see straight, but who has persevered just for me. I'm a very lucky lady.

166. The beginning of the sheep

'What's the best Christmas present you've ever had?' I ask Paul.

'Sheep.'

'I bet they were difficult to wrap and stuff in a stocking.'

When Paul was a little boy, his parents kept horses, cattle, sheep and goats. Paul couldn't drink cow's milk as a baby, so they got goats so he could have their milk instead.

When he was about ten, Paul decided he'd dearly love some sheep of his own. That Christmas, he received a letter from Santa saying he could pick two of the sheep out in the field, which would become his. The letter was accompanied by some rather charming sheep drawings. Nice one, Santa!

'How did you choose which ones you wanted?'

'I picked the prettiest ones.'

Fair enough.

Even at that age, Paul was prepared to work hard for the animals he loved. Thus, he did odd jobs at other people's farms and saved up to buy straw and all the other sheep paraphernalia he needed to care for them, knowing that one day, he wanted his own flock.

This story gave me hope and so I grabbed a pen and a piece of paper and started to write.

Dear Santa, for Christmas, please may I have a pair of goats?

And before you say it, I know I've not been a good girl this year, but it's worth a shot....

167. A New Year beckons

Most people can't wait to see the back of 2020, but I'll always regard it as the one of the best years of my life, because it was the one in which I married my gorgeous husband. It was also one in which a lot changed for me. I became a wife, moved country and took on a lot of sheep responsibilities!

Indeed, my old life seems as far away to me as England does, and I can hardly believe that I once had an office job, worked in a city and wore office clothes. I'm glad I trained as a journalist (and it's how I met Paul, after all) and I'm proud to have written for newspapers and magazines. I also hope I brightened the lives of readers via my work. But other than that, I don't miss it at all.

I look out of our living room window and see there's a mist rolling in. I wonder what's behind it, and what the new year will bring when it sweeps in? I don't know. But I'm ready to find out.

168. Thought for the day

The joy of knowing where you're going without needing a Sat Nav. Of seeing someone you know in the street and hearing them call your name. Being greeted by the local shopkeeper. Having someone asking after you and conveying good wishes to you and your family. I took all these things for granted before, but I never will again. Having these things happen to me in my new home country makes me happy. Maybe I'm becoming a local, after all.

169. The milkmaid's new clothes

I have a new set of navy-blue overalls which I wear to go milking.

In short, I feel like the bee's knees in my smart, clean attire, complete with gold buttons and zips and pockets for putting farming things in. Wearing them makes me feel as if I've completed my apprenticeship. I love my job and feel honoured to work with the gorgeous cows. Even if they do frequently poo on my head.

170. Please form an orderly queue

What a day! Our new foster calves arrived, shortly followed by our new office furniture. The yard was so busy I was seriously considering putting in a one-way system to manage the traffic. 'It's like Piccadilly Circus,' I mutter, which is one of my parents' favourite sayings.

I was just coming out of the calf house after settling the newbies in, when I spotted the delivery man, well, not exactly spotted. It wasn't the sort of van you could easily camouflage under a leaf.

I watched, mesmerised, as he emerged from his van with a box big enough to comfortably house both of our extended families, plus pets. I went to thank him but stopped when I saw him go back for another box, and another.

Later on, Paul and I open the boxes excitedly, and this, dear reader, is where I come into my own; having OCD is no picnic, but it does mean I'm *great* when it comes to flatpacks.

I check each component against the list and place each one neatly on the floor. Sometimes, for extra fun, I replicate the diagram exactly, so it looks as if the components have leapt from the leaflet straight onto our living room floor. I know, just hearing about my escapades makes you want to go and buy a flatpack right now, doesn't it? I should be named Lockdown Boredom Buster Minister for the UK.

We look from the array of wooden dowels, screws and fixings to the assembly leaflet and calculate that it will take us approximately seventeen days of manpower to put one desk together.

'Could we get the calves to put this lot together and save us a job?'

'Dunno if they're any good at DIY. Let's get them in and give it a try. They need to start earning their keep.'

'OK, you do that, I'll see if there are any construction videos they can follow on the internet. Which channel do you think the bovine friendly ones will be on? Moo-Tube?'

171. Cowering calves

The new arrivals look very pensive and are extremely quiet, so I go and have a little chat.

'We'll look after you,' I say, softly. 'The other calves we looked after all gave us good reviews.' I move a bit closer. 'It can be scary, being in a new environment, not knowing where you are or what to do. Trust me, I know. Maybe you're a bit homesick? Funny how it creeps up on you, isn't it? But it does get easier. And rest assured, you're very loved.'

Paul comes in during the middle of my monologue, smiles and wraps his arms around me as I put my head on his shoulder. 'Oh yes,' I smile, 'there's lots of love to go around. You can be sure of that.'

172. A frosty reception

Here's a tip: Don't clean your calf feeders by filling them with water and leaving them outside overnight. I speak from bitter experience.

'How are we going to defrost them?' I ask while staring at the two blocks of ice which used to be feeders. 'With hot water?'

'Na, brute force' Paul replies. 'Only joking.' And with that, he moves them onto the grass. 'The sun will move across in a while and thaw them out.'

Luckily, it works, and the calves get their lunch, meaning we've avoided a riot. This time.

173. Cold climate

Despite the fact I'm wearing three jumpers, a hat, gloves, two pairs of trousers and various socks, I'm still freezing. The chill feels like it's getting right into my bones and I can hardly speak for shivering, which gives Paul at least ten minutes of peace.

But while I'm trying my best not to die from hypothermia, the sheep are running around as if it's summer. Today, we're in the top field treating a lamb with sore eyes, or to be more specific, whose eyelids are turning inwards.

Now, I'm not usually squeamish, but I can't bring myself to look as Paul injects the lamb, so distract myself by counting sheep instead. The patient clearly isn't impressed either and is bleating blue murder.

'All done,' Paul says as he sets her on the ground, whereupon she's off like a shot.

Mission complete, I move off to feed the sheep in the other fields. As I walk, the sunshine breaks through the trees overhead, making the frost on the path shine like silver. The ice cracks and crunches under my feet and I can see the frost on my breath.

We then hit the road to check the sheep situated on the other side of the village. On the way, we stop off at the local ice-cream shop. I have chocolate coconut while Paul has strawberry ripple.

As we eat our cones in the warmth of the car, I state that I've never had ice cream in winter before, a revelation which astonishes Paul. As I look around the car park, I notice that lots of people are devouring ice cream. I don't know if it's a quirk of the area or what, but it's certainly something I could get used to.

'Should we get a couple of cones for the sheep?' I ask Paul. 'What flavour would they like? Straw-baa-ry, perhaps?'

174. Deck's growing up fast

D id I mention Deck's getting big now?
Deck's hanging out with his mates in the playpen, as cool as can be, which is nice, but makes me wonder if he's too grown up for cuddles now?

As if reading my thoughts, Deck looks straight at me and bounds over. As I kneel, he puts his hooves on my lap, as he did when he was a lamb, and we rest our heads together, just for a moment. Then, as if remembering his mates are watching, he dashes off. But I'm content; my little boy is still in there, despite being a teenager.

Meanwhile, Frazzle's trying to be all grown up too.

If he were a schoolchild, he'd be the smallest one in the playground, but with the biggest attitude. I can just imagine him strutting about in a bid to appear as tall as his contemporaries. If he could speak, he'd be saying 'I'm a big boy, I am.'

I think he's nervous around me because I keep picking him up for cuddles. He almost looks embarrassed whenever I do. I suppose it's the equivalent of me getting a handkerchief out and wiping his face in front of his mates.

He's so small compared to the other lambs, that I get a bit tearful as I watch him running about with them and trying to keep up. I feel like a mum who has dropped her child off at nursery for the first time and is watching nervously, hoping he's not being bullied and that he makes friends.

When they're young, the lambs will watch nervously from the corners of the shed while their mums eat from the troughs, as if they're not sure what to make of it all.

Then, as they get older, they run around in a group, like children on the dance floor at a wedding, all manic and jittery, as if their legs are on springs. Finally, as they grown in confidence and size, they follow their mums to the feeders and start nibbling.

We lay the troughs out in rows, meaning there's enough room for the sheep to all eat at the same time. The way they form neat, orderly lines puts me in mind of children eating school dinners. Except they don't have semolina. They can't stand the stuff.

175. Decked out

I'm genuinely gutted. Deck has stopped coming over to me now. He's all grown up, apparently. Well, that didn't take long.

Paul says this is a good thing as it means we've done our job properly. He's on his way to being a big, handsome ram. But it still makes me sad. Just like that, he's finished school, has graduated and is on his way to securing his first job. Where does the time go?

176. All power to you

I was asked to power hose the milking parlour today. 'No problem,' I said, even though I've never used a power hose in my life.

Despite this, I managed well enough and found it a very therapeutic and rewarding experience, working my way from one end to the other and making everything clean and bright.

Halfway through my shift, however, I had cause to text Paul: *The power hose hates me.*

His reply: *It can't hate you, it's an inanimate object.*

That may be so, but the power hose was giving it a good

go, nonetheless.

Every time I got started on cleaning one of the walls, the hose gave one good blast of water and then stuttered to a halt. I traipsed outside to the water source to check the pump was on, which it was, but I did the 'turn it off and on again' trick, just in case, and made my way back to the hose, but still nothing.

In the end, I gave up and asked one of the farmers for help. Obviously, they got it going for the first time of asking. Unbelievable.

177. You don't say.
Oh, but you do

I bought a bunch of daffodils today and was surprised to see a sticker on the wrapping which stated: This is not food. Do not eat these flowers.

I'll just leave that here for us all to contemplate.

178. On with the show(s)

I'm just sitting down to watch the 2020 Christmas special of *Call the Midwife*. And just for point of reference, it's now February 2021.

Believe it or not, this is the first opportunity I've had to catch up on programmes which were aired over the festive period, what with lambing and milking and learning to make cakes. Not that I'm complaining.

I put my feet on the sofa and pull out the Christmas TV guide. It's looking a bit dogeared now, but no matter. I flip through the pages, highlighter in hand and pick which programmes I want to watch, giving thanks for modern technology and catch-up services.

When I was little, I knew Christmas was just around the corner when Dad purchased the festive edition of *The Radio Times*. In my mind's eye, the picture on the front was always something jolly, like a family of snowmen and snowwomen, a reindeer or a rosy-cheeked Santa on a sleigh bedecked with presents. We'd sit together next to the Christmas tree (Mum would be in the kitchen making mince pies) and mark up our TV choices. It became a much-loved family tradition and is one I'm determined to continue in Northern Ireland. In February.

After an hour, I tick *Call the Midwife* off my list. One Christmas special down, six to go. At this rate, I might have watched all of my shows by June 2225.

179. Call me

It's my day off from milking and I'm having a lie-in, when my phone starts ringing. Once I've peeled myself off the ceiling, I groggily answer. 'Ello?'

'Hi Holly, is your Paul about?' It's one of our farmer friends. 'It's just I've tried his mobile and it's switched off.' I frown. That's odd. 'Hang on a second,' I croak, 'I think he's upstairs; I'll just get him for you.'

'Sorry,' Paul says when the call has ended, 'I didn't mean for you to get woken up.'

'That's OK. It's time I got up, anyway. How comes your friend couldn't get you on your mobile?'

Paul looks sheepish. Taking my hand, he leads me to the windowsill where his phone is artistically spread out in a variety of pieces.

'What happened?'

'It spent the night in one of the fields and got a good soaking. It must've fallen out of my pocket as I was feeding the ewes. I discovered it this morning as I was dishing out their breakfast.

'Ah.'

'I'm hoping it'll dry out and be OK. But that's why nobody can get through to me.'

'Good job the sheep don't have opposable thumbs,' I say. 'Otherwise, they would've been phoning premium numbers all night and landed you with a huge bill.'

I'm sure his phone will be fine. After all, its survived much more than a bit of a soaking. From being dropped in cow's milk and manure to falling, at some speed, from the roof of Paul's car. Most modern phones would've given up the ghost a long time ago, but his model is made of sterner stuff.

The incident reminds me of a friend of mine who works on building sites and is equally unlucky in the phone stakes. While working away on one particular site, she misplaced her mobile phone.

Her mate called her number to locate the device and, on hearing her chirpy ringtone, followed the sound into the next room, where it got louder. Venturing further, they crossed the floor and stopped when it became abundantly clear that the ringing was in fact, coming from below.

Realisation slowly and horribly dawned on them; the phone was in the footings, having fallen from her pocket while they were working. 'What are we going to do?' her workmate asked. My friend gave this due consideration before stating; 'Ah, bollocks to it. The battery will die soon. It'll be fine.' And it was.

180. Sheep scare

A gale is blowing and the rain pouring as I go to feed two ewes and their lambs.

The wind is skimming over the tops of the gates, making it sound as if someone's playing panpipes. I smile at the notion of a little pixie sitting under a tree and playing a tune to keep me entertained.

On entering the field, I see that the sheep and the lambs have decided, very wisely, to shelter under a hedge. I rattle my bucket, but they aren't interested today. I persevere, shouting louder and louder as I fight to be heard over the wind.

I walk a little further, but don't want to get too close for fear of undoing all the training of the past few weeks. If they want their snack, they're going to have to come over.

Eventually, one of the ewes raises her head and begins to show interest. She slowly gets to her feet and ambles over, head down against the wind. The nuts are too much for her to resist! Her lamb is right behind her, and the others follows suit. Except one.

In the distance, I can see a lamb lying down. I shake the bucket again, hoping against hope that she just hasn't heard me. Her head is tucked into her shoulder and she's right under the hedge, so it is possible. I step forward and make more noise. Nothing. Not even a flinch. My heart sinks and I start to move a little faster. Still no movement. I pick up the pace. 'Oi, lambie,' I call, trying to be jovial but not feeling it at all, 'what's up with you?'

I make as much noise as I can, but she doesn't muster. I go to call Paul, but realise I've left my phone it in the living room.

What could possibly be wrong with her? She was fine yesterday and from what I can see, she's not been attacked by anything. I shudder as I approach. I've heard of small lambs being attacked by crows and foxes, but surely, she's too big even for them to have a go at? I'm almost on top of her when, suddenly, her head jerks up. Blearily, she looks about. Thank goodness! She's just a heavy sleeper! I stop and giggle with relief.

The lamb, however, isn't impressed. Not only has she been rudely awoken, but she's also, as far as she's concerned, anyway, been abandoned by her mum. She shouts and shouts, getting herself, all worked up, as she spins in ever decreasing circles.

Having had a chance to calm myself, I walk slowly behind her until she's facing the right way and can see her mum, who is nonplussed and merrily stuffing her face on the other side of the field. It's like watching the sheep version of *Home Alone*, except this child isn't thrilled at having been left behind.

On spotting her mum, the lamb tears across the field, bleating all the way until she's by her side. Then she climbs into the trough and starts eating, all worries forgotten.

181. Yo-Yo

'Can you bring the yos in, please?'
    'The whats?'
'Yos,' Paul says. 'You know, woolly things, four legs. Say 'baa,' a lot.'
I narrow my eyes. 'Spell the word.'

'E-w-e-s'

'Oh you mean ewes as in, female sheep,' I splutter. 'Why didn't you say so?'

Paul blinks. 'I thought I just did.'

'No, you said yos.'

'Yos is how I say yos.'

'You mean yos is how you say ewes?'

At this point, my head starts to hurt. 'I'll just go and get the girls.'

Even after all this time, I still struggle with Northern Irish lingo. I love it, though.

182. One good turn deserves another

I love kind people, which is good, because many of them live in this pocket of Northern Ireland.

The farming community especially, appear to have each other's backs. If someone has run out of animal feed and hasn't time to the wholesaler, for example, a fellow farmer will happily give them some so that their animals don't suffer, happily stating, 'Sure, just return the favour when you can'.

Today, we ran out of calf feed for our new babies – the little tubs! Our delivery isn't due for a week and so, instead of having to run up the road before milking, we call a friend who is more than happy to let us have one of her bags. Such kindness is so refreshing. Or maybe it's just because I haven't lived in Northern Ireland all my life. Everyone is so friendly and helpful. It's beautiful to behold.

183. Tickets please

I 'm convinced it's a trap. The railway station car park doesn't have a ticket machine. Is it cunningly hidden in a bin or disguised as a bush, so I don't spot it? And if so, will I return to find my car plastered in fines?

My friend and I walk onto the platform and are even more bemused when we can't find a ticket office. All we can see is a man who looks as old as the hills, dressed in a smart suit with the words 'ticket officer' picked out in gold lettering on his jacket. A ticket machine is slung around his neck and he wears a peak cap. 'Over here,' he calls.

We approach with caution. 'Have we just gone through a time warp?' I whisper to my friend. I've never seen someone so smartly dressed, well, not in real life, anyway. Only in old films.

When we tell him we'd like two adult returns to Belfast, he smiles. 'That's sixteen pounds, please.'

'Each?'

'No, all together.'

I look at my friend quizzically. 'I don't think we're in Kansas anymore.' In London, you need to take out a small mortgage to get a return ticket to the city.

As we clamber on board and find our seats, we peer out of the window, convinced we've just seen a ghost. But no, the man is still there, happily chatting to other customers, which is something of a relief.

We had a great time in Belfast and on our return were delighted to discover that I hadn't got a parking ticket either! Apparently, car parks are free in this part of the county. I've said it before and I'll say it again, it's different in the country.

184. Confession time

OK, so I haven't written about this yet because it's a tough topic. But – takes a deep breath – here we go.

Yes, some of the sheep we keep are sold for meat. There. I've said it.

The harsh reality is that we have to make a profit, and therefore, can't keep every single sheep forevermore, much as I'd like to.

Funnily enough, on market days, I'm always busy doing something else. Anything else. I'd rather scrub the yard with a toothbrush than watch the sheep leave.

I'm also aware that I'm a massive hypocrite because I eat

meat, and therefore should either be at peace with where it comes from, or not eat it at all. But I'm not and I do. But at least I admit it.

I love seeing the new calves. I like stroking them and congratulating their mothers on producing such beautiful babies. And then I like to go to the supermarket to buy my nondescript box of beef, which bears no resemblance at all to the animal is once was, thank you very much.

In fact, I've never had any desire to think about where meat comes from, but I must think about it now, because we live in a farming community.

All the farmers I've met – and I've met a lot – love and respect their animals, look after them and care for them to the best of their ability, ensuring all their needs are met, from supplying fresh food and water to giving vaccinations and health checks.

The animals live in huge fields, hang out with their friends and ultimately, know nothing about what happens in the end. I think that's all anyone can ask for, really. And I know, I know, I'm still a hypocrite.

185. Light her up

'**K**eep her lit.'

'Sorry, what?'

Paul and I are taking a trip out and I'm driving. We're approaching a roundabout, but there's nothing coming, so I can go straight on. Then Paul says, 'keep her lit,' which confuses me, as nothing about the situation seems to suggest the need for naked flames, candles or the lighting thereof.

'No, I said keep her lit, as in keep going,' Paul explains.

'Oh, I see,' I say, not really seeing at all.

Sometimes, I'll be happily chatting away to the locals, when they'll throw in a slang term or phrase which is everyday parlance to them, but which confuses me.

Mind you, I'm also guilty of slipping in the odd phrase which is perhaps only used in my local area. 'He dobbed me,' being one such example.

I was animatedly explaining to a neighbour that Paul had 'dobbed me in' to my parents, probably for doing something naughty, like eating chocolate for breakfast.

'He what?'

'Dobbed me in, told on me, *squealed*,' I explained. Not for the first time, Paul has to translate. I hope he isn't charging me by the hour for his translation services. The bill would be astronomical.

186. Echoes

'**C**ome on, then.'

My voice echoes across the field and down the hill. I call again, making sure my shout reaches the far corners of this vast piece of ground. At first, the silence settles like dust but then, as if the message has finally come down the wire, there's movement: The flick of an ear, a flash of white among the green stalks of grass. I keep heading down the hill to meet my charges halfway.

Suddenly, as I call again, they come pelting across the fields apace, bleating excitedly. I like to think it's because they're excited to see me, but it's more likely because they've seen the bucket of food in my hand.

The wind's biting today. I have my scarf pulled up under my chin and my hat rammed so far down that only my eyes, nose and mouth are visibly. I shake the bucket again with gloved hands and slowly turn to make my way back up the hill.

As usual, the sheep, overtake me with ease. They bounce past and then stop to look down on me, as if to say, 'What's taking you so long, hooman?' And I explain that they have four legs, whereas I only have two, so they've got an unfair advantage.

Then, one will drop back and let me rest my hand on her for a second while I regain my balance on the slippery terrain. Sheep can be very considerate, you know.

As I make my way to the brow of the hill, I give one

more call to encourage the stragglers, and while I wait for them, turn, look out to sea.

For some reason, the view always takes me by surprise, as I've forgotten where I am geographically, and the sea has somehow snuck up on me.

The ewes react in a similar way when they've given birth. They'll get distracted by a bucket of food and take their eye off of their lamb for a few minutes. Then they'll turn around, look down, see a woolly little thing standing next to them and jump, as if to say, 'Whoa, a lamb. Where did a lamb come from? Oh yes, it's mine. I just gave birth to it.'

It's taken me a while, but I've mastered the shepherd's call now, I think. There was a time when I was timid and shy and wouldn't want to shout very loud for fear of causing panic, or making people think that something was wrong. Now, I frequently shout at a high frequency, and the sheep come to me. Or perhaps it's nothing at all to do with that, and everything to do with the fact that they've finally learned to understand my accent!

Getting the sheep to come when you call is vital, not only in terms of trust, but because it makes moving, treating or loading them into trailers so much easier. Indeed, shepherds have been calling to their flocks in this way for generations.

I can even whistle now. Admittedly, it still needs work, but it's better than it was. The cows especially, seem to respond to a good whistle when you want them to move down the line in the parlour.

As I stand on the hilltop and hear my own voice reverberating, I suddenly feel at one with this ancient land and I shiver, but it has absolutely nothing to do with the cold.

How many generations of people have stood on this hill and called to their flock, just as I'm doing now, I wonder? What were they thinking at the time? Were they happy with their lot, or aching for a chance to get away? Was the world at peace or at war? Was the sky clear overhead, or alive with the sound of aeroplanes? Were they just married and embarking on a new chapter? Or getting ready to retire and move on to pastures new?

Had manual work started to be replaced by machinery? Did they fear change or embrace it? Would they've been pleased to learn that the land in this area was still being used to graze animals and grow food hundreds of years later? Or surprised? I have so many questions which, sadly, will never be answered.

I hope they'd been happy to know that, in some parts of the country at least, traditions and family businesses continue to thrive. Others die out, of course, or change dramatically as people come and go.

Some live out their entire lives in one place, others leave and never return, or leave for a while. Others follow the ones they love to their homeland, because they'd rather uproot themselves and move five hundred miles than live without them.

Passers-by have and strangers alike, have now heard my voice ringing out from the fields. They may think that I'm a local, not knowing that I'm anything but.

'Look at that farmer and her sheep,' they may say as they watch me making my way to the gate where Paul is waiting, the sheep happily bouncing alongside. 'Nice to see the old ways preserved.'

They won't know that this is a new chapter based on old ways. Or that our family unit is different, but no less longed for or loved, than traditional ones. That we're building a new future based on the foundations of the past.

My call has now joined those which have echoed down the centuries. Sometimes, you can hear the voices of those that have gone before in the whistle of the wind, or in the crashing of the waves.

Who knows, maybe in the future, another young woman will stand where I'm standing now, excitedly contemplating her future as a newly married woman in a new land. Hopefully she'll be as happy as I am. If she is, she'll be very blessed, indeed.

187. Home time

As a journalist, I was more used to chasing deadlines than sheep. Now I do both, unbelievably.

I used to be a regular feature among the movers and shakers. Now I reside with the moo-vers and work with scrapers. And I wouldn't change it for the world.

As Paul and I finish feeding the sheep one afternoon, we lay down in the grass for a rest, and I share this thought with him, and we laugh.

'It's amazing how one's life can change in such a short space of time,' I muse as I take his hand in mine. 'When I was a little girl, I never thought my husband would be a veterinarian and farmer. I didn't think I'd ever be able to attract someone so clever and handsome.'

'Oh, shut up,' he laughs. 'I keep telling you that you're clever too, just in a different way. And beautiful and kind... I could go on, but we don't have all day.'

'When I was small, I remember saying to my mum that I didn't want to have a normal life.'

Paul grins. 'That's just as well, seeing as you're a cow-milking, sheep-rearing, lamb foster mum. Not to mention a journalist, writer and farmer's wife.'

I smile at the sky. 'It filled me with horror, the idea of being normal. I just couldn't see it. I never felt like I fitted in, but I never really wanted to, either.'

'A square pen in a round hole?'

'Exactly.'

'Well,' Paul says, rolling onto his side to look at me. 'Sure, I'm a square peg in a round hole too, so it's a good job we found each other at that congress. You do know most people come away from those things with a few new pens and a notebook, don't you? But you found a husband.'

'The best husband ever,' I say, reaching over and giving him a kiss.

I look at the time, which indeed does fly when you're having fun.

'After all, we're your flock now,' Paul says, as Deck, who has stopped being a teenager now, comes over and waits for head rubs, just like when he was a lamb.

Frazzle isn't far behind; he doesn't quite know what Deck is doing or why, but whatever it is, he wants some of it too, and soon, they're both rubbing their heads on me, which makes me cry with joy. My boys are back.

'Come on, my gorgeous husband,' I say, struggling to my feet after hugging Deck and Frazzle. 'Let's go home.'

Paul stops and stares at me, as a smile slowly spreads across his face. 'Mrs Crawford!'

'What?'

'You just said, "let's go home."'

'Yes.'

He scoops me into his arms and spins me around.

'Home,' he repeats, grinning broadly. 'You finally see it as *our* home, not just mine.'

I smile back, realising the enormity of what I've just said.

'Yes, my love,' I nod, taking his hand in mind. 'Let's go *home,*'

We stand for a bit, then wrap our arms around each other's waists as we walk slowly down the sun-dappled field towards the house, our sheep follow behind us, bleating happily all the way.

THE ~~END~~ *beginning*

Acknowledgements

I first wish to thank, first and foremost, my gorgeous husband, Paul for not only being the best husband in the world, but for proving that true love, gentlemen and chivalry still exist. Thank you for asking me to marry you; I am the luckiest, happiest and proudest wife in the world. You are the love of my life. Thanks for your encouragement, proofreading and veterinary expertise and for letting me share your sheep! Thank you for always believing in me. I couldn't have written this book without you. I believe in you, too. You are amazing and I will love you forever.

To the best mummy and daddy in the world. I am so proud to be your daughter. Thanks for your unconditional love and support, even though I'm a pain in the backside! Daddy, thanks for always reading me stories when I was a little girl and passing on your love of reading.

Mummy, thanks for giving me a love of words. Thanks to you both for all you do for me. When we went on holiday and explored bookshops, you would always say that one day, I would write a book. Thank you for never giving up on me. Can you believe you are holding my book in your hands? I couldn't have done it without you. Love you lots.

To Laura Cooke (Mrs C) the best English teacher in the world. Thank you for helping me fall in love with literature and introducing me to Murphy the dog from The Bell! You are amazing.

To my publisher James Essinger and the superb team at The Conrad Press for your hard work, for believing in this book and for making it a reality. A big thank you to Rachael and Nat Ravenlock for their typesetting skills and to our illustrator Susan Reed for her beautiful illustrations.

To my friends on the reading panel whose feedback and patience have been invaluable: Mary, Monica, Gemma and my soul sis Fee. To my lifelong friends, Glen, Loz, Amy, Hayley and Gemma; Thanks for sticking by me. To colleagues past and present and to my friend Carla, a vet nursing superhero! The aardvarks at Shepreth and their friend Liz.

To the staff at St Mary's High School in Cheshunt and Middlesex University, especially Phil Cowan.

To the Crawford family for making me feel so welcome, Monica, the best Mummy-in-Law in the world, Judith, David and Ruth and Alex Miller. To my family and friends, especially Auntie Helen and Uncle Andy. Love you all lots.

To the sheep, for being baa-brilliant and allowing me to write about them.

To Roberta, George and Jack for letting me milk your lovely cows – and to the cows for letting me milk them!

To my church family in Christ Church, Ware (big shout out to the Alpha girls) and to our church family in our hometown in NI.

To God, for showing me the way and for all my blessings, especially my husband.

And to you, the reader, for buying this book. I hope you've enjoyed reading it as much as I've enjoyed writing it.